POLITICAL CHAMELEON

In Search of George Thomas

Martin Shipton

ST DAVID'S PRESS

Cardiff

Published in Wales by Welsh Academic Press, an imprint of

Ashley Drake Publishing Ltd
PO Box 733
Cardiff
CF14 7ZY

www.welsh-academic-press.wales

First Edition - 2017

ISBN
Paperback - 978 1 86057 1374
eBook - 978 1 86057 1381

British Library Cataloguing-in-Publication Data.
A CIP catalogue for this book is available from the British Library.

Typeset by Replika Press Pvt Ltd, India
Printed by Akcent Media, Czech Republic

Contents

Acknowledgements

Although I was a constituent of George Thomas' for a year while taking a postgraduate course in journalism studies at what is now Cardiff University, I never met him. I am therefore particularly grateful to four people who knew him well for generously sharing with me their extensive memories and assessments of him: Lord Cormack, Gwynoro Jones, David Seligman and Lord Wigley. I also wish to thank Lord Elis-Thomas AM, Jane Hodge, John Osmond, Lindsay Whittle, Lee Wenham and, finally, the late and much missed Rhodri Morgan.

The seemingly inexhaustible George Thomas/ Viscount Tonypandy archive is held by the National Library of Wales. I made several trips to this rightly esteemed institution in Aberystwyth, where its staff were unfailingly helpful and courteous.

Some of the research for the book was undertaken with enthusiasm and efficiency by Louise Walsh, for which I am very grateful.

I also thank Tony Woolway of Trinity Mirror for locating many of the pictures, as well as Trinity Mirror itself for permission to reproduce some of them.

Ashley Drake of Welsh Academic Press is an admirable publisher who offers help and advice when it is needed, but allows authors the time and space to get on with the job.

I also thank my wife Kay and daughter Rhiannon for allowing me to indulge my George Thomas obsession. Hopefully it is now exorcised.

Martin Shipton
Cardiff
June 2017

In memory of my mother, June Shipton (1930-2017), who taught me never to be ashamed to be a member of the awkward squad.

Preface

I first met George in the autumn of 1967, a couple of months after I was selected as the Labour Party's Prospective Parliamentary Candidate for Carmarthen. During the first few years I found him to be a friendly, humorous and plain talking individual – especially when it came to talking about 'the Nationalists' and Gwynfor Evans – but even in those days he was full of gossip about fellow Labour MPs.

After that we would meet at Labour rallies throughout Wales, where he and I would be 'warm up' speakers for the then Prime Minister Harold Wilson. He was a good orator, full of humour and knew how to play the audience. In 1968, both of us had one thing in common which was taking the fight to Plaid Cymru and its leader, so I suppose he saw me as an important ally during his early period as Secretary of State for Wales. For instance, I recall writing a memorandum to him after the bombing at the Welsh Office in Cathays Park on May 25, 1968, on how to associate Gwynfor's emotive anti-London government utterances with what had taken place in Cardiff.

On March 1, 1969, at the behest of Jim Callaghan, I was appointed Research and Public Relations Officer for the Labour Party in Wales and this resulted in fortnightly meetings with George on a Sunday at his home in the Heath, Cardiff. The purpose of the meetings was for him to provide me with government material I could use for political campaigning by the Labour Party in Wales. It was then I began to notice the 'real' George, and that there really was a nasty side to his character which did not correlate with his public persona.

George would have done anything to advance himself. Anything. He was a man of no principle whatsoever. The only consideration was what would work best for George himself. That was his only guiding light in everything he did. His posturing as a good Christian was an effective cover for his rampant underlying ambitions.

After I became an MP my thoughts about him were crystallised further, not only because of how I saw him operate, but of what he used to tell me and others - at that Welsh table in Westminster - about various MPs.

George was a terrible gossip. He would wilfully damage any of us without compunction, particularly if it was about a Welsh-speaking pro-devolutionist MP: the 'crypto nationalists' as he described us. If he discovered something personal about you, he would enjoy spreading the 'tittle tattle', but what was George really up to?

Pointing the finger. Diverting the attention. Those are the impressions I always had about him. He disliked us all, but especially Cledwyn. He did not care much for Goronwy either and never trusted my good friend Elystan.

Elystan – in his autobiography, Atgofion Oes – recounts an occasion during his time at the Home Office when George, as Secretary of State for Wales, asked him to write a considered piece on a potential transport policy for Wales. Elystan spent months producing a detailed thirty-page policy document and dutifully presented it to George. One day in the House of Commons, Elystan was having a meal with a few people where, nearby, George was in conversation with some other MPs. Elystan overheard George saying, "Let me tell you a story, boys. I gave to that nationalist Elystan Morgan a task, and he wrote thirty-odd pages for me on a Welsh transport policy. So do you know what I did? I put it straight in the bin. Ha ha ha".

Mind you, the truth was that us pro-devolutionists had little time or respect for George either and that was widely known. In a biography of Cledwyn Hughes there is a reference to an article in the Manchester Evening News by the political columnist Andrew Roth, about Cledwyn's opinions when he was replaced by George at the Welsh Office in 1968. "Cledwyn Hughes could not help hating the idea of turning over Wales to George Thomas, a chirpy South Wales sparrow in Mr. Wilson's palm."

There was a serious element of malice with George and, if you got on the wrong side of him as I did following my time in 1969 as Chair of the working party preparing Labour's evidence in Wales to the Crowther/Kilbrandon Commission on the Constitution, you were in trouble. During the period of the Heath government, as shadow spokesman, he was a deeply divisive force, irretrievably damaging the party in the Welsh speaking areas, particularly with his regular column in the Daily Post. He poisoned Harold Wilson against people all the time. He was known as 'Harold's ENT': the Prime Minister's Ears, Nose and Throat!

I had a very good personal rapport with Harold throughout those years, having organised seven or eight of his meetings in Wales during his time as Prime Minister, and speaking at each one. However, I knew there was something preventing him from giving me some sort of recognition – a shadow junior role, or something similar. I had no doubt it was George weaving his web of distrust behind the scenes. In fact Fred Peart, the Minister of Agriculture after February 1974, confirmed to me that George had poisoned him against me: 'He's a nationalist. He's pro-Welsh language. He's pro-devolution. He would divide the party'. One can hear George saying these things, yet he projected the persona of being a great Christian.

Although I never witnessed it, there were references from time to time that George liked his drink, and yet he used to assert openly that he was teetotal, boasting and priding himself on it publicly. Indeed, I heard him say so from the pulpit when he was preaching in Tenby one summer.

You can be safe in the knowledge that he was a hypocrite and a rather hateful man, using religion to cover up his flaws. If you crossed George you had an enemy for life. Nobody could possibly claim that the following characteristics were not true: that George was anti-Welsh, anti-devolution and loathed the patriotic Welsh element within the Labour Party.

However, the bizarre thing is that he would probably have been more patriotic himself if he had been a Welsh speaker. It's his background, isn't it? George could say many, many phrases in Welsh. He could speak a bit of the language, and if he had stuck with it ... well, you never know.

He always resented Jim Callaghan. I can almost see his thought process. In the 1950s Jim, through the unions, gained power and got onto Labour's National Executive Committee. George was envious. Jim subsequently rose to a position of Shadow Minister and then Harold became Prime Minister, making Jim, Chancellor, Home Secretary and Foreign Secretary in succession. It must have driven George mad. He was full of enmity. In fact, he was a bit of a Trump-like character. It was all about him, and only him, all the time.

When anyone tells me stories about George, nothing surprises me whatsoever. He was a bad egg who managed to fool us all. He fooled elderly ladies like my grandmother. We had a house, where I was brought up in Foelgastell, with quite small rooms. In front of the fire, on a few occasions, he would sit with my mother and grandmother on one side of the fire and him on the other, pulling all the strings – tugging the heartstrings.

I do not know how many friends he had in the Welsh Labour Party. Not too many I would guess – not even those people within the party who might have agreed with George on policy issues, particularly with his general anti-Welsh stance. I never saw them consorting much with him. People such as Kinnock, Abse and Alan Williams from Swansea West: I believe they had little time for him. The one stand-out person was Barry Jones, the North Wales MP. It was apparent they were very close indeed – we used to refer to Barry as George's 'Parliamentary son!'

So I reckon he was a pretty lonely figure inside the Welsh Labour Party. Once he was not made Secretary of State in February 1974, his influence within the party in Wales was over. Even Harold Wilson eventually realised, following losses in the Welsh speaking heartlands, that it was George who had been the divisive, negative force for six years.

From then on the grand survivor turned his attention elsewhere – because he had hoodwinked and fooled the Tories for many years too. Many of them, including Mrs. Thatcher, were, I suspect, all starry eyed. He had a prodigious 'gift of the gab'. He was their type of Welshman, such a big 'establishment' man and a Royalist to the core. In his lounge of the bungalow in Cardiff would be a large picture of the Queen on one side of the fireplace and the Prince of Wales on the other.

Gwynoro Jones
Labour MP for Carmarthen 1970-1974
May 2017

Introduction

Although he never represented a south Wales valleys seat in Parliament, George Thomas decided he should be called Viscount Tonypandy when he accepted a hereditary peerage on stepping down as Speaker of the House of Commons.

No doubt he was inclined to believe that such a title secured for him an everlasting association with the mining town where he had been brought up. I took the train there from Cardiff to see what vestiges I could find of him.

Together with its satellite village Trealaw, with which it seamlessly merges, Tonypandy today is, for the first-time visitor, a surprisingly spread-out place. Built on the hills to both sides of the River Rhondda Fawr and the adjacent railway line, it takes a long time to walk around and get a feel for the town.

George Thomas lived in three houses in Tonypandy as a child and young man, only one of which has a heritage blue plaque.

The first is at 139 Miskin Road, Trealaw, a main road which can be reached from Tonypandy station by walking up a long flight of street stairs. George Thomas' parents could only afford to rent the so-called underhouse, a basement on a steep incline that today can just be made out through brambles from a muddy path below. In typical valleys fashion, the front door opens straight on to the street pavement. There's a brick façade and a white front door, with the '1' of the '139' stuck on by card. The view of the hill opposite is obscured by houses on the other side of the road.

The second house is not far away on another main road at 201 Trealaw Road, where Thomas lived with his mother, stepfather and siblings. It had been built by Thomas' maternal grandfather, a building contractor who had moved to south

Wales from Petersfield, Hampshire in 1872. Today the house, which also opens on to the street pavement, stands out from its neighbours. It's painted pastel red, has a mahogany-coloured stained door and its front wall has a blue plaque which reads: 'George Thomas 1909-1998, The Viscount Tonypandy, Speaker of the House of Commons, lived here'. In fact, he died in 1997.

To get to the third house, you have to walk over a bridge that crosses the railway line and the river. The bridge is defaced with, presumably adolescent, homophobic graffiti.

62 Ely Street is on the other side of the town centre, up a very steep hill. In social class terms it's definitely superior, with a gate and steps up to an elevated house with a large double-glazed window. There's a bracket for a hanging basket, a dark grey brick frontage and – on the day I passed by – a little white terrier sitting on the interior window sill.

The town centre has some historical board displays, now rather weathered, referring to the local mining heritage. But there's no reference to George Thomas or his later incarnation as Viscount Tonypandy. It defies the stereotype of a depressed post-industrial community, with the main shopping streets being quite bustling. The places of refreshment are well patronised, including Conti's Fish and Chip Bar, which actually has a wider remit as a Welsh-Italian café serving snacks and hot meals. A pensioner sitting alone eagerly eats an early lunch.

Conti's walls are decorated with old photographs of Tonypandy – the unveiling of the town fountain, the now abandoned colliery, the main street and other street scenes. But Viscount Tonypandy is not to be seen.

A shop displays sentimental gifts and cards in its window, including some that George Thomas might have felt inclined to give to his Mam, for whom he had a renowned sentimental attachment. In this category is an ochre brown bag with a message in the shape of a heart stating: 'Always my mother, forever my friend'. Another reads: 'I love you all the way to the moon and back again'.

If there was one place locally where George Thomas could expect to be accorded fulsome recognition, it would surely be the Lord Tonypandy pub. Some distance away from the town, it is accessible neither by public transport nor – legally – by foot. Getting there without a vehicle involves taking the train one stop back in the direction of Cardiff and then walking for several hundred yards along a by-pass prohibited to pedestrians. At lunchtime the pub is packed with diners who have driven miles to eat carvery meals featuring joints of roast meat and overcooked vegetables while listening to tacky cover versions by session musicians of hits from the 1960s. Some of the diners resemble what Elvis Presley might have looked like had he lived longer. None of them look as if they'd switch TV channels to watch Prime Minister's Questions. But given the pub's name, surely there would be some relic of the late politician in evidence.

As in Conti's, there are plenty of photographs on the walls – and as the building is so much bigger, I assume there's that much greater a chance of coming across a picture displaying the grinning visage of George Thomas in all his glory.

It quickly becomes apparent that there's no shrine to the former Speaker, perhaps displaying a replica of his robes, a photograph or two of him with the young Prince of Wales as well as a heart-warming homely scene with Mam.

But what about the pictures and other objects on the walls? What we can see are David Jason and Daffy Duck; a still from the film *Four Weddings and a Funeral*, featuring Hugh Grant; a photograph of the late comedian Norman Wisdom on a car bonnet; a framed record sleeve of Peter Noone's cover version of the David Bowie song, *Oh! You Pretty Things*; a black and white picture of the young Tom Jones; a colour photograph of the late comedian Les Dawson dressed as a woman, pouting; a picture of a pig wearing a necklace; another showing a cat with a computer mouse in its mouth; two standing poodles with an egg and spoon in their mouths; pictures of the Queen as a *Spitting Image* character and of the late Queen Mother drinking a pint of beer (albeit not in this pub); a photograph of Shirley Bassey; and lots of pictures of the comic actor Ricky Gervais.

After a fruitless exploration I concluded that I'd have to look for George Thomas elsewhere.

1

The Servile Welshman

Some would say that the autobiography of his or her subject is the last place where a biographer should look for assistance. I'm inclined to disagree, and in the present case, most certainly do. However self-serving an autobiography may be – and George Thomas' goes a considerable way in that direction – there are invariably insights to be had.

Thomas published his autobiography – *Mr Speaker, The Memoirs of Viscount Tonypandy* – in 1985, two years after he stepped down from the culminating role of his political career. We learn a lot about him by reading the first chapter, whose title is Invitation to a Wedding.

The wedding concerned is that of Prince Charles and Lady Diana Spencer in 1981, and Thomas drools with delight at having received a letter from the Archbishop of Canterbury, asking him to read the only lesson during the service in St. Paul's Cathedral.

In a few short paragraphs, where he describes a pre-wedding reception at Buckingham Palace hosted by the Queen and Prince Philip, Thomas manages to make cloyingly sycophantic references to the Prince and his fiancée, the Queen and her husband, as well as to the Queen Mother.

As he leaves the Palace, 'which must have seen one of the happiest parties ever to have been held in its awe-inspiring rooms', Thomas opines that the Prince and Princess of Wales 'are clearly a natural couple happy in themselves and with each other'.

Sitting next to the soon-to-be Princess at a lunch on the occasion when he first met her – again, hosted by the Queen – Thomas gives us a glimpse of the rapport he wants us to believe he quickly established with Diana: 'To my great joy I sat next to Lady Diana and throughout lunch we were sharing jokes, talking and laughing as we discussed our mutual interest in children and the things they do. We both saw Prince Charles look across clearly wondering what we were talking and laughing about.'

Thomas then launches into not just the kind of defence of 'the traditions of our country' (in other words, the monarchy) you would expect from a died-in-the-wool right-winger, but an attack on those who hold different views. He lambasts those Labour MPs who had said they would not be watching the Royal Wedding 'even ... on television'. He defends the monarchy as an institution, claiming the present Royal Family helps 'immeasurably' in the argument for one. And he tut-tuts at those who take the view that members of the Royal Family should not express opinions on current affairs, insisting on their right to do so, as long as they don't become party political. So far as Thomas is concerned, if 'the left wing' came out against the monarchy, they would get 'even less support than they do at present'.

In his description of the Royal Wedding itself, Thomas clearly relishes referring to the 'knee breeches, long black stockings and buckled shoes' he had to wear as part of his official costume. He is the centre of attention at the ceremony, at least in his own eyes, the proud recipient of praise whispered to him by the Cardinal Archbishop of Westminster for his reading of the lesson.

A reference to what he clearly saw as his humble origins

comes earlier in the chapter, at the moment he receives the invitation to read the lesson from the Archbishop of Canterbury. He writes: 'As I read the Archbishop's words, I looked at my mother's picture on the mantelpiece and thought, if only you were here now. She would have been as moved as I was that the Prince of Wales, who could have asked any crowned head in the world to read the lesson at his wedding, had asked me, a miner's son, to do so.'

These were the words not of a man proud of his origins in a south Wales coalfield community, but of one uncomfortable with who he was and who craved acceptance by those further up the social hierarchy. This craving was manifested in the deference he expressed towards his 'betters', the Royal Family. But in adopting such a fawning approach, he repudiated one of the traditions he purported to have such respect for: the tradition that the Speaker of the House of Commons is responsible for representing the interests of Parliament as a counter-balance to those of the monarchy.

George Thomas, however, belonged to a different and less distinguished tradition: that of the servile Welshman. The tradition goes back a long way.

Wales' position as the oldest colony of England and its subsequent incorporation into a British union meant that its people's relationship with power was not straightforward. Never a united country, the death of Wales' last native prince Llywelyn ap Gruffudd in 1282 ended what remained of it as a separate political entity. Llywelyn himself was killed as a result of an ambush perpetrated by noblemen related to him by blood and marriage – an early example of collaboration with the English that amounted to treachery.

Many members of the Welsh gentry enthusiastically joined the English armed forces, seeing it as a means of advancement for people denied progression in their own country. When Owain

Glyndŵr undertook his rebellion a little more than a century after Llywelyn's death, the support he gained in Wales was by no means universal and a large proportion of those fighting against him were Welsh. After the rebellion was defeated, and Henry V went to Normandy to fight the French, many of his captains and infantry were Welsh. It was the skill of Welsh bowmen that was most decisive in Henry's victory at Agincourt.

Shakespeare's Henry V contains the soldier Fluellen, a character who encapsulates the playwright's sympathetic, if patronising, portrayal of the Welsh. He is talkative to the point of long-windedness, yet comic, as well as courageous, honourable and good-natured. But his primary purpose was to entertain his English audience – and this he was happy to do.

To escape the harsh penal laws that affected Welshmen, those wishing to make their way in the world gave up rebellion and bought what were known as letters of denizenship which declared them to be English. Rejecting Welshness therefore became associated with seeking and obtaining material advantage.

Centuries later the satirical poet and balladeer John Jones, known more widely by his bardic name Jac Glan-y-gors, devised and mocked the character Dic Sion Dafydd, who in his desperation to ingratiate himself with the English rejected the Welsh language and Welsh culture. In his rousing anthem *Yma o Hyd*, which celebrates the survival of Welsh against all the odds, Dafydd Iwan alludes to 'Dic Sion Dafydds', the Welsh equivalent of an Uncle Tom.

George Thomas was certainly a servile Welshman, but one who used a folksy version of Wales to cultivate a personality cult of his own. His servility was supremely self-serving – and made him into a doyen of the British Establishment.

Fortunately for him, his humble origins provided the essential myth-making ingredients he needed.

2

Mam's Boy and Left Wing Activist

Despite being brought up in Tonypandy. Thomas George Thomas was actually born 23 miles away in Port Talbot on January 29, 1909. His parents, Zachariah and Emma Jane Thomas, had moved to the steelmaking town the year before, and didn't return to the Rhondda Valley until 1910.

Neither of his parents came from long-established south Wales valleys families. His father was a member of a family from Carmarthen who had moved east to work in the mines.

His maternal grandfather, John Tilbury, was a small businessman from a village called Clanfield in Hampshire. A staunch Methodist, whose relatives had founded a chapel in the village, he met George's grandmother, Elizabeth Loyns, while selling fruit in Bristol.

The Tilburys moved to south Wales in 1872 after hearing about the rapid expansion of the coalfield. After initially establishing himself as a greengrocer, Tilbury later became a building contractor. As Thomas put it in his autobiography: 'The fast-growing coal industry sucked in its manpower from England as well as from rural Wales, and grandfather set about building long rows of houses for the immigrant labour, soon establishing a highly profitable business'.

Yet his daughter's marriage to Zachariah Thomas when they

were both 19 did not turn out to be a happy one. The young miner was a heavy drinker, and as an infant George observed his father's drunken rages that sometimes involved smashing up furniture.

When the First World War broke out, Zachariah Thomas immediately enlisted in the Army and was stationed in Kent before being sent to Salonika. Some time later, George's mother found she was unable to claim her state allowance as a soldier's wife. It turned out that Zachariah had entered into a bigamous marriage with a woman he had met in Kent and assigned the wife's allowance to her. George's mother had to go to a tribunal to prove she was Zachariah's real wife before the allowance was restored to her.

George and his mother never saw Zachariah again. After returning from the war he stayed in Kent and died from tuberculosis in 1925.

His father's desertion of the family inevitably made George even closer to his mother and surely accounts for the fixation with 'Mam' that remained with him for the rest of his life.

While he appeared to have little curiosity about the Thomas family from a genealogical point of view, he was interested in his mother's family, the Tilburys. In his old age he kept an old Census return from Clanfield relating to his maternal ancestors.

It also seems likely that George's later hostility to the Welsh language had its origin in the bad behaviour of his father, a Welsh speaker. Writing of his father's family, he states: 'They were thoroughly Welsh, worshipping at the Welsh Congregational Church in Penygraig and speaking only in Welsh to each other. If only he had known it my father could have saved me considerable difficulties in my later political life when the militants in Wales were forever criticising my spoken Welsh.'

He writes that despite being asked by his mother to speak Welsh to the children, his father would never do so, taking the view that there was no point talking Welsh to the children if his wife couldn't understand the language. Without Welsh spoken at home, he claimed he had to get by the best he could when communicating with his paternal grandmother, who he said knew only one word in English: 'damn'. She died when he was six.

As a single mother with five children, money was extremely tight. They moved the short distance from Penygraig to 139 Miskin Road, Trealaw the village adjacent to Tonypandy. Their new home was quite grim, described by George Thomas as 'little better than a cellar'. He wrote: 'There was a small living-room with one window and a door that opened on to the pavement, and two pokey bedrooms with no windows at all. They were dark all day. We shared an outside lavatory – always referred to as 'the dub' – with three other families, and my mother did her washing on the pavement in a wooden tub balanced on two chairs'.

To make ends meet, his mother would do sewing and take in other people's washing, often working into the early hours.

His veneration of his mother was linked to the family's devout Christianity: after having a bath on a Friday evening, George and his two brothers would gather round her rocking chair and kneel to say their prayers.

However, the Nonconformist movement to which they belonged veered to the more radical side of politics. George tells how he grew up hearing stories of how Anglican Bishops supported hanging and flogging, keeping the workers in their proper station and how they had blessed the guns at the beginning of the war.

But this was not the only form of anti-establishment influence to which he was exposed. The town where George

Thomas was brought up holds a significant place in labour history because of the Tonypandy Riots of 1910, when he was a couple of months short of being two years old. The riots followed a lockout imposed on 950 miners who worked in a colliery at Penygraig after its owners claimed coal was not being extracted quickly enough from a new seam. This was a strange allegation, as miners were paid according to the amount of coal they produced, and there was every incentive for them to work as quickly and efficiently as possible. In reaction to the lockout, miners were balloted in all the pits whose owners belonged to the Cambrian Combine network of local mines, with the result that 12,000 men came out on strike. Rioting broke out in protest against the use of strike breakers in Llwynypia Colliery.

There was hand-to-hand fighting between the striking miners and the police. Home Secretary Winston Churchill – at the time a Liberal – was initially reluctant to send in troops, whose presence had been requested by the Chief Constable of Glamorganshire. Soldiers were held in readiness in Cardiff and Swindon, but Churchill did authorise the deployment of 270 mounted and foot officers from the Metropolitan Police.

Troops were used after a night where the looting of shops took place, but it was the police officers who have been described as behaving like an army of occupation. They were certainly extremely hostile to the strikers. One miner, Samuel Rhys, died of head injuries, it is believed after being hit by a police baton.

The strike wasn't settled until the following August, when the miners accepted a deal under which they returned to work on no better terms than they had been offered before the unrest began. There was an inevitable legacy of bitterness – and Churchill was reviled for his role.

What impact did these traumatic events for his home town

have on George Thomas? In his autobiography he refers to the Tonypandy Riots when he writes of the General Strike, which took place in 1926 when he was 17. He wrote: 'I was always told that the rioters came from over the mountains, but that it was our people who went to jail. The police behaved savagely; they brought in reinforcements from outside who could not even understand the Welsh accent, let alone Welsh ways. I used to hear stories of how they beat up people in their own homes, behaviour which caused a deep hostility and lack of trust that lasted throughout my childhood.'

Many years later, as Speaker of the House of Commons in 1978, Thomas would preside over an infamous exchange between Winston Churchill's grandson – also Winston – and Prime Minister Jim Callaghan, in which the younger Churchill demanded an apology from Callaghan for vilifying his grandfather.

In 1925 Thomas' mother married a friend from childhood, Tom Davies – an event the boy was initially sceptical about because he felt the family had been 'quite happy without him'. But he soon grew to respect his stepfather. Dad Tom worked as a winding engineer at the local colliery, lowering and raising the cage that carried miners and trucks of coal. They were able to move to a superior, three-storeyed home at 201 Trealaw Road, where George had a bedroom of his own for the first time.

That year, at the age of 16, Thomas took two decisive actions: he joined the Labour Party and decided, as he put it, to commit his life to Christ. Joining the party enabled him to accompany his mother to Tonypandy ward meetings, which she chaired, but the latter decision seemed of greater importance to him. Describing how he responded to a call from the Rev. W.G. Hughes at a Sunday youth service to give public proof of his commitment to Christ by walking up to the platform where he stood, Thomas wrote: 'I felt myself go hot and cold. The challenge seemed directed straight at me. I said a silent prayer, and stepped forward. It was the watershed of my life and ever since then I have started each day with a moment of silent prayer.'

In 1926 the General Strike and the continuing miners' strike, which lasted nine months, affected Tonypandy deeply, as it did all mining communities. But Thomas' family was cocooned from the worst because, as part of the safety team, Dad Tom was allowed to carry on working and draw his wages. Thomas was disappointed at not being able to join school friends at a 'soup kitchen' organised by volunteers including his mother that provided a free meal every day for the children of those who were not working.

Thomas wrote sympathetically of the plight of those forced to leave their communities to seek work elsewhere, describing tearful farewells at Tonypandy train station as individuals left for distant cities and towns in England, not knowing when they would be able to afford a trip back home. Around 300 valley girls found work as domestic servants in English houses, their clothes and train fares provided from a fund set up by the Lord Mayor of London. He says local people took the view that the girls were 'cheap skivvies for well-off people'.

But when the American-born socialite turned Tory MP Lady Nancy Astor arrived in Tonypandy after referring in the House of Commons to 'the ragged army of the unemployed', Thomas tells how he and other locals were captivated by her beauty and 'friendly nod'. Perhaps this was an early example of his deference to those he considered his social betters.

Summing up the impact of his environment on his childhood, Thomas stated: 'I realise now that to have grown up in the Rhondda Valley during the harsh years of the Depression was a good training for life. We were too poor to be subjected to most of the temptations that assail the present generation, and without the distraction of television we learned to rely on our own resources, to love good books and to make our own pleasures in singing and dancing.'

After leaving school, Thomas became a pupil teacher in Trealaw. In 1928 he got a job as an uncertificated teacher in a primary school at Dagenham in Essex, where he taught boys and girls aged about eight.

He returned after a year, leaving again to attend a two-year teacher training course at University College, Southampton. Money was tight, and he paid tribute to the sacrifices Mam and Dad Tom made to support him through his studies.

In a curious, throwaway paragraph in his autobiography he wrote: 'Two of my oldest and dearest friends in Tonypandy were Trevor Powell and Annie Thomas. The three of us had been inseparable in chapel activities but now I was becoming very fond of Annie. So before I left home the second time, I asked Trevor to look after her until I returned to Wales.'

This is the first time any kind of boyfriend/ girlfriend relationship involving Thomas and a girl or woman is hinted at. A few pages later, Thomas revealed something he said hurt him deeply at the time: 'Trevor had more than fulfilled my request to look after Annie and they were planning to marry'. He continued: 'They were obviously in love and it was right for them to marry. Happily they remained, and still are, very dear friends of mine.'

The biography *George*, written by E.H. Robertson, provides a little more detail: 'He entrusted his close friend Annie Thomas to Trevor Bennett [sic], who also had taught in Essex, and took his sad farewell. Twice a week he wrote to Annie. He was in love ... He soon discovered that Trevor had looked after Annie all too well. They were beginning to fall in love with each other, and eventually they married, to George's great concern and perhaps resentment.' Robertson managed to give Annie's husband the wrong surname.

In his autobiography, Thomas slips in a paragraph stating: 'There have been other women friends who have played an important part in my life but somehow marriage never seemed quite right and it remains my single greatest regret that I never had children of my own.'

This is the only statement Thomas made for public consumption about his personal emotional life.

Annie Powell became a teacher, an activist in the National Union of Teachers and many years later a Communist Party councillor. In 1979-80 she became Mayor of Rhondda – one of the very few communists to hold the post anywhere in Britain, and certainly the first communist woman. When she died in 1986, obituaries were published in newspapers ranging from the *Morning Star* to the *New York Times*.

While studying in Southampton, Thomas wrote home saying that all the other male students were wearing plus-fours – trousers or breeches that extend four inches below the knee and are associated with upper class sporting activities like game shooting. He knew his Mam and Dad Tom would scrape the money together that would enable him to buy some plus-fours, and that is what happened. When he went home to Tonypandy, he was wearing them as he walked along Trealaw Road. He was mocked by a group of miners, one of whom shouted out: "What's the matter, George? Are you working in water?" After this incident, Thomas was embarrassed, and said he never wore plus fours in Tonypandy again.

Another embarrassing incident he said stayed with him all his life took place in Southampton, where he volunteered to accompany a professor of education and other students on a visit to a local school for mentally handicapped children. He couldn't cope with their 'twisted bodies and over-large heads', left the school and vomited outside. The following day he explained to the professor why he had left. He was ashamed when he was told: "If everyone behaved as you did, think how hard life would be for people born with handicaps from which you do not suffer."

Thomas said that after this dressing down, he returned to the school regularly as a volunteer.

Both incidents revealed Thomas to be a rather naïve and self-absorbed young man who, despite being brought up in a deprived community, essentially saw himself as set apart.

After leaving college, Thomas was unable to find a teaching post in south Wales because of public spending cuts, but got a job teaching at Rockingham Street School near Elephant and Castle in south London. He relates how he would attend services at Central Hall in Westminster and go to weekly Methodist fellowship meetings there. He also used to queue up to watch debates in the House of Commons.

He tells how on one occasion in the autumn of 1931, as he came out of a religious meeting in Central Hall, he was 'caught up in a demonstration of chanting protesters'. To get away from them, he leapt over the railings surrounding the Houses of Parliament. There's some irony in a future Labour Cabinet Minister avoiding the demonstration, which was against austerity policies being introduced by the National government formed by Ramsay MacDonald mainly with the Conservatives after he had treacherously quit Labour.

His stay at the school in London was brief. When a job was advertised at Marlborough Road School in Cardiff, Thomas applied for it. Wearing a 'splendid new belted overcoat' that he borrowed from his brother, he attended an interview in Cardiff's City Hall, where he persuaded the committee to appoint him. He was on his way back to south Wales in time for Christmas 1931.

At the school he taught hundreds of boys to read and to sing, and inspired many of them to copy his rather flamboyant habit of having a handkerchief tucked into his sleeve to wipe chalk dust from his clothes. He claimed to have loved the boys, and that they loved him. He told how he paid for a boy called George Edgebrook to have milk after he fainted in class because his parents couldn't afford to feed him breakfast. However, he developed a reputation as a teacher who inflicted – and perhaps enjoyed inflicting – corporal punishment. Michael Foot alluded to this when he included an assessment of Thomas in his book *Loyalists and Loners*.

Many years later, in 1994, Thomas received a letter from Graham Birt, now living in Nottinghamshire, who was a boy when Thomas was a teacher at Marlborough Road School. Birt told how boys from Albany Road School attended Marlborough because they had no woodwork shop of their own in the late 1930s. Birt wrote: 'On such a day, at the end of morning break, one Mr. G. Thomas appeared on the school doorstep. His intent: to still the fearsome shrieks and marshal the wild horde back to classes. This was achieved by a blast on the whistle, normally causing instant silence and immediate total cessation of movement. However, a boy at the far side of the playground failed to hear this and continued to play. This resulted in a second whistle blast and although effective this time clearly required some strong indication of displeasure and authority. This was achieved by a resounding clip of the ears, not those of the offender, too far out of range, but those of the nearest (and innocent!) boy close to the door. That poor blameless lad of nearly 60 years ago was of course me! Since that day I have always had a very complete and sympathetic understanding of what the phrase a 'whipping boy' meant. However, I obviously bore no ill will as later during my time in college in Cardiff I canvassed and worked for you (and

Lieutenant James Callaghan) in the 1945 election. Neither did it affect my political inclinations as I have been an active Labour Party member ever since.'

Despite working in Cardiff, he carried on living in Tonypandy, from where he rode to school on a motor bike.

In 1932 the Thomas family moved to a bigger house again, at 62 Ely Street. While still having an outside toilet, it also had electricity – a first for George, who was to live there for 20 years.

Re-established in his home town, Thomas also studied to become a lay preacher, learning not just theology but the art of manipulating a crowd through emotive eloquence – something that stood him in good stead for a political career. His life settled into a pattern of teaching during the week, voluntary work at pupils' extra-curricular clubs on Saturdays and preaching on Sundays. Although his home chapel was Central Hall in Tonypandy, he regularly accepted invitations to preach elsewhere.

Preaching gave him status in his community and engendered pride in his Mam. He developed the persona of a God-fearing, clean-living, teetotal Christian – the identity to which he would default throughout his life, even if some people knew different.

Having joined the National Union of Teachers as a student, he quickly became an activist after returning to Wales, taking up the post of press and parliamentary secretary for the Cardiff Association of Teachers.

When a national march to London by unemployed workers from around England and Wales was planned, Thomas became joint organiser of the Tonypandy contingent. He tells how on the eve of the march, a police inspector told him that if anyone was observed collecting money, the organisers would be prosecuted for begging. It was common at the time for cash to be donated by sympathetic onlookers. After being told by

Thomas about the police officer's warning, one of the collectors moved among the crowd surreptitiously, taking donations in his cap.

In his autobiography Thomas gives other examples of how antagonistic the police were to left-wing activists in the community. Two of the best known British communists of the day – Harry Pollitt and Tom Mann – were arrested and charged with sedition after addressing a political meeting also attended by south Wales miners' leader Arthur Horner, himself a communist. The men were acquitted after a police officer gave evidence at their trial to the effect that any comments he disapproved of he regarded as seditious.

When British fascist leader Sir Oswald Mosley announced he was holding a rally in Tonypandy, Thomas called a meeting of the local Labour Party at which it was decided to boycott the event rather than join a protest outside the venue. On the evening of Mosley's event, Thomas went to see a film in the local Empire cinema. Despite not being present at the protest, he was accused by a police sergeant of having torn his cape during the fracas. Thomas was saved from prosecution by the cinema manager, who confirmed he had been watching the film at the time trouble erupted. Thomas wrote: 'I knew only too well what a narrow escape I had had, and realised that any left-wing sympathiser, no matter how non-violent, was at the mercy of trumped-up police evidence'.

In an illuminating aside which exposes both his political trajectory over the decades and the depth of his naïvety, Thomas later wrote how in 1981, when he was Speaker, he visited the Duke of Devonshire's home, Chatsworth, where he sat next to the Duchess' sister Lady Mosley (the wife of Sir Oswald), whom he described as 'a warm, compassionate woman', adding: 'If anybody had told me in the 1930s that I would thoroughly enjoy being with Lady Mosley, I would have been furious.'

Lady Diana Mosley was a personal friend of Hitler's who was given special permission to marry her husband in 1936 at the Berlin home of Nazi propaganda chief Joseph Goebbels, with the Führer as a guest. After the war, during which she and her husband were both interned in Holloway Prison, she claimed, despite an abundance of evidence to the contrary, that the British Fascist leader had not been anti-semitic. She did, however, make comments about Jews like: 'Maybe they could have gone somewhere like Uganda – very empty and lovely climate'. On the issue of non-white immigration, she said: 'Immigration has been a tragedy. Any number should have been allowed in to go to the universities and learn to be doctors and one thing and another – but not to settle.'

For George Thomas, however, Diana Mosley appeared to be a 'warm, compassionate woman'. Compassionate, as an aristocrat, in talking politely to him as her social inferior, even though he was Speaker of the House of Commons, was the sub-text of his comment.

Even as a boy, and despite the radical milieu in Tonypandy, Thomas was conscious of the need to defer to his social 'betters'. Referring to the marriage of his sister Ada May to William Webb, who worked for a Mr. Radcliffe as a farm bailiff, he wrote: 'The gap in social status was enormous. I always took my school cap off when I went there to buy a jug of milk'.

3

George the Draft Dodger?

In the run-up to the declaration of the Second World War, George Thomas went on his first trip abroad with a group from the International War Resistance Movement (IWRM), a pacifist organisation. He wrote: 'In the atmosphere of international violence in the 1930s, it was natural to have sympathy with organisations working for peace.' The group travelled by ferry from Harwich to Esbjerg in Denmark, but Thomas tells us simply about his seasickness and the fact that the couple he stayed with took him to see the local sights and enjoyed practising their English on him. We learn nothing about the IWRM event itself.

In his autobiography, Thomas claims that the declaration of war brought a personal crisis for him. He wrote: 'For some time my pacifist views had been badly shaken by Hitler's concentration camps and by Mussolini's incursion into Ethiopia'. But while the Italian invasion of Ethiopia began in 1935, the existence of Nazi concentration camps was not revealed until 1941. Such a mistake suggests he was not being candid about his position at the time, and may have been changing the facts in retrospect.

He continues: 'I went through an agonising period of self-examination, and decided not to go to a tribunal as a pacifist but to join one of the armed forces. I duly appeared before a medical board who declared me Grade C, meaning that I was not considered fit for military service – although they did not tell me why.'

It's stretching credulity for Thomas to claim that he didn't know why he was considered too unfit for military service. The mystery deepens when records held by the National Archives in London show that Thomas' name does not appear on the list of those who attended medical boards as volunteers and conscripts in the early months of the war, as he claimed. The files are not due to be released into the public domain until 2024 and 2025, but it is possible to seek a review which could result in an earlier release date being agreed. But an official of the National Archives told the author in relation to a sequence of files: "We have looked at these documents and unfortunately found no reference to the individual you have enquired about." One source speculated that strings may have been pulled on behalf of Thomas by an official of the National Union of Teachers, who may have had influence with the medical panel.

Gwynoro Jones said: "I think he would have been terrified if he'd gone to war. He was also a coward. It was self-preservation. He would have seen the war as potentially a danger for him. 'Maybe I'll be killed. Never mind about the war and fighting for your country. What about me in all this?' It was always back to George, every time. Whatever the issue, whatever you try to disentangle from the issue, go back to George himself and start your process from there as to why he did it."

Having been excused military duties, Thomas continued as a teacher but also joined the special police in Tonypandy – a decision he acknowledged himself was seen as odd by his Labour friends, given his past suspicion of police attitudes. He cited as another reason for the surprise of his friends the fact that Glamorgan Chief Constable Lionel Lindsay was 'openly hostile' to Labour representatives and had 'reduced public confidence in the police to zero'. In fact, Lindsay had already retired in 1937.

Thomas found the police work 'pleasant' and was quickly promoted to the rank of sergeant. On night patrol he could hear bombs raining down on Cardiff and observe the blazing of anti-aircraft guns in the night sky.

One morning he arrived for work at Marlborough Road school to discover it had been flattened in a bombing raid. Although the school had been empty, people had been killed in neighbouring houses.

He was transferred to Roath Park School where he became responsible for teaching scripture to all its pupils – a task he relished.

Already the president of Cardiff Teachers' Association, he was in 1942 elected to the national executive of the National Union of Teachers. He proposed that the union should be affiliated to the TUC – a move that did not endear him to some traditional members of the NUT, who believed it was unprofessional for teachers to mix with blue-collar workers.

Communists in the union wanted Thomas to stand for the presidency in 1943, but he refused to do so, saying he needed more experience. The following year he stood for the role, but was defeated.

As the war moved towards a conclusion, political parties went through the process of selecting candidates for the election that would follow. Elizabeth Andrews, the women's organiser for the Labour Party in Wales, asked Thomas to let her nominate him for inclusion in the approved candidates list. He agreed and was put on the list. A number of constituency parties contacted him, including Blackburn in Lancashire, which at the time elected two MPs. Thomas was selected, as was Barbara Betts, a *Daily Mirror* journalist who later became a formidable Cabinet Minister known by her married name, Barbara Castle.

Very soon after being selected as a candidate, however, Thomas had doubts as to whether he would be able to devote enough time to Blackburn in the run-up to the general election. A week later, after being invited to stand for selection in Cardiff South, he withdrew as candidate for the Lancashire seat.

Unfortunately for George Thomas, his wish to become Labour's general election candidate for Cardiff South was derailed by a glamorous outsider called James Callaghan. Callaghan was a naval lieutenant from Portsmouth who attended the selection meeting dressed in his gold-braided uniform. Despite being unknown in Cardiff, he managed to beat Thomas by a single vote. It was a huge knock to Thomas' ego: initially he didn't even know what his victorious rival's first name was as he had been introduced simply as Lieutenant Callaghan. The defeat coloured his attitude towards Callaghan for the rest of his life.

Not long afterwards, however, Thomas was visited by an old miners' leader called Meth (short for Methuselah) Jones, who asked him to seek selection in the neighbouring constituency of Cardiff Central. Although his confidence had been hit hard by the failure to get selected in Cardiff South, after talking the situation over with his Mam and Dad Tom he agreed to let his name go forward. This time he won the nomination.

Cardiff Central's retiring MP was Sir Ernest Bennett, one of a small number of Labour Members who had followed Ramsay MacDonald when he split the party and entered into a coalition with the Conservatives in 1931.

Victory was by no means guaranteed: there had been no Conservative candidate when Bennett retained his seat at the previous general election in 1935.

At the first public meeting he addressed during the campaign

George Edgebrook, the boy whose school milk Thomas had paid for years before after he fainted from lack of nourishment, got up and told the audience how grateful he was to the Labour candidate for his generosity.

Leading Labour figures including party leader Clement Attlee and Herbert Morrison came to support Thomas' candidacy in a pre-television era when public meetings provided the most common opportunity for voters to see politicians in action.

A 17-year-old called David Seligman, who many years later stood unsuccessfully as Labour's candidate in Cardiff West after Thomas' retirement, was in awe of him: "I first came into contact with George when I was not a member of the Labour Party. I was 17 years of age. It was in the 1945 election, and I acted as a runner from the polling station in Rawden Place in Riverside to the committee rooms, taking the numbers of those who had voted. That's when I first met George – he came to the polling station on polling day – and I thought he was a god. I was very impressed – he wasn't an MP yet. And then he became an MP and I went abroad for a while. I came back, joined the Labour Party and then had a lot of contact with George. I thought he was wonderful. I was very impressionable. I'd never met anybody who was a candidate for Parliament. And he was very nice. On the occasion when I was taking numbers he came up and asked what I was doing. He was very nice to me, and I really did like him."

For Thomas, the cornerstone of his campaign was to ensure the poverty of the 1930s did not return. His slogan was: 'I will fight to ensure that no mother suffers as mine has done' – conveniently fusing his mother fixation with a general political commitment. He told meetings that private enterprise should never again be allowed to put profit before people, explicitly linking such a view with his Christian faith. He later wrote: 'I wanted to use politics as a means of translating Christian values into practice, for I believed then, as I do now, that Parliament is one of the means for Christian people to make the world look like God's world – though I do not believe it is ever right for the Church to tell people how to vote.'

Thomas' comment was not random: a notice was pinned to the door of a Catholic church in the Cardiff Central constituency saying it was a mortal sin to vote for George Thomas because he was left-wing and chapel.

His most worrying moment during the campaign was when Winston Churchill came to address a meeting in the Ninian Park football stadium. Despite getting a very large proportion of residents to display his picture along the route taken by the Prime Minister, Thomas believed the wartime leader could galvanise support for the Conservatives.

He needn't have worried. The overall result of the general election was a landslide for Labour, and in Cardiff Central Thomas won with a comfortable majority of more than 4,500 over the Conservative candidate Charles Hallinan, a local solicitor.

Labour won Cardiff's two other seats as well, with Jim Callaghan securing a majority of nearly 6,000 in defeating Cardiff South's incumbent Tory, and Hilary Marquand nearly 5,000 votes ahead of the incumbent National candidate in Cardiff East.

When Thomas returned to his home in Tonypandy the day after his result was declared, someone had chalked on the pavement outside a message reading 'Congratulations George on your good work in Parliament'.

His work there had yet to begin.

Before taking their seats at Westminster, Thomas and Callaghan decided to introduce themselves to officials of Cardiff City Council. As they walked through the city centre, Thomas claims Callaghan suddenly asked him what he was going to do in the forthcoming parliamentary term. Thomas responded that he would do his best to look after his constituency. Then Callaghan said: "Before the end of this Parliament, I shall be in the Government." This didn't go down well with Thomas – but Callaghan was right.

There was a footnote to Seligman's youthful recollections, demonstrating that it was not easy to get excused from military service. He said: "I went to what was Palestine and spent a couple of years in a kibbutz there. The next time I met George was very interesting. I came back and I registered for National Service. But at the same time I enrolled in university in London. I asked for an exemption for the period I was taking my degree. I was refused. So I got in touch with George, and asked if there was any possibility that I might get an extension. I met him in the House of Commons and he introduced me to Ness Edwards [the MP for Caerphilly and Minister for National Service]. He put forward a case, but it didn't work. So I got conscripted and spent a couple of years in the Army, in the Royal Engineers."

4

Backbencher and Communist Fellow Traveller

The House of Commons that George Thomas joined was greatly different from the one that preceded it. Because of the war there hadn't been a general election since 1935. Many of the sitting MPs retired in 1945 and of the 393 Labour MPs elected, as many as 242 represented seats gained by the party.

Because the House of Commons chamber had been badly damaged by bombing – something which had not been announced at the time – MPs met in the chamber of the House of Lords. Attending his first session, Thomas sat next to Jim Callaghan and a man with a bad cold who turned out to be Michael Foot. Thomas told Foot he was a great admirer of his father Isaac, who had been a Liberal MP, adding: "Your father is a great Methodist – and a teetotaller." Foot responded: "My father is a good man, but I don't share all his views."

While Parliament was functioning, Thomas stayed in a 'friendly little Welsh hotel' called the Harlingford, near Russell Square. Maintaining the pretence that he was teetotal, he wrote in his autobiography: 'It suited me because it was completely temperance, and other members from the same sort of background stayed there too.'

In his description of conversations with great politicians of the day soon after he took his seat, Thomas displayed the fawning attitude for which he became well-known. He recounts meeting Anthony Eden, then the deputy leader of the Conservative Party and a future Prime Minister, outside the library.

Thomas, who liked being called 'Tommy' by the patrician Eden, wrote: 'Once when we met just outside the library, he said: "Hello, Tommy. Have you settled down yet?" When I replied, "This is a wonderful place, Mr. Eden, and there are some wonderful people here," he laughed outright. Then he said, "You are quite right, Tommy. There are wonderful people here, but there are also some of the other sort. The good thing is that we can choose our own friends. You be careful in your choice".'

Having been willingly patronised by Eden, Thomas sought out Churchill the following year on the eve of a ceremony in which the wartime Prime Minister was awarded the freedom of Cardiff. Thomas wrote: 'I was desperately anxious that the great man should not fail to recognise me in front of the Cardiff hierarchy, so I sought him out in the Commons smoking-room where I knew he liked to meet his colleagues.'

Thomas went on to tell of his sense of nervousness before he approached Churchill and said: "Mr. Churchill, you are coming to Cardiff tomorrow to receive the Freedom of the City and we are looking forward to welcoming you." Knowing Churchill had no idea who he was, Thomas said: "My name is George Thomas. I am the Member for Cardiff Central."

Churchill told him, "I look forward to seeing you in your own city", but at a small tea party in the Cardiff Lord Mayor's Parlour in City Hall the following day, Thomas recounts that Churchill looked at him and asked in a loud whisper, "Who is that?" Thomas wrote: 'I have never been able to resolve whether it was his sense of humour or whether I really had made no impression on him at all.'

For George Thomas, it seemed there was nothing shameful about sucking up to Churchill, whose antagonism to the miners of Tonypandy was not referred to, even tangentially. Thomas was much more preoccupied with gaining Churchill's attention. He must have been devastated at not securing it.

However, Thomas soon set out his stall as a representative of working people, saying: 'The people of south Wales have long since learnt that political democracy means little unless there is security, unless there is work and unless there are the general amenities that make life worthwhile.'

In his maiden speech he focused on the need for leasehold reform – a burning issue in Wales, where industrial expansion had been accompanied by the building of homes sold with 100-year leases. When the 100 years was up, families faced eviction by often merciless freeholders. He began a long campaign for reform which eventually succeeded more than 20 years later.

The following year he encapsulated his view on the issue during a Commons speech, telling his fellow MPs: "This is a question about which I feel deeply. The wretched ground landlord system is robbing the people ... Within the next 10 years the majority of leases in Cardiff will be falling due. It will only be possible for householders to keep their homes, and business people their shops, if these people are prepared to pay the prices which will be demanded of them by WGR (Western Ground Rents Ltd) or Mountjoy Estates, which is the estate of the family of the Earl of Bute."

The Labour government which Thomas supported had more urgent legislative priorities, however, like taking coal, gas and electricity into public ownership and setting up the National Health Service.

When Thomas asked the Minister of Health in a parliamentary question "whether he is prepared to introduce legislation to protect tenants in tied cottages from eviction, in view of the shortage of accommodation?", Aneurin Bevan's junior minister Charles Key responded: "No, Sir. The proper remedy for the tied cottage problem is in [Bevan's] view the provision of an ample number of free cottages by the local authorities and he is endeavouring to expedite this provision by every means in his power."

Thomas became known for singing the Welsh hymn *Cwm Rhondda,* in English, as MPs walked through the division lobbies, with many of his Labour colleagues joining in.

In the autumn of 1945, Thomas accepted an invitation to attend a World Peace Conference of Young People in Warsaw. It was organised as a propaganda exercise by the Soviet Union. In his autobiography Thomas claimed his decision to go stemmed from naivety – that he was a dupe of the communists. However, there are strong grounds to believe that in his early years as an MP he was not as naïve as he would have us believe and that he allowed himself to be influenced by colleagues who were sympathetic to and perhaps even controlled by the Soviet bloc.

Nevertheless, to play up the theme of naivety, Thomas tells how when talking with a group of young people in Poland, he noticed a six-figure number tattooed on the arm of one of the girls. He asked her why she had it, not realising that she was an Auschwitz survivor. The group stared at him in silence until one of them changed the subject. Afterwards it was explained to him that the girl with the tattoo still woke screaming from nightmares. He wrote: 'I still cringe when I remember my ignorance.'

On the same trip to Poland, Thomas visited Auschwitz and was deeply affected by the experience. Later in the year he went to Nuremberg to observe the war crimes trial of captured Nazis. He said his experiences confirmed for him that Britain had been right to wage war on Germany.

However, he did not agree with the Atlee government's

proposal to bring in compulsory national service and made it clear that he would defy a three-line whip on the issue. Summoned to a meeting, he was accused of disloyalty by Herbert Morrison, the Leader of the House of Commons. Thomas turned to Chief Whip Willie Whiteley, a fellow Methodist, and challenged him to deny there were occasions when a man must follow his own conscience. With Morrison getting increasingly angry at Thomas' show of defiance – not to mention his sanctimoniousness – Whiteley said the interview was over.

Thomas' stance gained him respect from pacifist groups across Britain. In common with 52 other MPs who opposed conscription he received a letter from the Wigan Christian Pacifist Group which said: 'At a meeting of the above group held recently, it was unanimously decided that we should send to you our congratulations upon your support of the amendment to the King's speech, opposing the imposition of military conscription in peacetime, and to offer you any support we can give in respect of this issue. We feel that there is a considerable body of opinion in the country that would wish you to continue opposition to this measure when the Bill comes before Parliament. We hope you will be encouraged to continue your resistance.'

The law to introduce conscription was, however, passed. Compulsory military service lasted until 1960.

Thomas' interest in military matters extended to concern about the implications of nuclear weapons. He kept an article from a pamphlet called *The New Commonwealth: The Rocket and the Future of Warfare*, which had been reprinted from *RAF Quarterly*. Its author, Flight Lieutenant A.C. Clarke, wrote: 'The inescapable conclusion is that the only defence against the weapons of the future is to prevent their ever being used. A country's armed forces can no longer defend it; the most they can promise is the destruction of the attacker. In such circumstances, the statement that the UNO is the last hope of mankind is literally and terribly true.'

Thomas was a resolute opponent of capital punishment, and wrote movingly about the callousness of Labour Home Secretary, James Chuter Ede, in refusing to commute the death penalty for a young man convicted of murder in controversial circumstances. By sheer coincidence, two murders were committed on the same night in the Aberavon constituency. In one case, a young girl was brutally assaulted and killed by the son of a woman to whom she was delivering 10 shillings borrowed by her mother earlier in the week. Her body was dumped at a nearby rubbish tip.

The other murder involved a 23-year-old man pressing his hands to the throat of his girlfriend as they had sex on a mountainside. The man had run down to a public telephone to call the police and say he had accidentally killed her. He was frantic with grief and Thomas wrote that his story 'had the ring of truth about it'. Thomas got involved in the case because the local MP had not been available when the father and brother of the condemned man visited Parliament to lobby for his death sentence to be commuted.

When Thomas went to see Chuter Ede to plead for clemency, the Home Secretary gave him a frosty reception and said: "You know there were two murders in the Aberavon constituency that night, and in each case a young man has been sentenced to hang. The young man you have come about is a Protestant, and the other is a Roman Catholic."

Thomas asked what on earth that had to do with it, and was told: "I am not going to offend my Catholics in South Shields [his constituency] by reprieving a Protestant and allowing a Catholic to hang."

Both men were hanged. Thomas recounted how, when

Chuter Ede left the Home Office in 1951, he said he had changed his mind about capital punishment following the Timothy Evans case in which an innocent man was hanged. Thomas reflected: 'I recalled my own unhappy dealing with him and wondered if the boy from Aberavon was also on his conscience.'

Thomas quickly took an interest in foreign, and especially colonial, affairs, asking a series of parliamentary questions about conditions in Britain's colonies.

On April 7, 1946, Hastings Banda, the future President of Malawi, known in pre-independence times as Nyasaland, wrote to Thomas stating: 'During my conversation with Dr. Hinden [of the Fabian Colonial Bureau] I learnt of your interest in colonial affairs. Dr. Hinden showed me a copy of the questions you had raised on Nyasaland in the House of Commons. I wish to thank you for the trouble you took in raising these questions. At the present, there are a number of subjects about which the Africans in the Protectorate are disturbed. One of these subjects is education, on which you so kindly raised questions in the Commons. Others relate to political representation in the Legislative Council, land laws and practices, Central African Council, protection of African women, colour bar etc. I fully realise that you are very busy but I shall greatly appreciate it if some time later you will permit me to send you a memorandum on these topics and any other information I may receive from home on any topic.'

Thomas responded saying: 'I am deeply interested in the question of the Colonies and would be pleased to have a chat with you about Nyasaland when you can spare the time to come to the Commons.' Banda subsequently wrote a detailed briefing note for Thomas, outlining the details of how the overwhelming majority of Nyasaland's people were excluded from the political process.

Thomas' next foreign adventure was by far the most dangerous he undertook, and nearly got him killed. In January 1947 he was invited by the communist-backed League for Democracy in Greece (oddly, in his autobiography, he attributes the invitation to the National Union of Students) to investigate the conflict between the Greek government and students at Athens University. He affected not to realise that he was blundering into a civil war.

When Thomas arrived in Athens, the Government had shut down the university. He was met at the airport by a Professor Georgiou, who took him to his home. Thomas claimed he did not realise that Georgiou was a member of the Greek Communist Party, whose military wing, the Democratic Army of Greece, was involved in a rebellion against the Government. The Government was backed by Britain and the United States, while the rebels were supported by Yugoslavia, Albania and Bulgaria.

The following day the translator who had been assigned to Thomas, named Christos, took him to visit a supposed cousin who had been imprisoned in shocking conditions. One man who was obviously very ill was lying on the floor, a fact which caused Thomas to become highly indignant about the Government's way of conducting itself.

Persuaded to travel to Macedonia in northern Greece, a region where some of the most intense fighting was going on, Thomas secured the help of the British Ambassador, who provided him with a military jeep and a cockney driver named George. Thomas was fitted out with a heavy white duffle coat and army boots.

Having been entertained and accommodated by the Mayor of Larissa, the largest city in Thessaly and on the way to Macedonia, he set off with Christos and George to a mountain village thought to be in the hands of the Government by day and held by guerrillas led by General Markos Vafiadis at night. About an hour out of Larissa, as they drove beneath a monastery set high on a hill, they found themselves caught in a gun battle. Bullets from the monastery whistled past them. The driver stopped the jeep, jumped out and rolled under it for cover, as did Thomas and Christos.

As the shooting continued, George the driver said the only sensible thing to do as to drive back to Larissa as quickly as possible. Thomas, however, was persuaded by Christos to continue with him on foot to a village ahead. The driver would have none of it, and took himself and the jeep back to Larissa. Christos and Thomas rolled into a ditch as the gunfire continued, Thomas thinking death could be near. He prayed and the shooting stopped after about an hour.

They walked on and as they approached the village some soldiers wearing British Army uniforms approached them, pointing their weapons at them. They were guerrillas, unimpressed that Thomas was a British MP and demanded his passport. The atmosphere became tense when he refused to hand it over.

The situation was defused, the villagers were welcoming, and Thomas was accompanied by the guerrillas on a two and a half day trek up Mount Olympus so he could meet their leader Markos at his headquarters. Even at this stage Thomas claimed not to realise that Christos was a communist.

When they arrived at Markos' headquarters, Thomas was greeted as the first Western parliamentarian the rebel had met. Marcos gave him a letter to take to the United Nations, then meeting in Athens, and invited the world's press to send representatives to talk to him and report on the activities of his guerrillas. In return for agreeing to deliver the letter, Thomas was given a guide to help him back down the mountain.

He had an anxious time walking with the guide and

Christos, but after leaving the guide at the edge of territory controlled by the rebels they found their way back to Larissa. The British Army were angry with Thomas, believing he had a prior arrangement to meet Markos and doubtless thinking it inconceivable that an MP would be so reckless as to undertake such a trip on a whim.

In fact, Thomas' disappearance had made world news and many had come to the conclusion that the guerrillas had killed him.

Again he was accommodated by the Mayor, although this time his host was sullen and unwelcoming, assuming that Thomas had been consorting with the rebels. Thomas felt his life was in danger as a result of the reputation he had made for himself, and he spent a nervous, nicotine-fuelled sleepless night thinking he was going to be assassinated.

He took the letter to the UN and went back to London, where he was in great demand as a public speaker at rallies organised by the League for Democracy in Greece.

Thomas spoke at a press conference organised by the League, declaring that Greece had all the marks one would expect to find in a fascist state. He said people could be tried simply for disagreeing with the authorities. While Athens had an uneasy atmosphere, he said things were worse in the provinces: "Outside of Athens I could only meet the Left in the dark, secretly, as though Greece was still occupied by the Nazis". He did, however, tell the press conference that he had gained a positive impression of real freedom in the territory controlled by the guerrillas and was not surprised to find their leader, Markos, a popular hero.

He told the press conference that the guerrilla movement was not a communist but a popular one, "a movement of revolt against tyranny – and if there was such tyranny within Britain, the British people would also go to the mountains."

From his own observations and talks with all types of political leaders, he had come to the conclusion that a new government should be formed under the centrist Themistoklis Sofoulis, in which the Left should participate.

A rally addressed by Thomas, other MPs and even a former chief of Britain's economic mission in northern Greece, Colonel A.W. Sheppard, passed a motion calling for the withdrawal of British troops from Greece and the implementation of recommendations from an all-party parliamentary delegation to the country.

According to the academic and historian of modern Greece, John Sakkas, the campaign waged by the League for Democracy in Greece represented the most potent challenge to the foreign policy being pursued by Britain's Labour government. The Foreign Secretary, Ernest Bevin, summoned Thomas and told him he was being used by the Communist Party. Thomas wrote: 'My pride was injured; no-one enjoys being told that they have been manipulated. I did not want to believe that I was an innocent abroad, and I reacted sharply to Bevin's lecture. Nonetheless, I began to look with a more searching eye at the people who surrounded me at the rallies. Soon I believed that Bevin had indeed been right, and I resolved to leave foreign affairs to people with greater experience. The whole Greek episode was a major political blunder on my part, and I was fortunate that Clem Attlee understood that my behaviour was due to naivety rather than malice.'

Obviously concerned for the MP's welfare, Attlee himself invited Thomas to meet him. The Prime Minister arranged for him to be seen by a doctor, who recommended he should go to Switzerland to rest for six weeks. Other MPs were prepared to pay for the trip, but Thomas felt he could not leave his constituents for such a period, even though a neighbouring

MP had been prepared to look after them in Thomas' absence. Instead, he agreed to rest at home for six weeks.

However, the Secretary of the World Federation of Democratic Youth wrote a letter of praise to Thomas, saying: 'You really have become very famous. We have just received the English papers out here in Prague of last Friday ... What I am really writing to say therefore is how very appreciative indeed we all are of your efforts in Greece, and how tremendously impressed we were with the letter you sent back to Paris.'

Another well-wisher wrote Thomas a letter saying: 'I must say I heaved a sigh of relief to read in the *Western Mail* this morning that you had safely arrived at Croydon once more ... Every good wish and heartiest congratulations on a good job well done.'

Nevertheless, such an escapade could have proved fatal to his career, but the press was kind to him. He had made sure he had good relations with journalists. The degree of friendly intimacy he had established with reporters was demonstrated in the tone of a letter sent to him in January 1947 by a *Daily Mail* reporter based in south Wales. The letter read: 'Alas and alack. Hear you will be in Greece when we visit in London. I put it to the boys and there was common consent that it would be a good thing for you to entertain us at lunch! ... Last news I had of you was that you were in the horizontal pillowed by a cushion more generally used to ease pseudo-Trotskian piles.'

A later letter to Thomas from Diana Pym, the communist secretary of the League for Democracy in Greece, underlined how perilous the trip had been: 'I thought that you would like to know the latest development about Betty Ambatielos' husband. I have today received a letter from her which says: "Yesterday morning [13.01.48] the press printed that Tony, together with two others, would be tried by Special Court Martial as a 'sabotage group' [This would carry a death sentence]. If the position weren't so serious, it would be comic! The one man [Hadji-Anou, a doctor] has only just returned from exile where he was sent in June after the mass arrests. The third is a lawyer – Flatsakis – who is completely unknown to us. As yet, there has been no official intimation of the charge and Tony only knows what he knows from the press".'

The letter went on to say: 'About the steps being taken, I was confident that you and our friends would all be on the job but we hear no reflection of it here – and I think it should be speeded up – you know how they rush things here, precisely in order to avoid pressure.'

Pym said she thought it would be 'very useful' if Thomas could pass information about the fate of Ambatielos to the Foreign Office or, if possible, refer to it in public speeches either in Cardiff or the House. She concluded: 'I hope that you will be able to come to the League Executive meeting next Wednesday at 5pm and am delighted that you had agreed to be Vice Chairman. [Up till then he had been a member of the executive council].'

Betty Ambatielos was a Welsh communist who was born in Pontypridd as Elizabeth Bartlett. Having trained as a teacher, she had joined the Communist Party in 1937. In 1940, by which time she was working in the party's Birmingham office, she was sent to liaise with the Greek Seamen's Union in Cardiff, where it was based during the war. Its secretary was Tony Ambatielos, himself a prominent member of the Greek Communist Party. The couple fell in love, married and after the war moved to Greece.

Ambatielos was sentenced to death, but after an international outcry the sentence was commuted to life imprisonment. His wife then spent years fighting a high profile campaign to get him released. He was eventually freed in 1964.

Thomas' adventure in Greece, undertaken while Parliament

37

was sitting, lasted a month. In the spring of 1948 Thomas went on a short break to Canada. When he returned to Tonypandy he found that his stepfather – Dad Tom – was close to death. He died shortly afterwards.

During the summer recess he was among a group of Labour MPs who visited Czechoslovakia, Yugoslavia, Poland and the Soviet Union, where they met Stalin.

In a broadcast talk for the BBC shortly afterwards, Thomas told how, during a meeting with the Soviet Foreign Minister Molotov, they were astonished to be told that while Stalin was 1,000 miles away, arrangements were being made for them to be flown to see him. We are expected to believe that Stalin would take the trouble to have such a meeting organised simply so that he could deliver a general homily about the need for international cooperation.

In his account of the trip that appears in his autobiography, Thomas contrasted the field marshal's uniform festooned with medals worn by the Yugoslav leader Tito with the plain drill suit worn by Stalin when they met him at his residence in Sochi on the Black Sea. It struck Thomas as odd that Stalin didn't send greetings to Churchill or Attlee.

In concentrating on such ephemera, Thomas sought to give the impression that he had a rather naïve view of what had been going on in Eastern Europe. The contents of his private papers, and the documents he chose to keep, tell a different story.

Thomas had material from the British-Czechoslovak Friendship League, the British Yugoslav Association, as well as from ZWM, the Union of Polish Youth communist movement. The first edition of its Bulletin, used as a tool of political indoctrination and dated January 1946, stated in English: 'The ZWM Central Administration summons the whole organisation to reinforce our ideological and educational offensive at all sections of Youth! The Central Administration lays a particular stress on the necessity of fighting all remnants of fascist ideology and of doing completely away with all influences of reaction in the ranks of Youth.'

Other Polish communist magazines and newspapers, including *Walka Mlodych* (Fighting Youth) were sent to Thomas via the headquarters of the National Union of Teachers.

By January 1948 Thomas had become chairman of the British Polish Society. That month also he received a copy of the Czechoslovak Communist Party's *Prague News Letter*, which contained a full-on ideological question and answer section involving party leader Klement Gottwald, who at the time was Prime Minister of a coalition government. Because of the Communist Party's waning popularity in the country, Gottwald had been ordered by Stalin to prepare the way for a coup in which all non-communists would be removed from the Government.

In the *Prague News Letter*, Gottwald answered several questions submitted to him by John Stuart, correspondent of the American Marxist magazine *New Masses*, including: 'What substantial difference is there between present and pre-war Czechoslovakia?'

Gottwald responded: 'The first substantial difference between present day and pre-war Czechoslovakia lies in the fact that before the war a handful of big capitalists, financiers and big landowners decided the fate of Czechoslovakia and disposed of her wealth, whereas today the fate and wealth of the country are in the hands of the working people of town and country.'

Yet in the Cold War climate of the late 1940s, many Labour MPs shied away from associations that could link them to the Soviet Union. One, Lyall Wilkes, wrote to Pym on March 15, 1948, saying: 'I do suggest to you that what is required is an organisation led and controlled by people who really do care for Democracy in Greece, and elsewhere, instead of by persons who are only too anxious to support executions and repression in Eastern Europe whilst fighting the same evils in Greece.'

It took Thomas until April 6, 1949, to write a similar letter and resign his post as vice chairman.

Despite claiming to have been persuaded by Ernest Bevin that he was being manipulated by communists during and after his Greek trip, Thomas was involved with a small group of Labour MPs who collaborated with the Soviet Embassy in London and the Embassies of other Eastern European countries in the Soviet orbit. On New Year's Day 1948 Thomas was sent a letter by the left-wing Labour MP Konni Zilliacus, in which the latter spelt out a public relations strategy aimed at proselytising on behalf of communist embassies that Thomas and others were expected to follow. The letter said: 'I am asking every one of us who was on the History Journey and will get some of the Embassy people in after dinner. I do hope you will be able to come. Harry White [Labour MP for North East Derbyshire] and Arthur Allen [Labour MP for Bosworth] have sent me very useful summaries of what they have been doing since we got back to educate our movement and public opinion generally about Eastern Europe and the USSR. I very much hope that you will feel like doing the same because I think, if we want to take ourselves seriously as missionaries of goodwill and understanding, and plan our collective activities for this year, it would be a good start for all of us to know what each has done so far. And I can see no objection and only advantages if copies of any collective note, prepared for our own use on the basis of the information you sent me, were given to our friends in the embassies of the four countries that we visited, just to show them that our claim that we were not just tourists but a working party was worth taking seriously! After all, this business of being missionaries of understanding and goodwill cuts both ways – we want responsible people in the countries we visited to feel that they can trust us and look upon us as friends, and that in spite of what the capitalist powers may be saying there is a lot of good sense and good feeling about Eastern Europe and the USSR in the Labour movement.'

Zilliacus – often known as Zilly – suggested a 'big meeting' in Cardiff to promote the cause. It's quite clear from this letter that Thomas was seen by Zilly as a politician who would go out of his way to support the Soviet cause in the face of criticism from others. It didn't take long for pro-active steps to be taken. The Soviet Ambassador visited Cardiff just two weeks after Zilly's letter and a meeting of the British Soviet Society took place in the City Hall. The *South Wales Echo* reported positively on the Ambassador's visit, saying: 'The official proceedings of welcome were notable for a first class speech by the Lord Mayor, whose pleas for a better understanding between the British and Russian peoples was echoed by the whole Assembly.'

Zilliacus was an intriguing figure of Finnish extraction. In 1947, George Orwell referred to him in an article for the *New Leader* about people he considered to have potentially Stalinist sympathies. He wrote: 'The important thing to do with these people – and it is extremely difficult, since one has only inferential evidence – is to sort them out and determine which of them is honest and which is not. There is, for instance, a whole group of MPs in the British Parliament (Pritt, Zilliacus, etc.) who are commonly nicknamed 'the cryptos'. They have undoubtedly done a great deal of mischief, especially in confusing public opinion about the nature of the puppet regimes in Eastern Europe; but one ought not hurriedly to assume that they all hold the same opinions. Probably some of them are actuated by nothing worse than stupidity.'

Orwell would not have been aware that Zilliacus was

coordinating a PR campaign for communist regimes in conjunction with their embassies.

There was an intriguing follow-up to Thomas' involvement with the Eastern bloc. It became a habit for him to make regular speaking and preaching trips to the United States. In November 1956 he spoke at the First University Methodist Church in Madison, Wisconsin. The brochure produced for his talk introduced him thus: 'This young legislator and church leader has travelled extensively in Europe, where he has had the opportunity – since 1945 – to meet personally with practically every head of state on the Continent, including the late Joseph Stalin of the USSR. Mr. Thomas this summer attended both political conventions (as a member of a four-man delegation of The World Methodist Council), met briefly with President Eisenhower, where mutual concerns regarding peace and religion were discussed. He is at present on a nationwide speaking tour under the auspices of the American Friends Service Committee to whom we are indebted for their cooperation in arranging this engagement for us.'

The American Friends Service Committee is a Quaker organisation originally set up to assist civilian victims in the First World War. During the Cold War it stood for Christian pacifism and at the same time backed the American civil rights movement. It also has a clear stance against the production and deployment of nuclear weapons. It has been accused of supporting communist activities and, like many similar organisations, has been monitored by the FBI and other government agencies.

Years later in 1969, following the death of Ben Parkin, another member of Zilliacus' delegation to meet Stalin and other communist leaders, Parkin's widow Pamela wrote to Thomas reminiscing about the trip. Enclosing a photograph of Parkin, Thomas and Zilliacus with lots of wine glasses on a table, she wrote: 'There is Zilly, Geoffrey Bing and so many other familiar faces. There is a beautiful portrait of Zilly – my son loved Zilly very much. He was always so kind, understanding and patient with small children and I have the happiest memories of Zilly spoiling Nicko in our Moscow hotel.'

Thomas responded: 'My warmest thanks to you for sending me a photograph of dear old Zilly. I was very fond of him and it is sad to think that he and Ben are no longer with us. I well recall the happy experience we had in 1948 when we toured the Eastern European countries. This was the occasion when we met Stalin and it was the time when Ben slipped and injured his hand. I shall value the photograph very much indeed.'

The general election held in February 1950 was not a repeat of the 1945 landslide, and Labour scraped home with an overall majority of just eight. But boundary changes saw George Thomas move to the re-jigged seat of Cardiff West, which was safer for Labour. The last line of his election leaflet read: 'Even the children want George Thomas back in the House of Commons.'

Thomas was very concerned about the lack of progress on leasehold reform. Getting legislation through Parliament that would provide secure protection for leaseholders was proving to be difficult and complex. He tabled a parliamentary motion calling for an immediate standstill order that would prevent the eviction of leaseholders whose leases had expired. Despite collecting the signatures of 125 Labour MPs prepared to back his proposal, he was unable to make any progress towards a vote before the summer recess. Over the summer he spoke to many constituents who were facing eviction orders. When the King's Speech was delivered in the autumn, there was at last a firm commitment on the part of the Government to legislate for a two-year protection period for tenants whose leases were about to expire. By Christmas the Leasehold Property

(Temporary Provisions) Bill was passed, affording temporary protection to those affected.

Thomas became a member of the Speaker's Panel of Chairmen, a group of MPs able to chair legislative committees and debates held in Westminster Hall. Thomas' biographer E.H. Robertson, whose view invariably reflected that of his subject, described the change in attitude this new status brought: 'There was dignity in his office and a member must live accordingly. George was still left-wing. Nye Bevan was still his man, and he felt close to such men as Harold Wilson and Tony Benn, but he never let himself go in debate in the way that they did. His rhetoric, of which he was eminently capable, was now always restrained by the dignity of the House.'

It is tempting to see this pledge to maintain 'the dignity of the House' rather than 'letting himself go' in debate like Bevan, Wilson and Benn as a retrospective attempt to justify being outshone in their different ways by all three. It's also an insight into an ultimately conservative mindset where commitment to an intangible ideal (the dignity of the House) becomes more important than a commitment to real and radical change. And thirdly, it could be seen as a way of kicking back against the communist influence he had been subject to in the realisation that it was not conducive to career advancement.

Years later he spoke to his friend, the Tory MP Patrick Cormack, about his involvement with Labour's hard left. Cormack said: "He did talk about this. I knew about Zilliacus. I didn't know about the embassies controlling things. But he did say these are dangerous and sinister people."

By the time he spoke to Cormack about his involvement with the hard left, many years had passed. It certainly wasn't in his interest to admit he'd been a willing fellow traveller. That would certainly have damaged his prospects of becoming Speaker.

5

Years of Frustration

After Labour's general election defeat in October 1951, George Thomas and his party colleagues were condemned to 13 years in opposition. He spent his time establishing himself as a mainstream politician who could one day hold ministerial office.

On St. David's Day, March 1, in 1954 the United States detonated its first hydrogen bomb at Bikini Atoll in what is now the Pacific nation of Marshall Islands. The 15 megaton nuclear explosion was about 1,000 times more powerful than the atomic bombs dropped on Hiroshima and Nagasaki in 1945. Thomas was, he wrote, 'deeply shocked' and attended a meeting organised by the veteran Labour MP Fenner Brockway in a Commons committee room. It was effectively the launch of the Campaign for Nuclear Disarmament, which, as he put it in his memoirs, 'in a way I helped to form'.

Together with a number of other Labour MPs including Fenner Brockway, Tony Greenwood and Tony Benn, Thomas advertised the formal launch of CND at a rally in the Royal Albert Hall by walking with sandwich boards from Victoria Station to Piccadilly via Westminster. The police insisted the marchers could not walk together and had to be 400 yards apart. As he walked alone, Thomas was persistently barracked by a large clergyman crammed into a small car who made comments like: "Go back to Russia, you communist".

Eventually Thomas shouted back: "If you don't go away, I'll lift this board and bring it down on your head." The clergyman responded: "There! I knew you were all men of violence inside."

Rather oddly, perhaps – though maybe in keeping with his wish to move away from his reputation as a left-wing maverick – Thomas decided not to join CND, but said he was always proud of having taken part in the walk.

The passing by the Conservative government of the Landlord and Tenant Act in 1954 was a blow to Thomas, because it failed to confer on leaseholders the right to buy the freehold of their homes. Months later he won a ballot to introduce a Private Member's Bill that would have given them the choice of renewing their leases or buying the freehold at a reasonable rate. But while the Bill got its second reading with a comfortable majority, there weren't enough MPs present on the Friday it was debated for it to go forward.

During the debate on his Bill, Thomas read out a letter he had received from an elderly leaseholder in Newport. She wrote: 'The lease of my house expires in 18 months and I am being asked £750 and all legal charges for the freehold. I pay three guineas (£3.15) per year ground rent. They therefore want 200 years' purchase price for me to have the freehold. I am a widow and have lived in this house 58 years.'

Thomas told those of his fellow MPs who were present: "There is something immoral and cruel about a system which allows an elderly person like that to be robbed of her home."

When Churchill stepped down as Prime Minister in April 1955 at the age of 80, Anthony Eden was appointed to succeed him. He called a general election for a month later.

The top policy commitment in Thomas' election address related to peace and disarmament. It read: : 'The menace of the H-bomb can only be removed by world disarmament which covers all kinds of weapons', adding in a personal statement:

'The leadership of Clem Attlee on this question has stirred the nation. The Conservatives are apathetic on the moral issues at stake. We call for the cessation of all further tests and experiments with the H-bomb.'

It also included a personal message from his Mam, which said: 'My son George is known to you all. No-one knows better than I do the care and the anxiety with which he fights for those who seek help. He brings his Christian faith to his public work. His entire life is given in service to other people. He is a man of principle. I urge you to vote for him because I know he will never let you down.'

By this time Thomas had moved Mam into a bungalow he shared with her in King George V Drive, Cardiff, overlooking Heath Park.

Attlee resigned as Labour leader after the 1955 general election, which saw the Conservatives increase their majority. There were three candidates to succeed Attlee: Herbert Morrison, Hugh Gaitskell and Aneurin Bevan. Thomas voted for Bevan, although he kept his vote secret at the time. The election was won by Gaitskell.

In 1956 Thomas was invited by the State Department to tour the United States. He decided to go for several months, during which he preached in every state except Florida.

In 1958 the Welsh Grand Committee was established, with Thomas as its first chairman. Essentially a talking shop with no policy making role, it provided a locus for MPs to debate Welsh issues.

Membership of the Commonwealth Parliamentary Association allows MPs to visit exotic parts of the world on the pretext of meeting politicians from other countries. In 1959 Thomas travelled under the auspices of the CPA to Kenya and the Seychelles with Paul Williams, the right wing Conservative

MP for Sunderland South who supported the white regimes in South Africa and what was then Rhodesia.

Thomas says that before undertaking the journey, Jim Callaghan, who was the Shadow Colonial Secretary, asked him not to ask to meet Jomo Kenyatta, the imprisoned black opposition leader. Callaghan told him such a request would not go down well with Kenya's whites, who held Kenyatta responsible for killings associated with the Mau Mau rebellion against British rule. In fact Kenyatta was not associated with, and had condemned, the Mau Mau campaign.

During a meeting with members of the white community, the chairman launched a verbal attack on Labour MP John Stonehouse, who had been declared a prohibited visitor in neighbouring Uganda after upsetting its whites. Thomas said he was not going to listen to such an attack on a parliamentary colleague, and both he and Williams walked out. As they walked towards their car, four sturdy young men ran towards them, and they thought they were going to be attacked. In fact the men wanted to press the white community's argument that Kenya should not be granted independence. For Thomas, the incident illustrated the tensions that existed as independence became increasingly inevitable.

The true gravity of the situation became clear when 11 black prisoners were beaten to death at the Hola detention camp in south east Kenya. Around 60 surviving prisoners suffered serious permanent injuries. The detainees, who were regarded as the most hard line Mau Mau prisoners were attacked by the guards after refusing to bend when they undertook manual labour as part of the punitive regime they were subjected to.

Thomas and Williams insisted on flying down to see what conditions at the camp were like. Thomas wrote: 'We were led in front of cages in which Africans were locked like animals in a zoo. One of the prisoners was stark naked, and kept making faces at us, and I was told he was mad.'

Thomas told the guard that if the detainee was mad, he should be in a hospital rather than a prison. He got no response from the guard other than 'a baleful stare'.

The atmosphere at Hola camp was frightening, said Thomas, with hatred filling the air and the temperature at 110 degrees Fahrenheit. Thomas said he was shocked by 'such stupid brutalities' committed by the British, adding: 'Anxiety about our reaction to what we had seen made the prison authorities ultra cautious in the conference that followed our visit'.

Despite expressing strong disapproval of the killings at Hola and the conditions under which the surviving prisoners were detained, Thomas did not appear to see the events in the wider context of colonial oppression.

As pointed out by Mark Curtis in *Web of Deceit*, a book in which he exposes Britain's deadly and duplicitous role in international affairs in the post-war period, the murders at Hola stemmed from a policy aimed at crushing Kenya's independence movement and maintaining white power. Four years before Thomas' visit, another Labour MP – Barbara Castle – had written an investigation report on what was happening in Kenya in which she stated: 'In the heart of the British Empire there is a police state where the rule of law has broken down, where murder and torture of Africans go unpunished and where the authorities pledged to enforce justice regularly connive at its violation.'

In fact, British repression had forced 90,000 Kikuyu Kenyans into detention camps like Hola surrounded by barbed wire and troops where they were subjected to forced labour.

Thomas, however, seemed more impressed by a visit to a graveyard in a Methodist missionary centre near Mombasa where six British missionaries were buried. Some had been murdered, while some succumbed to tropical disease. All were in their early 20s, and had travelled to Kenya from London in turn to succeed their dead immediate predecessor. Thomas commented: 'In the judgement of some people, these young men were wasted; but the strong Church in Kenya is lasting evidence of their success.'

The long years spent in opposition were a frustration for Thomas, who took consolation in the Methodist Church, preaching across Britain in nearly every city during the late 1950s and early 1960s. In a TV discussion with Rhondda West Labour MP Iorwerth Thomas, he reasserted his opposition to pubs being allowed to open on Sundays. Thomas wrote: 'My view was, and is, that anything that undermines respect for Sunday as our Sabbath Day undermines respect for Christian teaching.'

It wasn't the first time Thomas had pressed the case for keeping Sunday as a religious day. In 1951 he had openly criticised plans to open Battersea Fun Fair on Sundays during the Festival of Britain. Claiming that people from Scotland, Wales, Northern Ireland and Cornwall opposed Sunday opening, he personalised his attack on Herbert Morrison, the Deputy Prime Minister who oversaw the Festival, telling MPs: "My right honourable friend is sometimes described as a little Englander. He is not so, Mr. Speaker, he is a little Londoner, who does not appreciate the convictions of those who live elsewhere." Morrison subsequently wrote to Thomas, saying he would never come to Cardiff to speak again.

In July 1959 Thomas became vice president of the Methodist Conference, the first time an MP had held such a senior post in the Church. Shortly afterwards he went to a conference of the World Methodist Council at its headquarters in Lake Junaluska, North Carolina, before embarking on another preaching tour of the United States. In Georgia he encountered a problem when he found himself due to preach in a whites-only church. He agreed to preach at the church on condition that he could preach in another church on the same day that catered for black worshippers. He thought it inappropriate to denounce segregation from the pulpit of the whites-only church, but when accosted by a congregation member who said: "So you're another one-worlder", Thomas responded: "That's right sir. How many worlds do you believe in?" He was moved by his reception at the black community's church, where the minister said: "We are greatly honoured tonight to welcome Mr. George Thomas, a British Member of Parliament who is also a Methodist like us. His face is white, but his heart is as black as ours." Thomas said he never forgot the tribute.

George Thomas had a strong personal dislike for Hugh Gaitskell, and gave vent to this in his memoirs when writing about the 1959 general election which resulted in an increased Conservative majority. He wrote: 'Nowadays [his book was published in 1985] Hugh Gaitskell is being increasingly presented as a moderate man, but in fact he was anything but moderate. He stood way to the right of the Party, and could not be bothered with anyone who did not share his own views. In the members' tea-room he would sit only with his cronies, making it clear to everyone that he was content to lead a divided Party as long as his supporters were in the majority.'

He complained about Gaitskell coming to Cardiff to support Callaghan without notifying him (Thomas) in advance. Thomas had read about the visit in the Cardiff newspapers. When he was phoned by the Labour Party's organiser in Wales, Cliff Prothero, and asked to attend a press conference with Gaitskell at Transport House in Cardiff, he was inclined to refuse, partly through pique at Gaitskell's discourtesy in not telling him of his visit, and partly out of his sense that the party leader 'only wanted to lead half the Labour Party'.

After being begged by Prothero to change his mind, he agreed, but turned up late after holding a constituency surgery. In a conciliatory gesture, Gaitskell put his arm round Thomas and asked him to accompany him on a walk down Queen Street, one of Cardiff's main shopping streets. Angrily, Thomas responded: "I've seen you and Jim several times this week, and neither of you told me you were coming. If you want to lead half the Party, you lead it, but I'm not going to make it any easier for you."

The death of Nye Bevan in July 1960 confirmed Thomas in his view that Labour would never regain power under Gaitskell. The party was as divided as ever and Anthony Greenwood announced his decision to challenge Gaitskell for the leadership. This prompted Harold Wilson, now seen as the leader of the Bevanites, to come forward and stand himself. Greenwood withdrew. In the election Gaitskell won a comfortable victory among the MPs by 166 votes to 81, but with most Welsh Labour MPs backing Wilson.

Wilson was at first kept on as Shadow Chancellor, but later was shifted by Gaitskell to the role of Shadow Foreign Secretary. He was resentful of the move at first, but Thomas took the view it was the best thing that could have happened to Wilson, who shadowed Ted Heath as he conducted Common Market negotiations. Thomas, never a supporter of what was known at the time as the European Economic Community, made his views clear: 'At that time, Labour still had grave reservations about joining the EEC, doubts which I wholeheartedly shared. I was always a great supporter of the Commonwealth, and believed the Common Market could do it nothing but harm.'

Thomas made another push for leasehold reform, organising a petition and collecting signatures on five successive Saturdays at a table erected outside the St. Mary Street entrance to Cardiff market. People queued in their hundreds to sign, and the petition attracted the support of significant figures like the Archbishop of Wales.

Thomas deposited the petition, with more than 60,000 signatures, in a green bag behind the Speaker's chair. He was cheered by both sides of the House as he did so. Within a few days he was invited to meet Dr. Charles Hill, the former wartime 'Radio Doctor' who was Minister for Local Government and Welsh Affairs, and later became chairman of the BBC. Hill wanted to know what terms Thomas would agree to. When the latter insisted that leaseholders must be allowed to buy the freehold even against the landlord's wishes, Hill responded: 'You know this Tory government will never agree to that. Be reasonable, George, and settle for half a loaf now.' Agreeing there was no common ground between them, Thomas came to the conclusion that leasehold reform would have to await the election of a Labour government.

When he raised a motion on leasehold reform in the Commons in July 1961, Thomas used language that any Welsh nationalist would have approved of. He told MPs: "The Welsh national anthem begins with the words, *Mae hen wlad fy nhadau yn annwyl i mi* (The land of my fathers is dear to me). We ask the Government to accept the motion so that the land of Wales can belong to the Welsh people and not to finance corporations as at present."

Sir Reginald Manningham-Buller, the Attorney General, praised Thomas' "eloquence and charm", but said the motion "would give compulsory powers to private individuals, which is something that the House should be very reluctant to do".

Although the motion was rejected by 245 votes to 179, Welsh members voted overwhelmingly in favour of it.

The unexpected death of Gaitskell in January 1963 led to another party leadership election in which Thomas backed Wilson, the candidate of the left. The support of right wing

Labour MPs was divided between George Brown and Jim Callaghan. Supporting a candidate other than his Cardiff neighbour was 'embarrassing', according to Thomas, but he consoled himself by knowing where his duty lay.

Unproven stories damaging to the candidates proliferated during the leadership campaign. Thomas wrote a passage in his memoirs that in hindsight has additional resonances relating to himself: 'I never cease to marvel that whenever there is a major election amongst MPs, even the wildest rumours are repeated as though the gossips had proof of what they were saying. With their experience of the sorts of tales that are spread during dirty campaigns in general elections, it staggers me that MPs should either stoop to similar tactics themselves or take notice of the unscrupulous attempts at character assassination they hear. But they do.'

Thomas was approached in the members' tea-room by Percy Holman, a Labour MP from the right of the party who said it was strange that Harold Wilson's wife Mary was never seen with him and touched on rumours relating to his private secretary Marcia Williams, later Lady Falkender.

When Thomas mentioned the conversation to Wilson, he said Mary was very shy and did not like mixing in crowds. Wilson told him: "When Mary hears this, she will come with me tomorrow to the Abbey for Hugh Gaitskell's memorial service." According to Thomas, Mary Wilson conquered her shyness as a direct consequence of this incident and subsequently played a more significant part in Wilson's public life.

During the leadership campaign, Thomas was contacted by Callaghan, who wanted help with a sermon he was writing for delivery at Splott Baptist Church in his constituency. Thomas felt uncomfortable because Callaghan was not a preacher. Thomas met Callaghan at the Royal Hotel in Cardiff, where he was staying. Callaghan, as the Shadow Colonial Secretary, said the theme of his sermon would be brotherhood. He then asked Thomas to pray with him, and they knelt down to do so. Thomas prayed that they should be given strength and guidance to be worthy of their roles as MPs.

When they stood up – according to Thomas' account – Callaghan said he hoped he could rely on Thomas' support in the leadership election. Even after Thomas responded that he was already committed to supporting Wilson, Callaghan persisted, pointing out that they had been colleagues for nearly 20 years and saying he thought he could be sure of Thomas' vote. Not wanting to quarrel, and so he could leave, Thomas said he would consider his position over the weekend.

On the Monday morning, Harold Wilson drew Thomas' attention to a piece in *The Times* which said Thomas was switching his support from Wilson to Callaghan. Angered, Thomas called the editor of the *South Wales Echo* and made it clear he was supporting Wilson. An article appeared under the headline 'Cardiff MPs Divided'.

Callaghan came third in the poll and many of his supporters decided to back Wilson rather than Brown. After Wilson's victory, a new mood of optimism permeated the Labour Party. But if Thomas expected to get a front-bench role following his support for Wilson, he was disappointed. To underline his wish to bring both parts of the party together, Wilson appointed many from Gaitskell's camp to senior positions. Just before the general election, Labour's Chief Whip Herbert Bowden had a meeting with Thomas at which he said Thomas would be appointed Chairman of Ways and Means and Deputy Speaker if Labour won. Thomas declared himself delighted, but Bowden said if Labour's majority was very small, he couldn't be spared for such a non-voting role and the job would have to go to a Tory.

When Labour won the election with a majority of just

five, Thomas told his Cardiff West supporters he would be a backbencher again.

In August 1963 Thomas received a rather odd letter sent to his home in King George V Drive East from a Cardiff builder called Walter David Blakeman whose firm was called WD Blakeman and Co. Accompanying the letter was a document setting out details of a proposed housing development for people on lower incomes that the company was proposing to Cardiff City Council. The description of the scheme said hundreds of two- or three-bedroom houses could be built and sold for £2,200 each – less than the market price of between £2,500 and £2,700. It said: 'The company's proposed development may be adapted to almost any site in the city, either single blocks of various lengths or in complete streets or roads as required ... Lettings can be available subject to satisfactory negotiation with building societies. We have interviewed a great number of would-be purchasers and in all cases have been met with great enthusiasm. Applications for mortgages from Cardiff City Council and private societies would be subject to their approval.'

One example proposed by Blakeman was for 600 three-bedroom homes, a further 100 two-bedroom homes and five blocks of flats to be built in the adjacent districts of Grangetown and Riverside with revenue totally £1,397,200.

Such a scheme seemed unobjectionable in principle. What was strange was the letter to Thomas which accompanied it. It read: 'Dear Sir, We would be most grateful for an opportunity to discuss the enclosed scheme with a Labour member, and if possible for the members of the company to join the Labour Party. The scheme is in the hands of the City Housing Manager, and it will be seen that only the best materials and workmanship are to be used.'

For a developer who wants planning permission to write to a

Labour MP at his home enclosing details of a proposed housing development and suggesting that he wants to join the party is at least suspicious and raises concerns about an improper motive.

Thomas kept a copy of the city council minutes which showed that three months later another Blakeman scheme involving the building of new homes in Pentrebane and Trowbridge, different districts of the city, was approved.

By this time Thomas was a significant celebrity, and a letter dated November 29, 1963, informed him: 'The National Portrait Gallery have the honour of informing Mr. George Thomas that it is their wish to include his photograph in the National Record of Distinguished Persons. He is to give a sitting to Mr. Walter Bird.' Bird was the official photographer for the National Photographic Record, initiated by the National Portrait Gallery in 1917.

Thomas' 1964 general election leaflet contained the usual message from Mam. On this occasion she said: 'Dear Friends, During the years that my son George Thomas has represented you in Parliament, I have watched him give his whole life to public service. No-one knows better than I do the care and the anxiety with which he fights for those who seek his help. Whether he is sharing in the life of a youth club or relaxing in the fellowship of a pensioners' meeting or whether he is entering into some other activity in the constituency, he always has the same deep concern for people. I know that he will not let you down.'

At the beginning of the election campaign Thomas wrote a letter to Harold Wilson expressing concern at the possibility that an incoming Labour Education Minister might scrap the obligation on schools to provide Christian education. Wilson responded: 'Dear George, Very many thanks to you (and Mam) for your good wishes at the beginning of the campaign. For good measure I am beginning the election campaign as I began a year last February – in Cardiff – so I hope to be seeing you. I am glad the mood in Cardiff is so good and that our leasehold policy has been so effective. Re the rumour about Minister of Education. First, I do not know who I will be appointing, we have got to win first, but, secondly, there will be no question of a change about religious instruction.'

6

Junior Minister

It was Jim Callaghan who rang George Thomas on the Sunday after the 1964 general election to tell him he was to get a ministerial appointment, although the new Chancellor said it was up to Harold Wilson to let him know the details.

After being teased by Wilson about the job he was to be offered, saying it required humanity and compassion, Thomas wrongly guessed that it involved National Insurance or the health service. In fact he was being appointed Parliamentary Under-Secretary of State at the Home Office, with responsibility for immigration.

The Home Secretary was Frank Soskice, a lawyer who represented Newport in south Wales. He held reactionary views on race and immigration, and was not comfortable with the pressure exerted on him by the Parliamentary Labour Party to introduce legislation making it an offence to discriminate against anyone on the grounds of race. This was rather strange, given that Labour candidates had stood on a manifesto – titled *The New Britain* – that included a commitment to make racial discrimination illegal. But the party was not in favour of a wholly open-door immigration policy, and the manifesto also stated: 'Labour accepts that the number of immigrants entering the UK must be limited.'

At a conference in the Home Office where some of those present advocated easing immigration controls, Soskice said:

"If we do not have strict immigration controls, our people will soon all be coffee-coloured." Thomas said his protests were brushed aside.

Nevertheless, showing there were limits to his own progressive outlook, Thomas endorsed another of Soskice's positions, writing: 'As for legislation against racial discrimination, Frank would have none of it. He thought such legislation would add to our problems, and in that I agreed with him.'

As well as immigration, Thomas was responsible for the police, drink, gambling and Sunday observance. His remit also extended to the nationalised brewery at Carlisle – a facet of his portfolio he didn't dare disclose to Mam.

Throughout his parliamentary career, he sought strict controls over gambling and the sale of alcohol, as well as being one of the strongest supporters of Sunday observance. One day, while he was in the members' tea-room, Harold Wilson came up to him and said: "Is it true that you are responsible for drink, gambling and Sunday observance?" When Thomas answered in the affirmative, Wilson raised both hands above his head and said: "Heaven help us! We face enough troubles without that."

Thomas said it was immigration that caused him more heartache than anything else as a Home Office minister. It made him feel 'ill with worry' when he had to order 'some poor man' back to his own country. On one occasion a man being sent back to Africa from Heathrow committed suicide by cutting his throat as the aircraft flew over Rome. Thomas noted that it was an immigration officer, rather than himself, who had made that deportation decision.

In 1965 he wrote a personal note railing against gambling clubs and casinos: 'It would be fair to say that when the Government made gambling clubs legal in the Act of 1960, it could not have been foreseen that in so short a time they would have become a scourge and a real black spot in our social system. In fact, many of Britain's gambling clubs are "places of evil" where all kinds of illegal practices are carried out.'

Thomas thought it was wrong that clubs were allowed to advertise and saw the rules of roulette as loaded against gamblers: 'When a ball lands in a zero hole on a roulette wheel, all bets are invalid and the punters lose their money ... Another aspect of the conduct of certain clubs which is very disturbing is that of engaging 'hostesses' whose purpose is to 'pick up' men and bring them to the club. Usually such men are from out of town and the hostesses receive from the management a 'cut' in respect of losses incurred by any man they bring along.'

In March 1966, with Ted Heath now leading the Conservative Party, Wilson called a general election. Wilson's purpose in calling the election was to secure the healthy majority that had been unattainable in 1964.

Mam, whose health was declining, wrote her now customary message in Thomas' election address, saying: 'This is the first general election in which I shall not be able to accompany George to his meetings. I send you all my greetings and my heartfelt thanks for your concern in my illness. My son George has dedicated his whole life to public service. He has never spared himself in trying to help those who seek his aid. Whatever he undertakes to do, he never fails to remember that people matter. I know that in his work as a Home Office Minister he has tried to bring compassion and care to every case. He will never let you down.'

A slogan on the leaflet described Thomas as 'The progressive Labour candidate who has devoted his life not only to this division but to mankind as a whole.'

On the eve of polling day, Thomas had his customary lunch with Jim Callaghan, who told him he would be promoted after the election. The swing to Labour was greater than expected, and the party ended up with an overall majority of 110.

Callaghan was well-informed and Thomas was appointed Minister of State at the Welsh Office, which had been set up after the 1964 election. Thomas did not approve of this, writing: 'I soon discovered that the department's major preoccupation was to look for issues that we could say were specifically Welsh. By setting up the office, the Labour government had opened the floodgates for nationalism.'

Cledwyn Hughes was the Secretary of State, and Thomas wrote: '[His] nationalist fervour led to periodical tensions between us. Despite a genuine pride in my Welsh heritage, and my eagerness to advance Welsh culture, I have never believed in Welsh nationalism.'

He said his mother had nurtured in him a deep affection for her parents' home counties, Somerset and Hampshire, and 'the anti-English sentiment always just beneath the surface in Welsh-speaking areas jars on me ... Anyone listening to my strong Welsh accent could be forgiven for assuming my attitudes would always reflect the views of the Welsh establishment. It was often resented when people discovered that this was not so.'

Describing the contrast between Welsh-speaking and non-Welsh-speaking Wales at the time, he wrote: '[The] Welsh language was very much in decline. Industrial south Wales was almost entirely English-speaking, for in the counties of Glamorgan and Monmouthshire most people have English or Irish as well as Welsh blood in their veins. Three quarters of the population of Wales live in these two counties and it is a fact of life that English is their first language ... In reality, there are two separate populations in Wales: the vast majority in the English-speaking areas, and the small Welsh-speaking minority, who are widely scattered over the rural areas.'

Thomas could hardly have been clearer. So far as he was concerned, his priority was to look after the majority of the population who could not speak Welsh. He regarded the minority of Welsh speakers as a troublesome group who were anti-English and should be given no quarter.

Despite being a Welsh Office Minister, Thomas expressed his contempt for a Welsh Language Bill that originated in the House of Lords and was taken forward by Cledwyn Hughes, the Secretary of State himself, in the Commons. The Bill, which Thomas said had been 'inherited' by Hughes from the first Welsh Secretary Jim Griffiths, had just two clauses – the first allowing people to give evidence in courts in Welsh if they wanted to do so, and the second granting Ministers the discretion to introduce forms and official documents in the Welsh language.

Thomas, who erroneously stated in his memoirs that the Bill was enacted in 1966 when it was in 1967, said: '[Within] months of the measure receiving the Royal Assent, its weakness was exposed. The Welsh Language Society understandably seized with both hands the stick given to them to knock the Government. Every department in Whitehall was subjected to demands for bilingual publication of its documents. Local government came under the same pressure. Nothing had been done by the Welsh Office to pre-empt these demands, for the simple reason that no-one had given any real thought to how the Bill would work. Overnight, the Welsh language became a divisive issue.'

Thomas gave no credit at all to the motives of those who were promoting the Bill. In introducing the Bill to the House of Commons on July 17, 1967, Cledwyn Hughes set out the moral case on which it stood.

He said: "The Welsh Language Bill honours the pledge made in the Welsh Grand Committee on December 14, 1965, [by

Jim Griffiths] to introduce a Bill to remove the existing legal obstacles to the use of Welsh and to repeal or amend those Acts which at present prevent or limit its use. The Bill will do away with the remaining legacy of those legal restrictions in the fields of public administration which have beset the Welsh language since Tudor times ... The Act of 1536 passed by Henry VIII declared: 'henceforth no person or persons that use the Welsh speech or language shall have or enjoy any manner of office or fees within this realm of England, Wales or other of the King's Dominions upon pain of forfeiting the same offices or fees unless he or they use and exercise the speech or language of English.' That the language has survived despite such legislation and that it still shows such vigour over four centuries later are facts to ponder upon."

In his speech, Hughes quoted one made by Herbert Morrison, who as Home Secretary introduced the Welsh Courts Act 1942. Morrison told a wartime House of Commons: "The Tudors ... suffered from the mistakes of their age, and one was the belief that before we can have national unity we must have national uniformity ... I am all in favour of that national spirit which takes pride in its individuality, in its culture, its literature, but which is not so exclusive and intolerant as to require the repression of all other forms of language, literature and culture."

Hughes praised Morrison's words, stating: "I can only echo these sentiments and admire the faith in the future shown by Parliament at that time of crisis during the last war in devoting time to legislating about the rights of the oldest language in the UK."

The 1967 Act extended the provision of the Welsh Courts Act, which had allowed individuals to give evidence in Welsh only if their English was inadequate, so that in future all who wanted to could use Welsh.

The other clause gave discretion to Ministers about what forms and documents should be produced in Welsh. Hughes made it clear that the legislation did not mean all documents should be available bilingually because of the cost that would be entailed. But George Thomas' friend Leo Abse made a speech in which resentment against the Welsh language shone through. He said: "Every man has his prejudice and I have mine; a certain diffidence towards the notion that it is irrevocable that language must be the depository and the sole means of containing the wisdom of nations."

Brushing aside Hughes' throwaway description of Welsh as 'the language of heaven', Abse said: "If we look at the myths of heaven, or of golden ages, there is one feature of these myths which is bound to be relevant when we are discussing a Bill of this kind. I was brought up ... to regard the number of languages which burden the world as a curse and not as a blessing, and there is the old story of the pride of man, symbolised in the Tower of Babel, which brought great vengeance upon those people replete with conceit. The great tower crumbled, and the men and women building it were lost in the confusion that resulted from the divisive consequence of so many languages."

There can be no doubt that Thomas approved of every word uttered by Abse. In retrospect it is quite extraordinary that a Minister in the Welsh Office had such a jaundiced view of an important piece of legislation promoted by his own department.

When it came to a proposal to shut the mine at Glyncorrwg, at the head of a long valley leading down to Port Talbot, the local community had Thomas' sympathy – not that he was in a position to help much in a practical sense. Decisions over the closing of pits were handled by the Department of Fuel and Power, although the Welsh Office had a right to express its view before decisions were taken. Strangely enough the local MP, John Morris, later Secretary of State for Wales and Attorney General, was Parliamentary Secretary for Fuel and Power, although under parliamentary protocol he would not have been allowed to participate in a decision affecting a mine in his own constituency.

Thomas made representations to Lord Robens, chairman of the National Coal Board, who disappointed him deeply by his attitude and his refusal to give the pit a reprieve: 'Over the years he had proved to be a compassionate and kindly man, but at the Coal Board that side of his nature was not evident,' wrote Thomas.

There was, however, something for the Cardiff West MP to celebrate. Tony Greenwood, the Minister for Housing and Local Government, introduced a Leasehold Reform Bill along the lines advocated by Thomas for many years. It was on the statute book by autumn 1967 and leaseholders were at long last able to buy the freehold of their homes.

7

The Betrayal of Aberfan

George Thomas' role in one of the most shocking disasters ever seen in Wales was both inglorious and disgraceful – although he did not recognise that himself.

The deaths of 116 children and 28 adults at Aberfan when a colliery spoil tip collapsed on to the village primary school were caused by extreme negligence on the part of the state-owned National Coal Board. The Aberfan disaster, which happened on October 21, 1966, was not just the single most appalling event in modern Welsh history. What happened also represented a multiple betrayal of a whole community.

If the tragedy had been the result of a tragic and unavoidable accident due to natural forces – what insurance companies refer to as an Act of God – it would still have been profoundly shocking. But the criminal negligence of the National Coal Board (NCB) in failing to remove the tip that collapsed, coupled with the callous post-disaster treatment of the community by political leaders, made the loss of life even more heartrending.

Unlike the Hillsborough disaster or miscarriage of justice cases that took years of persistent campaigning before the truth was recognised, the negligent conduct of the NCB was quickly exposed. When he was appointed to chair the tribunal inquiry that investigated the disaster, Lord Justice Edmund Davies stressed that he would not be party to a whitewash – and he was true to his word.

The inquiry report made it clear where responsibility lay. It said: 'Blame for the disaster rests upon the NCB. This blame is shared (though in varying degrees) among the NCB headquarters, the South Western Divisional Board, and certain individuals. There was a total absence of tipping policy and this was the basic cause of the disaster. In this respect, however, the NCB were following in the footsteps of their predecessors. They were not guided either by Her Majesty's Inspectorate of Mines and Quarries or by legislation. There is no legislation dealing with the safety of tips in force in this or any country, except in parts of West Germany and in South Africa. The legal liability of the NCB to pay compensation for the personal injuries (fatal or otherwise) and damage to property is incontestable and uncontested.'

But what made the negligence even worse is that from the time the tips began to accumulate there were compelling signs that they posed a significant danger.

Complaints were made to the NCB by local residents and by the local Merthyr Tydfil Borough Council more than three years before the disaster, yet remedial action was not taken.

The negligence went further, with evidence of earlier problems emerging both during the course of the tribunal inquiry and later.

Some 30 years after the disaster, in 1996, a paper written for the *Quarterly Journal of Engineering Geology* called 'Rapid failures of colliery spoil heaps in the South Wales Coalfield' identified 21 significant incidents over a period of 67 years to 1965. The earliest incident – reported in the *Western Mail* at the time – occurred on November 3, 1898, when five houses were demolished in Bailey Street, Wattstown, Rhondda, below the National Colliery tip.

The tip slide happened at 1am, when residents were woken by its noise. The flow of mine waste was halted temporarily by a high retaining wall, but within a couple of minutes the wall gave way, and with a tremendous roar the huge mass rushed on to the houses. The residents just managed to escape, but domestic animals and possessions had to be left behind.

With all these precedents, it's difficult to explain the inertia that seemed endemic in the NCB when it came to the overriding need to safeguard the lives of people living and working beneath the tips. Perhaps the number of incidents coupled with the lack of fatalities engendered complacency.

Such negligence that led to the loss of so many lives is impossible to excuse. It would have been unforgivable if the Aberfan disaster had occurred at a time when the collieries were privately owned, and decisions not to remove the tips were taken for cost-cutting reasons. But that wasn't the case.

The tips were the responsibility of a nationalised industry which was supposed to be dedicated to the collective good in mining communities which themselves were founded on the finest of humane principles. In betraying the people of Aberfan, whose lives were cruelly dismissed as insignificant and unworthy of protection, the NCB also trashed the ideal of social solidarity on which the common ownership of the mining industry was built. But if the criminal negligence that led to the Aberfan disaster betrayed the whole community, the aftermath compounded the betrayal. Not only did the bereaved have to cope with the knowledge that no-one received the slightest punishment for the 144 deaths, but an appeal fund for the villagers was plundered so what remained of the lethal tip could be removed.

Although the inquiry report laid the blame for the disaster squarely with the National Coal Board (NCB), no NCB employee or board member was demoted, dismissed, or prosecuted, nor did the board face any corporate sanctions after the disaster.

There was no prosecution either for manslaughter or for any regulatory offence.

Lord Robens, the former Labour Minister who chaired the NCB, remained in post. For public consumption he offered his resignation, but papers released decades later showed this was a sham and that he'd been assured his job was safe. Incredibly he was subsequently appointed to chair a committee that made recommendations to the Government about health and safety legislation.

It's difficult to understand why nobody, including Robens, was held to account for the NCB's negligence at Aberfan. Perhaps the best explanation has been offered by Professor Iain McLean of Nuffield College, Oxford, whose tenacious research threw light on many aspects of what happened.

He wrote: 'The NCB and its senior officers escaped scot-free because the governments of the late 1960s and early 1970s needed their help in the 'high politics' of running down the coal industry without provoking a national strike. There was no concept of 'making the polluter pay' in British public administration at the time, and a nationalised industry was treated as if it were a government department. Therefore, policymakers thought that it would be futile to make the NCB pay the environmental (or even the direct) costs of the disaster, as such a payment would merely increase its deficit, which fell to be funded out of general taxation in any case.'

At a political level, too, there was a wholly inadequate response.

Successively Minister of State and Secretary of State for Wales, George Thomas' chapter on Aberfan is the shortest in his memoirs. He sought to portray himself as a man of compassion and empathy, but when it came to the crucial issue of making the community safe for the future, he sided with those who wanted to betray Aberfan again.

Within an hour of the spoil tip's collapse, Merthyr Tydfil's Town Clerk was on the phone to Thomas in his office at Cardiff. Within another hour Thomas was in Aberfan, helping the Town Clerk and the Chief Constable plan relief work. Miners and other local people were digging frantically to see if anyone could be found alive, but the news was desperately grim.

Cledwyn Hughes, Secretary of State for Wales at the time of the disaster, arrived by helicopter from north Wales at tea time, and Prime Minister Harold Wilson came later to Merthyr Town Hall, where he said all government agencies and the armed forces would be deployed if they were needed. In a characteristic display of one-upmanship, Thomas made the point in his autobiography that while Hughes went to spend the night at the Llantwit Major home of Welsh Office Permanent Secretary Goronwy Daniel, he, as a valleys man, could not bear to leave Aberfan that night. He rang Mam to say he would not be coming home to the bungalow they shared in Cardiff.

Thomas visited grieving relatives in their homes – everyone was in deep grief. At 2am he was requested to return to the police station at Merthyr, where the Chief Constable told him Lord Snowdon, the Queen's brother-in-law, would soon be arriving. At first Thomas and Snowdon went to the Bethany Chapel, where the bodies of the dead were being laid out. Three surviving teachers were putting name tags on the children's bodies so their parents could be taken straight to them. Snowdon asked who else was working in the chapel and was told members of the Red Cross and the Salvation Army were there. He said: "If they can undertake that job, I can go in to thank them."

Afterwards they went to the site of the disaster, moving between more bodies that were waiting to be identified by a teacher before being taken to the chapel to have their faces and hands washed.

Thomas and Snowdon then went to visit the homes of the bereaved. In the first house, a pregnant mother and her husband were awaiting news of their daughter, who was under the rubble. The father, feeling the need to say and do something, asked: "Will you have a cup of tea?" Snowdon chipped in, saying: "Yes, I would like a cup of tea, and the Minister can do with one also." As the young miner moved towards the kitchen, Snowdon pushed forward, saying: "Let me do it. I'm used to making tea."

When Snowdon returned with the tea, Thomas couldn't resist giving vent to his notorious royal sycophancy, saying: "Here is the Queen's brother-in-law waiting on us."

The mother looked Snowdon straight in the face and said: "How would you feel if your child was under the tip?" He responded: "That thought has been in my mind ever since I heard of the disaster. That is why I am here. I could not stay away."

Thomas spent three weeks after the funeral visiting the homes of each bereaved family.

In terms of the aftermath, Thomas wrote: 'The people of Aberfan were left not only with their unassuageable grief, but also with the threatening shadow of the remains of the tips that loomed above their village on the mountainside. Every time a shower of rain fell, their remaining children would be called indoors, or taken from their beds to huddle around the fire downstairs.'

The big issue was making the area safe, so that nothing similar could ever happen again. But who was to pay for that?

Thomas wrote: 'The fight to get the tip removed from the hillside above Aberfan continued bitterly and continuously for nearly three years and was to confront me very painfully when I became Secretary of State for Wales in 1968.'

He said he was advised 'by all the experts' – local authority engineers, National Coal Board (NCB) engineers and government engineers – that the tip was absolutely safe, and it was therefore unjustified to ask the taxpayer to pay £1m for its removal. Thomas went to the Treasury, had an argument, but failed to persuade them to change their minds. He described as 'a dreadful experience' his having to tell the people of Aberfan they mustn't worry about the tip because the experts said it was safe.

During a meeting at the Welsh Office in Cardiff, Alderman Tom Lewis – leader of the Aberfan delegation – stood up and said: "Secretary of State, I never thought to hear such words fall from George Thomas' lips. I thought you understood the problems of Aberfan. That tip is a nightmare for our people. You can say that it is safe, but we were told that before. Nothing could do as much for the peace of mind of Aberfan as moving that tip."

Others in the Aberfan delegation used less polite language, shouted and were very angry. Thomas promised to take the matter up in London.

He went straight to the station and got the next train. In his memoirs he said that when he got to his flat, he phoned Harold Wilson immediately, telling him that the tip had to be removed. Thomas went to 10 Downing Street and was present when Wilson rang Roy Jenkins, the Chancellor of the Exchequer. Within five minutes a formula was worked out according to which the Aberfan Fund – launched to help the bereaved families – would contribute £250,000 towards the cost of removing the tip. The NCB would contribute another £250,000 and the remaining £500,000 would be made up by the Government. Later the contribution required from the disaster fund was reduced to £150,000.

Thomas thought this was a good solution, but unsurprisingly it went down badly with the trustees of the Aberfan Fund. He wrote: 'I thought that all would be well, but I had a rough ride from some of them. I made it clear that I was not asking for a penny of the fund that had been contributed by the public but only for the interest that had accumulated. I withdrew to allow them time to consider the offer.'

His private secretary looked out of the window and told him that S.O. Davies, the Merthyr MP who had championed the rights of the villagers, walked out of the meeting – held by the trustees – to discuss the offer. Thomas wrote: 'It was the best sign so far, as it meant that the committee was moving my way. Throughout the controversy, Davies was determined that no contribution should be made from the fund.'

Shortly afterwards, agreement was reached on the terms Thomas put forward. He wrote: 'It was deeply satisfying for me when the Aberfan people held a dinner in celebration of the moving of the tip, and they made my mother and me the chief guests.'

Thomas was deluding himself. The members of the committee had only capitulated because they felt backed into a corner. They worried that unless they handed over the money demanded by Thomas, the tip would remain and pose a continuing threat to the community.

The Aberfan Fund had received donations from all over the world, raising £1.75m – a huge sum at the time. Villagers may have disagreed over how exactly it should be spent – whether it should be distributed to the families who had lost children or whether it should be used for community projects and a memorial – but all felt a sense of great injustice at the way they had been forced to pay towards the tip's removal. It was a profound insult to the memories of those who had died, and quickly a campaign began to get the money returned.

In her book *Aberfan*, school survivor Gaynor Madgwick tells how her father Cliff Minett, who lost two other children in the disaster, was arrested after displaying outside his bungalow a makeshift banner made of a bed sheet which read: 'Bereaved afraid to say anything about the fund'.

At the police station Minett was told by a police officer: "You are a troublemaker, you are. You are trespassing and causing trouble in Aberfan." He spent a night in the cells and was only released after it was established that he was campaigning at his own home.

It was 30 years before a new Labour Welsh Secretary, Ron Davies, returned the £150,000 to the fund and another decade before the Welsh Government gave the fund £2m, to make up for the lost interest. The campaign and the feeling of deep hurt that accompanied it – would not have been necessary if George Thomas had been more forceful in his representations to Harold Wilson about how plainly wrong it was to expect the Aberfan Fund to pay towards the tip removal. For Cliff Minett and many others, the demand for a contribution was no less than the biggest insult in political history.

8

At the Commonwealth Office

In June 1967 Thomas was transferred to the Commonwealth Office – at the time a separate department from the Foreign Office. He later described his brief stint as Minister of State there as the most exciting ministerial office he held.

In the role he acted as a kind of ministerial fireman, visiting Commonwealth heads of government to dampen down problems that had cropped up between them and the UK Government. His first involvement was with Ghana, where the nation's first post-independence president Kwame Nkrumah had been ousted the previous year by a military strongman, Lieutenant General Joseph Ankrah. Ankrah was unhappy at Britain's refusal to extradite a former Ghanaian High Commissioner accused of corruption. Roy Jenkins, the Home Secretary, was adamant that extradition couldn't happen for political reasons.

Harold Wilson told Thomas it would be possible for the ex-High Commissioner to be prosecuted in England. When Thomas met Ankrah in Ghana's capital Accra, the general launched into a tirade of abuse against the UK Government and Roy Jenkins in particular, accusing the latter of taking bribes to refuse the extradition order.

Thomas remonstrated, saying Jenkins was a pillar of rectitude. Ankrah carried on with the abuse, but calmed down when Thomas mentioned he was a Methodist and gave his word that the matter would get a proper hearing in Britain. It turned out that Ankrah had been educated by Methodist missionaries. The general insisted on sealing the deal with a glass of champagne – something Thomas claimed that in the circumstances he had no choice but to go along with, despite being teetotal. A civil servant sent a telegram report back to London which mentioned the champagne drunk by Thomas, and he was teased about it by Harold Wilson for months afterwards. The fact is, he wasn't teetotal at all, but felt it necessary to maintain the pretence that he was.

The next significant overseas trip undertaken by Thomas was to Nigeria, where the country was about to be torn apart by civil war prompted by a declaration of independence by the oil-rich eastern region, which called itself Biafra. Thomas met Nigeria's military leader Yakubu 'Jack' Gowon, who was anxious to buy 'planes and bombs' so he could end the civil war as quickly as possible. Thomas told him that while Britain's usual supplies of weapons and ammunition to Nigeria would continue, it was not regarded as acceptable to provide planes and bombs to be used against citizens of a Commonwealth country.

Gowon said that if he couldn't buy weapons from Britain, he would be forced to buy them from the communist bloc. But Thomas told him firmly that he couldn't get what he wanted from the UK Government, and this decision was ratified by the Cabinet after his return to London.

Years later, Thomas wrote that in retrospect he considered the decision wrong: 'Nigeria had relied on the UK for her arms and ammunition, and there seems no difference in moral principle between supplying bombs and cannon. The war would have ended much sooner if we had met Gowon's demands. A side issue was that we allowed the French ammunition industry to exploit our decision. They had no scruples in supplying arms both to Biafrans and to the Nigerian federal government.'

Thomas said that at the time he agonised over whether he should resign from the Government, feeling hypocritical as a pacifist for condoning the sale of arms of any sort. He claimed to have stayed on because he didn't want to provide a propaganda coup for the Biafrans. But he continued to question whether his failure to resign was motivated rather by a desire to stay in ministerial office.

The fact is that up to three million people died as a result of the civil war in Nigeria, with more than two million perishing from starvation due to the federal government's blockade. Thomas never faced up to his share of responsibility for what happened.

When his boss at the Commonwealth Office, Herbert Bowden, was on holiday in August 1967, a crisis occurred in Uganda over white people being beaten up by soldiers. President Milton Obote seemed indifferent to protests. Roland Hunt, the British High Commissioner in the country's capital Kampala, was angered to a new level when a white woman was made to get out of her car by soldiers and beaten with canes. He made a public protest. Obote was furious.

Thomas decided that Hunt should return to London for 'consultations', the usual way for governments to signal disapproval, with the official going back after a suitable interval. But Obote said he didn't want Hunt to return at all. Thomas went out to Uganda, armed with a suggestion from Harold Wilson that Hunt should return for one month to Kampala, after which he would be transferred elsewhere. To give himself negotiating room, Thomas increased the month to two months. After some brinkmanship, Obote settled for six weeks.

In Kenya, Thomas defused a row over financial matters

with the 'old and irritable' President Kenyatta by introducing himself as from Cardiff. Many years before, Kenyatta had lived for a period in Cardiff docks when only the Labour Party would have anything to do with him. He had much affection for the city, saying: "Those choirs ... and the cups of tea ... and the Welsh cakes!" The row between the two governments was quickly resolved.

Next stop was Malawi, where the veteran leader Hastings Banda lectured him on how Britain was 'very foolish' not to look after her own interests in Rhodesia – where the whites-only regime had declared its independence from the UK two years before – and how it should forget the 'clamour' about racial discrimination. Banda also thought that Britain should regard the *apartheid* regime in South Africa as a friend rather than as an enemy.

But although he liked Banda and respected his achievements in Malawi, Thomas didn't share his views on such matters. Apart from his principled objection to *apartheid*, he had been made aware of the pettiness of its application in practice. A black woman minister he had met in the company of the president of Botswana and his wife told Thomas how many black South Africans limped because they could not try on new shoes before they bought them. The same rule applied to other clothes like hats, and the woman told how she had been obliged to try on the hat while on the pavement outside a store rather than in the store itself.

When he visited South Africa, Thomas found that the British Ambassador was himself sympathetic to the *apartheid* regime. Arriving at Johannesburg Airport, Thomas and his Principal Private Secretary, Donald MacLeod, were met by the Third Secretary at the Embassy – a snub to a visiting minister in itself.

When they arrived at the mansion used as the Ambassador's

residence, there was little sign of life. Thomas came upon the Ambassador, Sir John Nicholson, and his wife drinking cocktails in the garden. Nicholson didn't bother to stand up to shake hands, and nodded towards a chair that Thomas could sit in. MacLeod had to find another chair for himself.

As they took their places for dinner, the Ambassador said: "You know, Minister, *apartheid* is not as bad in practice as it is in theory."

He repeated the comment after Thomas told him if that was how he felt, they were poles apart.

Silence ensued, and the Ambassador's wife said: "From what part of England do you come, Minister?" Thomas' curt response was: "I do not come from England."

MacLeod sought to defuse the situation by stating that Thomas came from Wales. "Oh, Wales!" said Lady Nicholson in a disparaging tone.

Back in London, Thomas told George Brown, the Foreign Secretary, that he didn't consider Nicholson a suitable person to represent the views of the British government. The Ambassador retired two years later.

During a trip to Pakistan, Thomas was charmed by the military dictator General Ayub Khan. He described him as 'a cultured man with a keen sense of humour that appealed to me, and I found it hard to remember that I was in a country where there was no democracy'.

In what was clearly a stage-managed series of visits, Thomas was flattered at being garlanded with flowers and regaled with 'stories of increased crops and improved drainage and water supply'. Moving on to India, he acknowledged that he had already 'fallen under the spell' of the Prime Minister, Indira Gandhi. He wrote: 'Her dark eyes seemed to carry the suffering of India's millions. Her femininity was expressed in her fantastic saris, and her passionate concern for the young.'

In Colombo, capital of Sri Lanka, a Buddhist priest's call to public service reminded Thomas of his chapel days in Tonypandy. He was thrilled when Colombo's Methodist Church was full when he preached a sermon based on the text 'Abide in me'.

Thomas' musings on his Commonwealth trips are those of a man who saw himself as the centre of attention. While his principled opposition to *apartheid* was commendable, he was too susceptible to flattery and seemed unable to comprehend the scale of the appalling tragedy that was unfolding in Nigeria.

9

Secretary of State for Wales

In April 1968 Thomas was summoned to see the Prime Minister: a Cabinet reshuffle was taking place.

So far as Thomas was concerned, he and Wilson had been friends since their first day in Parliament in 1945. But he knew that friendship was not the basis on which Prime Ministers choose Cabinet Ministers.

Wilson came straight to the point, telling him he was being appointed Secretary of State for Wales, that he was to be made a Privy Counsellor and that he would be a member of the Inner Cabinet. Thomas' new responsibilities did not prevent him from pressing causes that tied in with his religious beliefs. A month after being elevated to the Cabinet, he wrote to Harold Wilson to say: 'I am deeply concerned about the rumour that the Government proposes to give time for further discussion on the Sunday Entertainments Bill [which would have made it lawful to charge admission to shows and sporting fixtures on Sundays]. So far as Wales is concerned, this would be an act of political stupidity, difficult to exaggerate. It would present the Government as lining up with that small number in the House who are determined at all costs to change our Sunday. Several Welsh MPs have already made indignant proposals to me and we can expect an ugly reaction if, at any time when parliamentary business is severely crowded because the timetable is so full, we can find time for a measure of this sort.'

In June 1968 Thomas was made an Honorary Member of the Gorsedd of Bards – a strange accolade, perhaps, for someone whose approach to the Welsh language could be so hostile. Responding to a letter from Henry Edwards from Rhondda, Thomas set out his objection to Welsh nationalism: 'I see that I have aroused the wrath of the Welsh nationalists but this for me is encouraging for it is an indication that they are aware that I shall never be reluctant to enter into a fight with them. I am a firm believer in a unitary system of government for the United Kingdom and I regret the policy of hatred of the English so consistently advocated by the Welsh nationalists as a danger to our best interests.'

While Thomas became notorious for his sycophancy towards the Royal Family, he had many sycophants of his own. One, Ivor Jones of Cardiff, was in the city's St. David's Hospital when he heard he was to receive the British Empire Medal from Thomas. He wrote to Thomas in these terms: 'No finer person than George Thomas could have the honour of presenting this medal. Because you were my choice. I have followed your wonderful life and your good mother. Two marvellous people. It's quite an honour for me to have an eminent minister of the Government like you to do the presentation. Oh it's wonderful news. Your letter in hospital to me was just wonderful. I could not wish for a finer person than George Thomas for the presentation.' Sycophants aside, the Labour Party in Wales was not in good shape.

Gwynoro Jones was brought in by Jim Callaghan to be the party's research and public relations officer. Jones had also been selected to stand in Carmarthen at the next general election when he would be seeking to win the seat back from Plaid Cymru president, Gwynfor Evans, who had won it at a by-election in July 1966 to become the party's first MP. He said: "I had the shock of my life – how totally on its knees the

83

Welsh Labour Party was. One of the first things I decided to do was visit every constituency in Wales. I knew how to do it, because Carmarthen was on its knees after the by-election – literally decimated. There was no party. So we had to build it up from where it was in the past – there used to be a lot of branches, a lot of union branches, women's sections, and plenty of young socialists. All of this had been shattered by Gwynfor Evans' victory in the 1966 by-election. The same had happened to Labour in Wales because of further near defeats in the Rhondda and Caerphilly by-elections. I told Emrys Jones, the organiser, that I was going to go round every constituency. I went to every local executive committee: in the valley seats you'd be lucky to get four or five people turn up in places like Abertillery, Caerphilly, Rhondda. They ran their councils, but they didn't run their party.

"It transpired that part of the job was to propagate what the Labour government was doing. So it was agreed for me to meet George in his home every Sunday night at 8pm. George would give me the papers from the Welsh Office – whether he was allowed to I don't know – that I could use to turn it into a newsletter for the constituency parties and the members in Wales, and they would distribute it. Then very soon after that I created a newspaper called *The Radical*.

"When I saw George in action at that time, I thought, 'Hang on a minute this can't be normal'. His mother would be sitting in a corner and every time he got up to go and get something from his room – where the governmental papers were kept – he would kiss his mother. He'd walk over as he was going to the room. 'Oh Mam' he'd say, as he passed her. Then, as he came back, he'd say 'Mam', and kiss her again. Every time. He never missed it.

"He also had two big pictures of the Queen and Prince

Charles on either side of the fireplace. He was a right royal sycophant."

The two men did, however, make common cause in trying to make Gwynfor Evans feel uncomfortable: "He and I agreed a lot – when I was a candidate – on how to approach Gwynfor," said Jones. "He loved baiting Gwynfor, and so did I, to be fair. We used to pour scorn on Gwynfor, sometimes embarrassingly. I remember once when Gwynfor was an MP – this would be 1968 or 1969 – and Carmarthenshire County Council had sent a delegation to see the Secretary of State for Wales, led by Gwynfor, obviously, as the county's MP. So, in the Welsh Office in London, the delegation was welcomed in, and I was asked to come as well, to keep the balance between Plaid and Labour: George probably would have insisted on that, without me knowing. George said to Gwynfor, 'You see the photo I have behind there' – it was the Queen and Prince Charles – 'I put that there especially for you'."

"These visits lasted 18 months or so, until I became an MP. I also devised a system of writing letters to newspaper editors, from the office in Cardiff, and sending them to 40 or 50 party activists across Wales, and they would send those letters to the local papers."

Soon after appointing him as Secretary of State for Wales, Harold Wilson told Thomas he would be responsible for Prince Charles' Investiture as the Prince of Wales on July 1, 1969, at Caernarfon Castle. As Thomas put it: 'This had become a highly controversial issue, and a minority of Welsh nationalists seemed to think that if they created enough noise and caused enough violence, we might be persuaded to drop the ceremony.'

Cledwyn Hughes had established an Investiture Committee and meetings had already been held. Early one morning when such a meeting was due to take place, a bomb explosion damaged the Temple of Peace and Health in Cardiff. Hughes and Lord Snowdon, as Constable of Caernarfon Castle, were due to be present. When news of the explosion emerged, Thomas made a speech in which he accused the nationalists of having created a monster which they could no longer control.

Thomas took charge of the Investiture Committee, and quickly laid down a marker so far as use of the Welsh language was concerned. He wrote: 'There had been one uneasy meeting of the committee at St. James's Palace before I took over. A Welsh minister of religion had insisted on speaking in Welsh, and Cledwyn acted as interpreter. I let it be known that if anyone wished to speak in Welsh while I was there, they would be quite free to do so, but there would be no translations. In the event, that crisis never occurred again.'

In Thomas' mind, there was a huge contrast between the troublesome types who tiresomely insisted on speaking Welsh, and the likes of the Duke of Norfolk, who took over the chairmanship of the Investiture Committee meetings because of his responsibility for all state ceremonial involving monarchy. Thomas, who acted as vice chairman, wrote: 'I liked the Duke from the start. His dry wit and Edwardian attitude fascinated me.'

Giving examples of the Duke's 'dry wit', Thomas tells how when asked if he wanted a cup of tea, the Duke replied: "Never drink the stuff"; when asked if he wanted an alcoholic drink, he responded: "Wrong time of day".

Thomas was obviously in awe of the Duke, although was unable to help when he wanted to spend an extra £50,000 on the Investiture beyond the £200,000 that had been allocated by the Government. The Duke sought a meeting with the Prime Minister, and wasn't pleased when it was also attended by Thomas. Harold Wilson confirmed that no more money would be made available, in spite of the Duke 'pulling no punches'.

Referring to how he had been told by the Duke that they

were to call each other by their first names, Thomas wrote: 'I never found it so hard in my life to call any man Bernard'.

As Thomas recognised himself, the run-up to the Investiture would not be trouble-free. Not everyone in the Labour Party was happy about the Government spending £200,000 on such a ceremonial occasion. Emrys Hughes, the left-wing Labour MP for South Ayrshire who was born in Tonypandy, told the House of Commons that the Government had got its priorities wrong.

Far more troublesome, however, was the opposition to the Investiture shown by Welsh nationalists. At the time, Thomas was receiving death threats at the rate of almost one per week. On one occasion when he was due to attend a procession at Cardiff City Hall, he received an anonymous letter telling him he would be able to walk to the venue, but would have to be carried away. He looked around the crowd wondering whether a would-be assassin was present. Special Branch officers guarded his flat in London, and sometimes a police constable was on duty outside the Welsh Office in Westminster, signifying that a further threat had been made.

At home in Cardiff, Thomas' mother, now 88, was often woken up in the middle of the night by anonymous telephone callers threatening his life. He changed his home phone number and went ex-directory to protect Mam from 'mindless extremists'.

Thomas was advised to change the route of Prince Charles following the Investiture ceremony, when he was due, the next day, to visit the residential education centre of Urdd Gobaith Cymru – the Welsh language youth movement – at Glanllyn, on the banks of Llyn Tegid (Bala Lake).

Goronwy Daniel, Permanent Secretary at the Welsh Office, wrote to Thomas' Private Secretary Geoffrey Diamond saying: 'The Lord Lieutenant [of Merioneth] advises against going on the road to Glanllyn at all on the grounds that it goes past Tryweryn [the site of Capel Celyn, a Welsh-speaking village in Meirionnydd where the local people were forced out of their homes - against the wishes of the inhabitants, most people in Wales and all but one of the Welsh MPs – by the Liverpool Corporation so that their valley could be flooded to provide water to the northern English city] which was the scene of demonstrations when the new reservoir was opened and because the road could be blocked by a party wishing to present a petition or make a fuss. The Director of the Urdd [R.E. Griffith] has written a very friendly letter congratulating the Secretary of State, assuring him of the fullest co-operation of the Urdd, looking forward to seeing him at the Urdd Eisteddfod and to the Prince of Wales' visits etc. He would undoubtedly be very upset if the Prince's visit to Glanllyn were dropped. The issue which these two letters raise is of course whether the Prince should try to get to know and to endear himself to the youth of Wales – particularly the Welsh speaking part of it – or whether this section of the electorate should be allowed to become dominated by extremist opinion. Both the Founder of the Urdd and its Directors are very much in favour of the former and it would certainly seem to me most regrettable if the second alternative were adopted.'

Daniel suggested re-routing the Prince's route so it didn't pass Tryweryn – a proposal agreed by Thomas. The Permanent Secretary described Urdd Gobaith Cymru as 'a sane, reasonable and non-extremist movement'.

In his memoirs Thomas wrote: 'The Welsh language press was both bitter and malicious. Even the so-called religious newspapers became political, and included regular personal attacks on me. There was a period when Mam was included in the tirades, which I thought was reaching the lowest level of political activity. I was even attacked from the pulpit on occasion, and came to the conclusion that there were some people in Nonconformist Wales who had replaced the worship of God Almighty with the worship of the language. This was the kind of malevolence I was subjected to every week, without the great majority of people in Wales even knowing that the bullying was taking place.'

Thomas did not favour the idea of sending Prince Charles for a term to University College of Wales, Aberystwyth, where he took lessons in Welsh. This was seen by Thomas as 'patronising' and 'unnecessarily provocative'. Shortly before the term was due to start, Thomas received a letter from the college principal, Dr. Tom Parry, expressing grave fears about the atmosphere in Aberystwyth, and indicating he could not accept responsibility for the Prince's safety. Thomas considered this to be a serious problem: if the Prince couldn't go to Aberystwyth, there could be no Investiture in Caernarfon. He stated: 'I felt it would be a terrible thing if there was any part of the UK which had to be declared closed to a member of the Royal Family.'

After raising the issue with Harold Wilson, who was also concerned, advice was sought from the Chief Constable of Dyfed, who said he was confident the Prince would be safe.

Former Plaid Cymru president Dafydd Wigley commented: "Gwynfor Evans had won Carmarthen and we'd given Labour a close run in the Rhondda and Caerphilly by-elections. So George was put into the job [as Secretary of State] to keep Wales clear of the 'Nats'. He therefore decided to use the Investiture of the Prince of Wales, quite ruthlessly to my mind, in order to propagate the unionist side of things.

"He'd every right to be a unionist, the Prince of Wales has every right to be a unionist, but for George to be using the Prince of Wales in that capacity – running through to the Investiture in 1969, which was the backdrop to the election in 1970 – was, I felt, totally wrong. I thought that he abused the Prince of Wales – in a political manner – for doing that, and had he not done so, the Prince of Wales wouldn't have had quite as difficult a time as he experienced at that time: I felt quite sorry for him."

In the event, most people in Wales supported the Investiture. The Prince was widely praised after making a speech, in Welsh, at the Urdd Eisteddfod.

Nevertheless there was very tight security in advance of the Investiture, given that the whole British establishment, including every member of the Royal Family, was going to be at the ceremony. The run-up to the event brought a lot of correspondence to Thomas. He preserved that which was favourable to him.

To Tom Nightingale of Glandŵr Hall near Barmouth, who had backed the Investiture and offered to accommodate some of those attending, Thomas wrote: 'It is encouraging to get a helpful message like yours. It appears that the general rule is that abusive correspondence comes in greater measure than words of encouragement. I suppose this is inevitable because a minority often makes a noise trying to appear to be the majority; yet I am absolutely convinced that the great majority of the Welsh people support the point of view that you put forward.'

The organiser and secretary of the Freedom from Hunger Campaign wrote to Thomas saying: '[I] would like you to know that I have been very concerned about the attitude towards you of certain people in Wales. I refer to the ungratefulness of those connected with the Aberfan Disaster and also those who acted so unkindly towards you at the National Eisteddfod. However, thank God, these people are only a very small minority and that the great majority of people of Wales appreciate what you are doing and will remember your outstanding efforts with gratitude.'

Even a future Plaid Cymru AM – the 15-year-old Lindsay Whittle – had positive words to say about Thomas in a letter kept by the Secretary of State in his correspondence archive: 'Dear Mr. Thomas, Forgive me for not answering your two very nice letters you posted to me, but I had examinations at school, then the Caerffili by-election and then the holidays. However, I feel that I must write to congratulate you on your brilliant piece of work on getting the Aberfan tip completely removed. Wales is proud of you. I am sorry I was out canvassing for Plaid Cymru when you called at my house, while you were canvassing for the Labour Party. I would have loved to talk to you. I was very pleased to see Mr. Gwynfor Evans MP and yourself walking side by side at the Eisteddfod. I hope you are friends now. I feel I must apologise to you when it was stated in the press that you blamed Gwynfor for the bomb explosions and I walked to your office in Cardiff. I see from the official Hansard that you are completely innocent. You should let Wales know this and I feel you have been mistreated by us. If you look in the *Welsh Nation* next month, you will see where I will try and prove you innocent. Once again congratulations on getting the tips removed. I repeat Wales is proud of you.'

Thomas responded: 'Dear Lindsay, My warmest thanks for your very kind letter. I deeply appreciate your kind words about the Aberfan tip complex. It has not been an easy matter to settle and I find it tremendously encouraging to receive a letter like yours. When I was at Caerphilly, I had a very pleasant conversation with your mother. You are clearly a fortunate lad to be growing up in a good home. This is an asset that money can't buy. When our routine has returned to normal after the parliamentary recess, I would like you to come down to the Cardiff office one day: you could bring a friend with you and have a cup of tea with me and discuss the future for Wales. I am quite sure that we are united in our desire to get the best we can for the Welsh people. Please give my kindest regards to your parents.'

Whittle says the visit to Thomas' office never took place. " I was only 15 at the time and my mother made write a very polite letter to George Thomas. She didn't approve of my involvement in politics at that age and stood over me as I wrote. Looking back and knowing what I know now, I wonder whether he was trying to entice a 15-year-old boy into his office."

More support for Thomas' general approach came from the editor of the *South Wales Argus* in a leader article after a student drama group from Cardiff was barred from taking its production of Beckett's *Waiting for Godot* to Turkey because of the Turkish authorities' concern about student troublemakers. The leader said: 'Already it is clear that the bomb outrages which have been perpetrated in Wales are beginning to act as a disincentive to investment in the Principality, with all that this means in restricting opportunities for expansion and employment. It can only be a matter of time before they hit tourist figures, which have been rising as a result of imaginative leadership at the Wales Tourist Board. The image which a noisy, half-cracked minority is projecting abroad does nothing but harm to Welsh aspiration and endeavour, and the distortion it represents in the long run may have a serious effect on economic development as well as the recognition of Welsh achievement.'

Thomas wrote to the editor of the *Argus* to say: 'I have just read your leading article entitled 'A Distorted Image'. I wish I had seen it before I spoke in the House on Welsh Day because I believe your article ought to reach all the people of Wales. In a very succinct way it reveals the price that we are paying for our stupid extremists. You will appreciate that it is difficult for me to write you a public letter of appreciation, but I was anxious for you to know how deeply I appreciate the wisdom of what you have said, but I intend to use it in a speech at an appropriate time.'

On September 10, 1968, a bomb exploded at RAF Pembrey in Carmarthenshire, seriously injuring a warrant officer named Bill Hougham. The bomb consisted of eight sticks of gelignite in a shoe box with a time control. Hougham lost an eye and had blurred vision in the other. Press reports stated that surgeons might only be able to save two of his fingers. The shoebox was found on a table in the radio room of Number 2 control tower at the range. The attack was strongly condemned by Plaid Cymru and The Free Wales Army denied responsibility.

Thomas visited the man in hospital on a regular basis and the following February, Hougham wrote to Thomas thanking him for his kindness and for a generous contribution towards the Mayor of Kidwelly's appeal fund for him. At the time Hougham was in an RAF Rehabilitation Centre, awaiting another operation on his hands.

In the midst of preparations for the Investiture, Thomas wrote a letter of resignation as Secretary of State to Wilson as a result of his unhappiness at not being allowed to announce proposed local government changes. The letter read: 'My dear Harold, The decision that I shall not be allowed to proceed with the announcement of my proposals for local government reform in Wales has placed me in an impossible position. Both backbenchers and Ministers know that I was going to do so in answer to [Labour MP] Arthur Probert's PQ [Parliamentary Question]. My position in the Government and in Wales is made quite untenable and I have no course open to me but to resign my office. It has been a great privilege and honour for me to serve under your leadership and this is the saddest letter I have ever had to write. You <u>know</u> that my loyalty to you will be as real on the back benches as it has been during my service as a minster. You are more than P.M. to me: you are a man who

93

I would trust with my life. I look on you as a valued friend so you need have no anxiety about my conduct in exile. I do not want my resignation letter to you to go to the papers. Thank you for all your many kindnesses to me. PS: I shall release the news to the press in time for the 6am news. G'

But Thomas won his battle. His resignation letter was dated November 20, 1968. On November 21 he announced his proposals, including the creation of new counties of Gwynedd and Clwyd in north Wales in response to Probert's question. The change relating to north Wales council boundaries was enacted by the future Tory government in 1972.

As the date of the Investiture grew closer, Thomas' references to Prince Charles became increasingly sycophantic. He wrote to the senior civil servant Sir Eric Roberts on February 12, 1969, stating: 'I was with the Prince of Wales this morning at our Investiture Committee meeting. He is very Commonwealth minded and will undoubtedly want to see a great deal of the Commonwealth for himself once his Cambridge days are over. We are fortunate to have such a wholesome and intelligent young man as heir to the throne. Throughout Wales there is a growing warmth towards him and preparations are well under way for the ceremony in Carmarthen on July 1.'

In the main, Thomas did not keep letters of criticism and/ or abuse that were sent to him. He did however keep one from a Mrs. Irene Fletcher from Cambridgeshire who wrote to tell him: 'I want to express my sickening disgust at your calling upon God to bless parasitic Charles. I thought Jesus condemned parasites and all those who live on other people's labour ... Not only have you betrayed the people of Wales but all the working people of the British Isles.'

When Thomas went to Caernarfon Castle two days before the Investiture was due to take place to see how preparations were going, two young men leaned in through the open window of his car and spat *"Bradwr"* ["Traitor"] at him.

On Investiture day, the royal train – due to arrive at a specially built station two miles outside Caernarfon – was delayed for two hours after signalling wires were cut at Crewe. Two men had also blown themselves up trying to put a bomb on the railway line.

Thomas rode in a horse-drawn coach with the Prince at the head of the procession, and was surprised to be told it had been used by Queen Victoria. "I hope she was more comfortable than I am," he said.

As they rode along, a bomb exploded in a nearby field. Asked by the Prince what the noise was, Thomas said it was a royal salute. When the Prince said it was a peculiar royal salute, Thomas responded: "There are peculiar people up here, Prince Charles."

In the ceremony, it was Thomas' responsibility to read the Letters of Proclamation in formal Welsh. He wrote: 'I thought particularly then how I wished my father had taught me Welsh.' Idwal Jones, the then MP for Wrexham, had recorded what Thomas had to say, and he went over it with him many times.

The Investiture went off without further incident, and Thomas praised the Duke of Norfolk for his organisation of the ceremony. Most people in Wales warmed to the Prince, exhibiting the same kind of royal sycophancy as Thomas himself.

In his memoirs Thomas couldn't resist a broadside at Plaid Cymru leader Gwynfor Evans, who had refused an invitation to the Investiture on principle, but after the Prince's popularity had become evident had queued to be presented to Charles when he visited Carmarthen on a triumphant tour of Wales. Evans had been encouraged to change his stance by his agent, who apparently panicked when he saw how popular the Investiture was. For Thomas this was an act of humbug which did not go down well with the public. At the following year's general election, Evans lost his seat.

Nevertheless, says the former Tory MP Patrick Cormack, he did distinguish privately between Evans, whom he described as a democratic nationalist, and the 'hotheads'. Cormack said: "He thought there were some very bad people. He always used to rejoice in the fact that there were not as many bad people in Welsh nationalist circles as there were in Irish. He also felt that people were too anxious to bend over backwards for Welsh language people. George, of course, didn't speak Welsh – he knew the odd word or two."

There was an interesting footnote to Thomas' association with the Duke of Norfolk. His papers show that the day after the Investiture, on July 2, 1969, Thomas wrote to the Duke saying: 'I write to offer you my warm and sincere congratulations on your scintillating success at the Investiture. I told the Queen at the end of the day that I thought you were a gift for the Nation! It has been a real joy for me to work with you over the past 18 months.'

Thomas went on to suggest a potential lunch engagement at the Travellers Club, concluding the letter with a sycophantic reference to the Duchess: 'I was glad to see the Duchess again; she plays the regal role to perfection.'

The Duke responded: 'Thank you for your letter. I was writing to you today to say thank you for all your help and understanding over the past months. It is a relief it is over but it did go really well and that makes all the difference.'

Later, a note from a secretary to Thomas said: 'Secretary of State, Some time ago we arranged a lunch between you and the Duke of Norfolk which he had to cancel. His secretary promised to come back about a new date but hasn't done so. Do you wish us to pursue this?' A handwritten note from Thomas said: 'Forget it.'

Four days after the Investiture a 10-year-old boy, on holiday from Chalfont St. Giles in England, was seriously injured by a bomb planted by nationalist extremists in Caernarfon. Ian Cox's right foot had to be amputated after he disturbed a package while retrieving a football from a garden along the Investiture route. Thomas wrote to the boy's parents saying: 'I am writing to express to you my deepest sympathy for the tragic accident to Ian. I know I need not tell you that this senseless violence is caused by a very small minority in Wales, although I know that this can be of no consolation to you in your distress. I pray that your son recovers soon from his grave injuries. When he is well enough I would like to visit him. Perhaps you would let me know if I might do this? All Wales is shocked at the senseless act which led to this tragic accident.'

Months later, in the run up to Christmas, the *Western Mail* reported on the boy's progress, with Thomas saying his plight 'ought to be on the conscience of every decent Welshman'. He added: 'It does not appear to have been generally appreciated that he not only lost his right foot but sustained quite serious fractures to his left leg and lost all the flesh off the lower part of that leg mainly through gangrene.'

In a private letter, Thomas wrote: 'My dear Ian, I am very glad to hear that you are not going to have to spend Christmas in hospital, though I know you will have to return there after Christmas. I hope that you have a very happy Christmas at home and that you are able to pay a visit to Rhymney [the birthplace of the boy's grandmother]. We are all very interested to hear of your progress, Ian, and the whole Welsh Office sends you their warmest good wishes for Christmas and the future. I am sending you the enclosed token so that you can visit Smith's some time and make your own choice of a present. Please give my kind regards to your Father and Mother.'

Thomas felt impelled to write to the novelist Kate Roberts about an article she had published in the Welsh language weekly paper *Y Faner*. Translated as 'Observations on the Investiture', she wrote: 'Yes, I received an invitation to the ceremony, but I did not accept it. I did not see it either on the television, I saw photographs in the newspaper the following morning and were it not for the tragedy of the previous night, I would find the thing terribly amusing. Two young men lost their lives as they were going to show their protest – possibly – and the words of Mr. Saunders Lewis became true: Welsh blood was spilled. The observations of the Secretary of State on the subject were cruel: he who speaks so sentimentally of his mother, being able to hope that this would be an end to the bombing, indeed to maintain it would be so. Apart from their being cruel, it was a stupid thing to expect from that quarter, and having seen all the servility that was shown in the photographs, little men hobnobbing with the Royal Family, all the kneeling, and the presenting of the English Prince to the Welsh Nation, it is difficult for even a pacifist not to raise a din!'

Thomas wrote to her: 'Your tendentious article in the *Faner* astounds and disappoints me. Although we are political opponents, I have hitherto respected you as a fair minded person with pronounced Welsh nationalist views. I just cannot believe that you have read my comments on the Abergele tragedy. I enclose a copy for you to see: they were the only remarks I uttered in public about this sad affair. If you had been with me when I was told the news privately you would know that my first words were about the tragedy of those bereaved. Your written remarks are at once unjust and inaccurate. No impartial person would agree with you that my remarks are 'cruel'. Your reference to my mother is typical of Welsh nationalists' propaganda jibes. It is a strange way to conduct political debate.'

His enclosed statement read: 'This is a dreadful tragedy. While enquiries into this shocking incident are still continuing, it would be unwise to arrive at any hasty conclusions. But to those of us who have repeatedly warned of the ultimate outcome of such incidents involving explosives, it is a grim fulfilment of our worst fears. I hope this will mark the very end of the lamentable course of events which we have witnessed in recent months.'

Roberts responded: 'What I heard of your statement on the Abergele tragedy was the last sentence only on the BBC news, Radio 4, taken out of its context, without any reference to the families, it was cruel. And there was a shade of difference in meaning in the translation. You more than anyone will understand the harm done by quoting out of context, but you will never understand the bitterness of the Welsh nationalists on account of the injustice Wales has suffered from all English political parties, and you will never understand what I suffered personally at school because my parents and the community in which I lived were monoglot Welsh people. On occasions like the Investiture this bitterness wells up. At other times I think I have been fair minded enough.'

Later in July 1969 a Church friend from Worcestershire wrote to Thomas raising concerns about alleged marital infidelity on the part of Prime Minister Harold Wilson. Thomas' reply is interesting in the context of his own troubled private life: 'I was very disturbed to read what you had to say about the Prime Minister. I know him as a personal friend as well as the leader of the Government in which I serve. I believe he is the victim of a most malicious slander campaign. Every day of his life he is working from early morning until 2am or 3am. I think it fair to say that he very rarely has 10 minutes alone. I happen to know that he and Mrs. Wilson are devoted to each other and it is diabolical that these wicked stories should be spread about him by people. I sometimes wonder if they would like to have their private life under a searchlight. The Prime Minister has no private life. It is one of the sacrifices the office calls for. Politics being what they are, I suppose it is expecting too much to hope that these unfounded and scandalous stories could be checked. I never cease to be astonished how people without having a shred of evidence on which to go are prepared to believe the worst of other people simply on the basis of gossip.'

Thomas gave a speech at the *Western Mail*'s Centenary Banquet which attracted sycophantic praise from T. Mervyn Jones, chairman of the state-owned Wales Gas Board: 'My dear Secretary of State, Will you let me tell you what all of us, your hearers, felt last night and that is the highlight of the *Western Mail* Centenary Banquet was your admirable speech. It had all the ingredients of excellence for such an occasion, humour, pertinent but always kindly, charm, because warmth of feeling, yet with all real significant purpose. My table included such oratorical gourmets as Sir Trevor Evans, David Cole, young Bill Lloyd George, Emlyn Hooson and a Colonel of the Welsh Guards. We vied with each other in words of praise and commendation. This calls for no reply, know how proud we all were of our Secretary of State.'

Thomas' response was suitably gratified – and as a bonus provided an insight into the closed world of Welsh public appointments: 'My heartfelt thanks to you for your very kind letter following my speech at the *Western Mail* Centenary Banquet. I cannot tell you how encouraging I found your message. You have always been a very faithful friend of mine and I shall value your letter more than you might realise. I am looking forward to working with you when you assume the chairmanship of the Wales Tourist Board.'

In January 1970 he wrote to Hywel Roberts of Cyncoed, Cardiff, rejecting a suggestion that clemency should be shown towards the folk singer – and future Plaid Cymru president – Dafydd Iwan after his conviction for a bilingual road signs protest. Thomas wrote: 'Dear Hywel, Thank you for your letter concerning Dafydd Iwan. I am afraid I do not share your views on this young man's behaviour. He deliberately flouted the law and then took the decision that he would not pay any fine imposed. Thus the fact that he is in prison is by his own decision. The law would break down completely if people of this sort feel they are somehow above the law and militancy can force their wishes on the rest of the community. I cannot lend my support to any appeal for Mr. Iwan to be released. I am sorry that we do not see eye to eye on this matter.'

The following month he again wrote to Roberts, this time taking issue with comments made by Plaid Cymru president Gwynfor Evans: 'Gwynfor Evans went to the Far East and came back and said the Vietcong were like the Welsh Nationalist Party fighting for their national independence. Any reasonable person would interpret that as an encouragement to hot-heads to take action in Wales. He has also referred to Wales as 'an oppressed country' which in my judgement is a lot of poppycock. Far from being oppressed Wales is being given every encouragement to enrich and defend its culture and I am very proud of our record.'

In April 1970 Thomas received a note from Harold Wilson, congratulating him on being awarded the Freedom of Rhondda. The PM commented: 'This is a splendid and well deserved tribute to you personally.'

Responding to a note from the wife of a key worker who had moved from London to Neath to work in the nearby Ford vehicle plant and found themselves subject to racist comments like 'English wogs', Thomas wrote: 'Thank you for your letter. I was deeply sorry to read of the experiences that you have suffered. I believe they are not typical of the attitude of Welsh people to those who come to live and work amongst us. The United Kingdom is too small for us to be able to afford the luxury of disagreements between our various peoples. I earnestly hope that as the days go by you will feel that things are better.'

During his period as Secretary of State, the National Coal Board embarked on a programme of pit closures. In a precursor to the huge struggle that occurred a decade and a half later, the Labour government of which Thomas was a member had decided it was right to shut down 'uneconomic' mines. He acknowledged that every pit which closed would result in the loss of between 500 and 1,000 job losses, and that new factory start-ups rarely employed more than a couple of hundred workers. This made the task of solving the unemployment problem appear insurmountable. In a backhanded compliment, Thomas wrote: 'Strong leadership by Glyn Williams, president, and Dai Francis, secretary, of the South Wales NUM was of enormous help at this time. They fiercely resisted some closures but ensured that law and order prevailed once a firm decision had been made.'

For George Thomas, strong leadership by the NUM officials entailed keeping a lid on resistance to pit closures.

Dafydd Wigley characterised him as a "wily" Secretary of State: "There's the story about the railway line running from Carmarthenshire up to Shrewsbury – the Heart of Wales line. Beeching had been closing all the railways, and this line was down for closure. George was Secretary of State for Wales. By that time in Carmarthen there had been a couple of by-elections and there was some debate in the Cabinet or at a Cabinet committee that the Prime Minister needed to remember that the line ran through at least four marginal constituencies. That intervention is reputed to have saved the line, which is still open. It was very unusual for that line to have survived the cuts. Far more viable lines than that didn't survive."

With the polls swinging in Labour's direction, Harold Wilson was inclined to call a general election, nine months earlier than he needed to. He asked all Ministers sitting round the Cabinet table if they agreed, and they did. Thomas and the rest expected a great victory. The electorate, however, decided otherwise, giving the Conservatives a 30-seat majority. It seemed that Tory leader Ted Heath's promise to cut prices 'at a stroke' had gone down well, especially with women voters.

Thomas was interested to see who would be appointed to succeed him as Secretary of State for Wales. He wasn't impressed when Heath chose Peter Thomas, the MP for Hendon, who combined that role with the party chairmanship. There was an outcry, with Peter Thomas being described as 'the part-time Secretary for Wales'.

George Thomas was Secretary of State for Wales for little more than two years. It was the only Cabinet post he ever held and his time in office was dominated by the Investiture, and by events that flowed from it.

Some Welsh nationalists have mythologised the Investiture as a gross insult to Wales as a proud nation, with Thomas as the Quisling puppet of colonial England, while others saw it as a calculated and politically motivated action designed to re-assert the dominance of the monarchy and 'Britishness' during a time of growing support for Plaid Cymru, the concept of self-rule and sympathy towards those taking direct action to defend the Welsh language.

Knowing that the great majority of Welsh people supported the Royal Family and – once announced – the Investiture, the moderate nationalists voiced their opposition but, apart from acting as an effective recruiting tool for the republican minority, it was in general a futile cause as the nation embraced the occasion wholeheartedly: an inconvenient fact that continues to confront the nationalist narrative.

A very small and militant wing of Welsh nationalism – disowned by the moderates – fought against the Investiture with violence and it is difficult not to feel uncomfortable about the way two bomb victims – RAF warrant officer Bill Hougham and 10-year-old Ian Cox – have, to a considerable extent, been airbrushed from the history of the Investiture. Both suffered life-changing injuries as a result of what can only be described as terrorist activity.

During a period of heightened political tension, and despite the perceived colonial slight he'd 'imposed' on Wales, the threats and abuse directed at Thomas and his mother were intolerable in a democratic society.

In many ways this enabled Thomas to play-up his role as the victim and for him to generate the additional sympathy he arguably didn't deserve. If the Investiture was, for the growing national movement, a symbol of Wales' conquest by a foreign country, the way the more militant nationalists behaved denied the now increasingly numerous, moderate and peaceful wing of Welsh nationalism represented by Plaid Cymru – which totally opposed the Investiture – from occupying the moral high ground, as many in the media and the general population could not distinguish between the two.

10

Back in Opposition

Following the unexpected general election defeat, Thomas was appointed by Wilson to the Shadow Cabinet as Shadow Welsh Secretary. With the departure of a number of longstanding Members including Jim Griffiths, Welsh Labour MPs were now split into two camps: one led by Cledwyn Hughes and Goronwy Roberts who were strong supporters of devolution; the other, largely non-Welsh speakers like Thomas, who were fiercely against it. Thomas nevertheless stated that he considered it his responsibility to keep a united party.

At this time he was worried about what he described as the 'increasingly vocal' Welsh Nationalist Party. He said: 'It was not difficult to get men like Cledwyn Hughes, Goronwy Roberts, John Morris and Elystan Morgan to make moderate speeches on devolution, even though they felt strongly on the issue; but Will Edwards and Tom Ellis were a different cup of tea. They went their own way and fanned the flames of nationalism at every opportunity.'

Thomas will also have been unhappy with Edwards because of a speech in which he argued that Julian Hodge's Bank of Wales should be nationalised. Hodge was a great friend of Thomas, and both Thomas and Jim Callaghan were directors of his bank.

It didn't take Thomas long, after the general election defeat, to turn his guns on Plaid Cymru, some of whose supporters had not taken their party's own disappointing results gracefully. The party's president Gwynfor Evans had lost his seat, and there were no successes elsewhere.

At a Labour rally in Newtown on July 4, 1970, Thomas said: "In their marginal constituencies the Tories' best allies were the Welsh nationalists. This general election has given a clear message to the Welsh separatists who shelter under the misnomer of Welsh nationalists. Their philosophy is rejected. In 25 seats out of 36, that is in five out of every seven seats in Wales, the nationalists lost their deposit. Gwynoro Jones' spectacular triumph in Carmarthen was not only a great personal victory, it was a damning indictment of Welsh nationalism. It is not often that I address a message to the Welsh nationalists, but I am bound to say that if they want to contest parliamentary seats, there are some important lessons they have to learn, not least of which is how to take defeat. The disgraceful behaviour at the declaration of the count in many parts of Wales was resented by decent minded people in all parties.'

He also hardened his line against Welsh language activists' campaign for bilingual road signs. In a briefing written for Labour in advance of a formal submission to the Bowen Committee, set up to look at the issue, Thomas wrote: 'The provision of bilingual road signs cannot be regarded as of the same priority as the need to review and strengthen the effective teaching of Welsh in schools, the provision of modern aids to such teaching, including varied and attractive reading matter. The time scale for the introduction of bilingual road signs may well be prolonged. Questions of safety, of traditional and current linguistic usage, the views of democratically elected local authorities, as well as financial priorities must be properly considered. There are cases where a place has never had a Welsh or an English name (Shotton, Neyland;

Pontypridd, Aberystwyth). In such cases the extant usage is in reality the bilingual form. In such cases there would seem no point in translation from one language to the other. In conclusion, evidence to the Bowen Committee on behalf of the Labour Party should clearly indicate our condemnation of the partisan and divisive methods of agitation used by the so-called Welsh Language Society. If the language is to survive, let alone flourish, it can only be on the basis of the good will of the Welsh people as a whole. Present methods of agitation are increasingly estranging the sympathies not only of those among us (and they account for three quarters of our people) whose first language is not Welsh, but also of many who are themselves Welsh-speaking. The Labour Party is determined that all the people of Wales should share in the fashioning and implementation of constructive policies to preserve what is a common heritage of us all and not the monopoly of a partisan few.'

Cledwyn Hughes and Thomas had adjoining rooms in the Commons and often spoke together about what the future held for them. Hughes tried to persuade Thomas that he should stand down as an MP and go to the House of Lords, where he would have a chance of becoming a Minister again. The idea began to appeal to him.

Others, however, simply saw Thomas as two-faced.
Gwynoro Jones said: "I remember to this day: there was a Welsh table in the House of Commons. It doesn't matter which party you belonged to, that's where we'd sit, in the tea room. In the corner would be all the Welsh papers – *Daily Post*, *Evening Post*, *Western Mail*, *Argus*, *Gazette*, *Merthyr Express*, etc. – and that's where we'd gather.

"This particular morning, I remember it well, there were six or seven of us around the table and George started pontificating about Cledwyn. 'I'll tell you what Cledwyn said last night.

Terrible isn't it, the things he says about the pro-language Welsh side?' And so he went on, and on, and on, during which, by the entrance door, I could see Cledwyn come in – I was sitting at the end of the table. Somehow George sensed it. Within five or six feet of him, Cledwyn now appeared. So George got up on his feet – very typical of him – and exclaimed, 'Cledwyn – I was just telling the boys how marvellous you were last night.' He was completely two-faced; he could do it like that.

"After experiences like that, you realised George couldn't be trusted. He might try get you on his side with something, only to find out he only wanted information from you. As a result – in those days – he had a nickname amongst us Welsh speaking MPs: Harold Wilson's ears, nose and throat – 'ENT'. He would go, with any 'tittle tattle', back to Harold. Wilson relied heavily on him for gossip, from the Commons. That's how Wilson survived, really. He had a machine of his closest guys and George was one of those."

Nevertheless, Jones had a high regard for Thomas' oratorical skills: "I have to say, mind, that in the early days when I was an MP, it was great to listen to George speaking in Parliament," he said. "George was a very good debater, particularly when winding up a debate. He'd have a few drinks beforehand, but he'd wind up a debate well. The House was full, with MPs quite full of wine after the various dinners and occasions, and George would be in full *hwyl*, mocking the Tories. He and Michael Foot were star turns with things like that."

Jones was appointed to chair a working group that would recommend how the Labour Party in Wales should contribute to the Crowther/ Kilbrandon Commission, which was examining whether there should be changes to the UK constitution, perhaps involving devolution to Wales and Scotland.

He recalls: "I gathered round me a group of enthusiastic

Welsh devolutionists: Alun Michael; Paul Flynn; Wyn Thomas, who stood as the candidate in Montgomery; Bruce George, who was a farmer in Monmouth at the time and went on to become an MP for Walsall; and Barry Jones of Cardiff University. We came out with a lot of papers for the Welsh Executive. The MPs really got concerned, because we were now going for a directly elected Council with much wider powers than they had ever envisaged. They had assumed the policy would be a nominated body for Wales. So all hell let loose.

"That was the start of the disagreement and the division between George and myself, because George didn't want any of that. Actually, he was furious with us. Jim Callaghan must have regretted the moment he suggested that I became involved, because he now realised this guy must be a nationalist, which is what George called us – the crypto-nationalists: Cledwyn, Elystan, Tom Ellis, myself, Will Edwards, that's how he used to refer to us.

"I was feeding George papers on what those in the nationalist wing were saying but it fell apart politically, not personally, once the question of an elected Council for Wales appeared on the agenda. In the end, however, we won, and we won the argument because Gwyn Morgan was Assistant General Secretary of the Labour Party in London. He became a major ally of us – devolutionists in Wales – and persuaded the UK party and the UK executive to go along with it.

"I remember going to meetings with Welsh MPs at the end of the 1960s and they were wild. Leo Abse, Ness Edwards, Gwilym Davies from the Rhondda but the one that surprised me most was Ivor Davies of Gower. I honestly thought Ivor would be sensitive to devolution, but he wasn't. So there was now a big division, but the policy was approved – much against the will of the Labour MPs at the time."

Thomas' thoughts of stepping down increased when his

mother died on April 21, 1972, after which the prospect of staying on in the Commons had no attraction for him. It seemed to him that his ambition had died with Mam, who had only been admitted to hospital a week before her death. Losing her was a shattering blow to him, and he briefly doubted his faith. Two months later his younger brother Ivor – his last family link with Tonypandy – also died.

"He absolutely adored Mam", said Patrick Cormack "and I remember how cut up he was when she died. He was really very, very shaken. He was devoted to his mother – he thought she was the most wonderful person he'd ever known. The least he said about his father the better. I was aware of the basic circumstances – he'd walked out and gone off with somebody else. That he made plain. But he talked about Mam a lot."

Thomas remained depressed for at least a year, and he discussed his feelings with Callaghan, who told him he should inform the Prime Minister it was his intention to retire at the next general election. Wilson reacted sharply, saying: "Why do you want to go? You'll be Secretary of State for Wales again." Thomas said he was concerned that he'd be appointed for just one year and then be dropped for a younger man, making it appear he had been sacked for incompetence.

Shortly afterwards, the prospect of Thomas' retiring was leaked to the *Western Mail*, which carried the story on the front page. He had to make a quick decision: either to confirm the story and watch what authority he had with his colleagues ebb away, or deny it and insist he intended to stand again at the next election. He chose the latter course.

At the February 1974 general election, Thomas put out an election address which succinctly explained Labour's view on the political choice facing Britain. It was called by Heath during a miners' strike which had led to power cuts and saw the country's businesses reduced to a three-day week. Thomas' personal message to voters read: 'This election will decide the sort of government we shall have for the next five years. The miners' strike is a phoney issue. It will be settled within weeks of the general election. Mr. Heath hopes you will be diverted from giving judgement on his three and a half years in office. He has brought Britain to its knees. Food prices have rocketed despite his 1970 promise to halt increases 'at a stroke'. Rents have been doubled and ordinary families are priced out of the market for purchase of homes. The Common Market has proved to be a disaster on the terms of entry Mr. Heath accepted so willingly. Only a Labour government can change them. Mr. Heath is a prisoner of his own agreement with M. Pompidou [The French president]. This is your chance to effect a change. The Conservative government proposes to pursue the same policies for the next five years. Labour's new policies are directed to putting Britain back on its feet.'

Labour won more seats than the Conservatives, though without an overall majority. Wilson returned to Downing Street. Thomas was looking forward to a return to the Welsh Office and another stint as Welsh Secretary. He was to be disappointed.

11

The Road to the Speaker's Chair

When it became clear that Wilson would form a new government, Thomas began thinking about what he would do at the Welsh Office when he returned to his old post. Expecting all evening to be summoned to Downing Street, at 9.50pm the phone finally rang. It was Wilson himself, asking Thomas where he had been, as his office had been trying to contact him. Thomas said that was odd, as he had been sitting four inches from the telephone.

Wilson told Thomas to come to Downing Street at once. He got a taxi and arrived as Big Ben was striking 10pm. Wilson's secretary Marcia Williams was there, together with MPs Fred Peart, Gerald Kaufman and Peter Shore. Wilson suggested they watch the News at Ten to see the events of the day before he and Thomas went for a talk in the Cabinet room.

Wilson's opening gambit was: "George, you have been a good friend to me". Thomas replied that they had been good friends to each other and had been loyal to each other. Wilson then asked him whether he would like to be Deputy Speaker and Chairman of Ways and Means. Thomas responded: "What, Deputy Speaker and not Secretary of State for Wales?"

Seeing he was upset, Wilson said: "Before you get agitated, remember how old Selwyn Lloyd is". Selwyn Lloyd, the sitting

Speaker, was 69 at the time, and the clear suggestion was that Thomas could be the new Speaker when he stepped down.

Thomas agreed to take the Deputy Speaker's role 'if that's what [Wilson] wanted [him] to do'. But when he asked Wilson who was going to get 'his' job at the Welsh Office, the Prime Minister claimed – almost certainly falsely – that he hadn't yet decided. In fact it was to be John Morris, a Welsh speaker who was pro-devolution.

Thomas was the only former Cabinet Minister not to go back into the Cabinet. He later came to realise that his anti-devolution views embarrassed Wilson, writing: 'There is no doubt in my mind that many senior Labour politicians had impressed on Harold that devolution was unlikely if I was still in the Cabinet.'

In fact, he was aware that during Labour's years in opposition a number of Welsh Labour MPs had met Wilson privately and complained about his views, especially as expressed in a weekly column he had in the *Daily Post*. These columns had, in Thomas' words, annoyed some of his parliamentary colleagues because of his 'strong resistance' to Welsh nationalism.

They had also annoyed members and supporters of Plaid Cymru. "After he stopped being Secretary of State," recalls Dafydd Wigley, "he was the scourge of the Nats with his newspaper articles – in the *Daily Post* – which used to be published, if I remember right, on a Wednesday. He had a long column down the side of a page. Anyway, he used to get up the nostrils of Nats in a big way. I asked him about the columns – I got to know him when I got into the Commons. 'Oh it was like this, Dafydd,' he said. 'I'd write my article on the Sunday morning. I'd show it to Mam. Mam would say 'Oh George, you can't possibly write that!', and I'd say, 'Oh yes I can!' So I put my article into the envelope, I'd go down and catch the lunchtime post, and then I'd wait. I'd wait until Wednesday morning. I wouldn't go to the Welsh table [in the Commons tea room]. I'd go to one of the tables in the far corner, and I'd sit there reading *The Times*. And I'd wait. And I'd see Cledwyn [Hughes] coming in, I'd see Goronwy [Roberts] coming in, and going to the Welsh table, and picking up *my* paper' – he called it 'my paper' – 'and turning to my page and reading my column. I'd see them getting redder and redder, and I'd sit there laughing to myself'.

"What do you do with that? He clearly enjoyed it. He created quite a lot of mischief – for those in his own party – in the Welsh-speaking west and north who were having to deal with Plaid. I remember Dafydd El [fellow Plaid Cymru MP Dafydd Elis-Thomas] and I going into the tea room on our second or third morning there. George used to hold court in the tea room and he'd have a whole phalanx of Labour MPs sitting around and he'd be leaning back and telling stories, as he could. There would be people like Ioan Evans and Alec Jones – the valley MPs, Donald Coleman. Neil Kinnock didn't frequent the Welsh table quite so much; he was more an occasional visitor to the Welsh table. I wouldn't say those who were there were his acolytes, but George treated them as his audience, and he would be holding court. Of course he didn't do so much of that afterwards, because once he was in as Deputy Speaker, and particularly as Speaker, he was then in his own corner of the House doing his own thing.

"Anyway, Dafydd El and I went in and we wondered what the hell we were going to do with this guy who'd been 'whipping' us up and down the valleys, as it were. So we thought we'd better make some peace. So we said 'Congratulations, George', and he leant back and said, 'Thank you. You know, nothing will give me greater pleasure than seeing you two boys entering the chamber (we thought God, the revolution's happening – but he hadn't finished) and having to bow to me'.

"He was full of vanity – sometimes he would use self-deprecating humour as a ploy where he didn't intend to be self-deprecating at all. But the mock modesty that came from doing that gave him one step up, as it were. He had an enormous chip on his shoulder, I reckon. Part of that chip was probably related to being one of the youngest boys in the family, and the older ones all spoke Welsh."

Wilson told him he had sent the small delegation away with a 'flea in their ear', but advised Thomas to be more on his guard.

Subsequently, Thomas dismissed rumours that John Morris would be appointed Secretary of State, believing it unlikely that Labour would be elected, and that even if the party returned to office Wilson would not 'lend himself to the intriguers'. Thomas had underestimated the degree of pressure that had been brought on Wilson to stop the returning Prime Minister reappointing him to the Welsh Office. MPs Gwynoro Jones and Tom Ellis were among those who told Wilson that Thomas' stance was losing Labour votes and seats in Wales.

"He had this column in the *Daily Post* which caused havoc," commented Gwynoro Jones, "because he would say the most outrageous things about the language; about the National Eisteddfod. I remember telling him once, 'George, for God's sake man, do you know who are the biggest supporters of the National Eisteddfod?' It was Labour Party workers and MPs, back in the early 1900s. It was the working class people. It's not a Plaid Cymru movement, it was a Labour movement, but he didn't see that. He had a lot of those chips on his shoulder.

"I got on to Clive Betts of the *Western Mail*. I said there was a big row coming up in the party in Wales about the Early Day Motion on devolution. 'We're going to have a debate about it in the party, and I'm going to release to you who supports and who doesn't'.

"After the story was published, an inquiry in the Welsh

parliamentary party was established to discover who was behind the leak. We all turned up. Even Jim turned up: one of the rare occasions in my time there he ever turned up. They knew who had done it. There was only one guy with the expertise with the press – from my professional background – but they could never prove it and I held my ground with them. There was a hell of a row about it and, after that, George didn't trust me whatsoever.

"Then came the election of February 1974, when Goronwy Roberts lost his seat, Will Edwards lost his seat, and Elystan Morgan lost his seat. Tom Ellis and I got back but Wilson only had a majority of three. The day we reconvened in Parliament we asked immediately to see Harold, the Prime Minister. Very little has ever been said about this, but it's true. Tom and I went to see Harold and said: 'Look, you've got to drop George as Secretary of State. He is causing havoc. He is dividing the party. You don't need to listen to us. Look at what happened in those three Welsh-speaking seats'.

"That was when John Morris came in. John became Secretary of State. I'm not saying – at all – that we helped John to be Secretary of State, but we do claim – Tom and I – that we put the knife into George. We automatically thought it would be Cledwyn, but it wasn't, it was John Morris. I suspect old Harold, being the guy he was, realised it would be too much to accept that Cledwyn would be the Secretary of State.

"When we went to see him, Harold listened more than he spoke. He would never give any commitment. Pretty much like he was with Robin Day on television. He'd get his pipe out and spend half the time lighting it up, which gave him time to think and less time to talk. He didn't give us any commitment, but he obviously took our comments on board. There was no need for anyone to guess about whether George was causing trouble: just look at the record, look at what had happened in the election. Why had it happened? George was anti-Welsh, George was anti-devolution, George was writing these things in the *Daily Post*: he was causing havoc inside the party in Wales. Three Labour MPs had gone. Three very experienced people and two of them were Ministers; Elystan and Goronwy Roberts. How many more did they want to lose? I was next, wasn't I, six months later in the October 1974 election.

"To be fair, Harold came to Carmarthen twice that summer to speak. But George and I hardly looked at each other then. I think he rumbled that something had happened. He realised that someone had put the knife in. Whether he knew about Tom and me and that incident I don't know, but he obviously zoned-in on the crypto-nationalists, and he was right."

During the February election campaign, Thomas saw nothing unusual in the fact that he was asked by party officials to appear in an election broadcast alongside Morris. And his constituency neighbour Jim Callaghan gave him no hint that he was aware of any threat to his position as a future Welsh Secretary.

After Morris' appointment was announced, Thomas bumped into Callaghan behind the Speaker's Chair and asked him whether he had known before the election that he was not going back into the Cabinet. "Yes, I did," responded Callaghan in what Thomas described as a manner without any sympathy.

In his memoirs, Thomas wrote: 'Politics can be a squalid business. I never have been able to understand the mentality of those power-seekers whose friendship is worthless when the going is hard. During all the intrigue that preceded the election, the participants maintained their pretence of friendship with me and never gave even a hint that danger signals surrounded me. It is easy in retrospect to see how much my views on devolution were an embarrassment to people like Cledwyn

Hughes, Elystan Morgan, John Morris and Tom Ellis, who lived in a world of their own cocooned by nationalist aspirations.'

When the 1979 referendum on setting up a Welsh Assembly resulted in a decisive rejection of such an idea, by a vote of four-to-one, Thomas couldn't conceal his delight. He wondered why Callaghan and Wilson had vastly miscalculated the desire for an Assembly. He wrote: 'I was thrown overboard because both of them fell into the trap of mistakenly believing noisy nationalist propaganda to represent the views of the majority in Wales.'

By the time the referendum took place, he had been Speaker for three years. He phoned Cledwyn Hughes to crow at the victory of those like himself who opposed devolution. When Hughes complained that he was supposed to be impartial, Thomas responded: "Oh yes. As Speaker I am entirely impartial: but on this issue I know on which side I am impartial!"

After being elected Chairman of Ways and Means, Thomas resolved that his involvement with party politics was over – a strange conclusion, given that in that capacity, rather than as Speaker, he would still have to seek votes at a general election as a Labour candidate. Resentful at the way he had been blocked from returning to a Cabinet role, he wrote: 'From then on I gave my wholehearted loyalty to the House of Commons and not to the Labour Party. It was not for me to allow the Labour government to use me as a parliamentary pawn to get their own way.' From then on, he made no party political speeches in public, but to keep in with Cardiff West Constituency Labour Party he made a speech once a month to its management committee.

The first change that struck him after taking on the role of Chairman of Ways and Means was the need to wear morning dress around the House of Commons. He claimed initially to be embarrassed, but reconciled himself to the fact that it was effectively a uniform for the job.

In 1975 Thomas was made a Freeman of the City of Cardiff. The same honour was bestowed on Jim Callaghan, who was Foreign Secretary and invited US Secretary of State Henry Kissinger to the ceremony. So far as Thomas was concerned, inviting Kissinger was no more than an exercise in one-upmanship by Callaghan.

Thomas got on well with Selwyn Lloyd, the Speaker, another closet homosexual who was also a Methodist. They developed a friendship, with Thomas able to indulge his propensity to be deferential towards his social betters. Selwyn Lloyd was educated privately at Fettes College in Edinburgh – where Tony Blair was later a pupil – and was a Cambridge graduate. Earlier in his career he had served as Foreign Secretary and Chancellor of the Exchequer.

After postponing his intended retirement date several times, Selwyn Lloyd stepped down on February 3, 1976, opening the way for the election of a new Speaker. While Thomas quickly received good luck messages from MPs who came up to him in the Commons, he took nothing for granted, and described the period before the election as the longest 10 days of his life. He needn't have worried, and was elected Speaker with the support of MPs from all parties.

The following day, as protocol dictated, Thomas had to receive the approval of the Queen in the House of Lords – a ceremony that required much bowing and doffing of caps. He loved it, naturally. Almost certainly, he got masochistic pleasure out of uttering the newly elected Speaker's standard verbose response to the monarch's message of confirmation: "My Lords, I submit myself with all humility to Her Majesty's Royal will and pleasure, and if, in the discharge of my duties and in the maintenance of the rights and privileges of the Commons

House of Parliament, I should inadvertently fall into error, I pray that the blame may be imputed to me alone and not to Her Majesty's faithful Commons."

Reflecting on his election as Speaker In his memoirs, Thomas reveals himself again as someone with the psychological default mechanism of a natural conservative: 'Now I was really Speaker in a tradition that goes back nearly 700 years, a thought that always makes my blood tingle. There are people who want to change the ways we do things in Britain and in the House, but very often change is just for change's sake. Traditions that have endured through the centuries must have something about them and you need a very good reason to tamper with them. If there were such a reason then they would probably not have survived as long as they have. And at the very least, they give a sense of continuity and security – not complacency – which so many other countries have good cause to envy.'

Such comments give a clue to his approach to the Speaker's role over the next seven years.

12

Falling Out With Labour

Shortly before he was elected Speaker, Harold Wilson had confided in Thomas his intention to resign as Prime Minister. So when Wilson's resignation was announced on March 16, 1976, he was one of the few people in the country not to be surprised. Conspiracy theories abounded at the time about Wilson's sudden departure, but the fact was he had become aware that his mental powers were failing. It later emerged that he had early onset Alzheimer's Disease.

Although he had been a friend of Wilson's for 30 years, Thomas believed the decision to give him advance notice of the resignation was entirely attributable to his role as Speaker.

Wilson was succeeded by Jim Callaghan, with whom Thomas had a much cooler relationship, despite the proximity of their constituencies. Thomas put it like this: 'I had always found Harold to be open in his dealings, while Jim was much more guarded.'

By the time Callaghan took over, Labour had lost its overall majority – a development which made governing more difficult and put a greater spotlight on the Speaker in mediating between the Government and the Opposition.

In the last week of April, David Steel, then the Liberal Chief Whip, asked to see Thomas on a matter of urgency. With Steel looking as if he was about to burst into tears, Thomas came to the conclusion that Jeremy Thorpe had decided to resign as party leader. Thorpe was at the centre of allegations that he had conspired to murder Norman Scott, a former male model who had long claimed to have had a gay relationship with Thorpe at a time when homosexuality was illegal. Three years later he was acquitted of conspiracy to murder Scott, but compelling evidence emerged that Thorpe had been involved in diverting money, donated to the Liberal Party in good faith, to a hit man.

Thomas, obviously feeling a resonance with his own position as a closet gay open to blackmail, made clear his sympathy for Thorpe in his memoirs, writing: 'He [Steel] was clearly upset and I knew before he said a word that Jeremy Thorpe had at last given in to the cruel campaign that had been conducted against him ... I expressed my sadness at the cruel sacrifice of a first class member of the House of Commons'.

Thomas then opined: 'My feeling has always been that Jeremy Thorpe was destroyed by his parliamentary colleagues as much as by the press campaign against him. The Liberal MPs behaved very badly by showing disloyalty just when their leader needed it most. Jeremy had been in dire trouble for a long time and had a right to expect far greater loyalty from those around him than he received.'

Harold and Mary Wilson and their son Giles came to dinner with Thomas that night. Wilson said he had been in touch with Thorpe that weekend to encourage him to stay and fight, but Thorpe said further lurid newspaper stories coupled with a broadcast attack on him by Liberal MP Richard Wainwright had left him with no choice but to resign.

For Thomas, even in hindsight when writing his memoirs years later, the 'disloyalty' shown to Thorpe by party colleagues was of greater importance than the criminal conspiracy Thorpe participated in.

Thomas had a major falling-out with the Labour government

over his handling of the Aircraft and Shipbuilding Industries Bill, a piece of legislation aimed at nationalising large parts of the aerospace, shipbuilding and ship repairing industries. Labour had a manifesto commitment to take the legislation forward, but there was fierce opposition to it from the industries themselves and from the Conservatives.

Tory MP Robin Maxwell-Hyslop, an expert on parliamentary procedure, argued that the Bill was 'hybrid' – in this case not dealing fairly and equally with every shipyard concerned – and should not proceed.

Thomas, who promised to give a ruling on Maxwell-Hyslop's submission within days, came under great pressure from both sides. A Tory delegation comprised Sir Michael Havers, the Shadow Attorney General; Humphrey Atkins, the Chief Whip; and other frontbench spokesmen. Labour's delegation was led by Michael Foot, the Leader of the House; Eric Varley, the minister responsible for the Bill; other ministers; the Attorney General, Sam Silkin; and the Government draftsmen responsible for drawing up the Bill. Thomas wrote: 'Both sides argued their case with passion, but the meeting with Labour was particularly tense as they argued why I should rule in their favour. I think it was only then that they realised just how impartial I intended to be.'

Maxwell-Hyslop drew Thomas' attention to one of the definitions in the Bill, which stated: 'For the purposes of this Bill a ship is anything that floats and has a hull.' The Tory MP then showed Thomas a picture of an oil rig, pointing out that it had a hull and floated. Oil rigs were not included in the Bill, and the shipyards which built them were not to be nationalised. Because some ships and shipyards were included in the Bill, it was therefore hybrid, claimed Maxwell-Hyslop.

Thomas was persuaded there was 'no doubt' the Bill was hybrid. When left-wing Labour MP Eric Heffer, who represented a Liverpool seat, told him that if he ruled against the Government thousands would be made unemployed, Thomas responded that would be 'a grievous thing indeed', but he could not make a decision on that basis. He wrote in his memoirs: 'I told him it was simply a question as to whether it was right or wrong so far as the House was concerned. I had to keep to the rules of the House as it was the only way to be fair.'

After he formally ruled that the Bill was hybrid, Thomas claimed Harold Wilson told him it was "the right ruling and a very courageous one".

For Thomas, 'once you put the Speaker's wig on your head, you feel differently'. He added: 'I think the party as a whole understood what I had to do, but I am sure that Jim Callaghan and the rest of the Labour leadership never really forgave me.'

Shortly afterwards, when Cardiff City Council requested a picture of Callaghan and Thomas together, Callaghan initially refused. He only agreed to have the picture taken when Thomas said he'd otherwise have to tell the council that the Prime Minister wouldn't cooperate. Thomas said that Callaghan never forgave him. When, after his retirement, Thomas was at a dinner in Cardiff with Sir Julian Hodge, their mutual friend who founded the Commercial Bank of Wales, Callaghan approached the pair and said to Hodge: "It is you who should be the viscount, not him."

In the case of the Aircraft and Shipbuilding Industries Bill, the Labour government decided to press on despite the Speaker's ruling. The Conservatives put forward an amendment that the Bill should be referred to a committee of examiners. The vote on the amendment was tied, with 303 votes in favour and the same number against. Thomas therefore had to give a casting vote. Before he did so, the future Labour leader Neil Kinnock shouted out: "Vote Labour, George!" Basing his decision on a

19th Century precedent, Thomas voted against the amendment, the result of which was that it fell. There was then a need to have a vote on Labour's substantive proposal to set aside standing orders so the Bill could continue despite the Speaker's ruling that it was hybrid.

The atmosphere in the House was electric and hostile. Michael Foot said: "Nothing could do more injury to the House of Commons than for the people outside to hear that the jobs of workers in the shipbuilding and aerospace industries are put in jeopardy by a semi-drunken Tory brawl." Thomas responded: "It is not in order to accuse anyone in this place of being drunk. To a man in my position, to be semi-drunk is as bad as being drunk." Foot withdrew his words, but added: "Yesterday many opposition members tried to stop me speaking in the House when they were sober and tonight some have tried to stop me speaking when they are in a different condition."

When the vote was taken, the Government somehow found an extra vote, winning by 304 to 303.

A group of Welsh MPs including Neil Kinnock sang *The Red Flag*, emphasising the word 'here' in 'We'll keep the red flag flying here'. Some Conservative MPs responded with mock Hitler-type salutes.

Amongst scenes of general disorder, opposition frontbencher Michael Heseltine famously grabbed the mace – the ceremonial symbol of royal authority – and swung it around over his head. Thomas suspended the sitting initially for 20 minutes, deciding it would be 'grossly unfair' to name – and suspend – Heseltine, without taking the same action against those who had sung *The Red Flag*. He then suspended the sitting until the next morning, when he told MPs: "I have been in the House for 31 years. I have witnessed many occasions when tempers have become frayed and right honourable and honourable members have said and done things which they regretted afterwards. I hope that the

House will remember that any action which undermines the dignity of this House undermines its authority both here and outside."

Years later he wrote: 'It had been a truly disgraceful night in the Commons but I still believe the action I had taken was the best in the circumstances, with so many members in breach.'

With the Tory opposition believing that the Government's single vote victory had been achieved by a Labour MP reneging on a pairing arrangement, unremitting hostility broke out between the two main parties. This increased the pressure on Thomas as Speaker, and he believed it was inevitable that he would have more trouble with the Government than with the Tories.

In June, Thomas had a visit from Michael Foot and Michael Cocks, the Labour Chief Whip. They asked him how he would vote if there was a tie on the Opposition's motion to get the Shipbuilding Bill referred to a committee. Thomas considered Foot to be in a belligerent mood – he was insisting that the Government needed a guillotine to force the Bill through. Thomas told Foot and Cocks he would be governed by precedent. This meant he would vote against the Tory motion if there was a tie – but if there was a tie on the guillotine vote he would have to vote against the Government. Foot objected and put forward other interpretations of rules of the House. But Thomas insisted he would follow precedent, later stating: 'I was a servant of the House and the House alone'. In a significant passage in his memoirs, Thomas wrote: 'It became clear to me then that whereas the struggle of my early predecessors had been to protect the rights of the Commons against the monarch, a modern Speaker's struggle is to be independent of the Government ... I believe passionately that the Speaker's role is to confine himself to protect the rules of the House and not to take sides in the battle'.

He said he resolved to maintain his integrity and vote regardless of past loyalties. And he added: 'I felt a real sense of shock at the way Michael Foot had behaved in trying to influence my vote.' To demonstrate that he did not always side with the Opposition against the Government on procedural issues, Thomas makes the point in his memoirs that he upset the Conservatives by allowing the Government to approve a guillotine motion on five Bills in the same day. A delegation of front benchers including John Peyton, Humphrey Atkins and Sir Michael Havers pressed him to rule the guillotine motion out of order, with Peyton making the point that the Opposition would be very angry indeed if they didn't get their way. He stood firm.

Weeks later Atkins came to see Thomas again and told him senior Tories believed he was too friendly with Cledwyn Hughes and the Prime Minister. Atkins denied there was any implication that he performed the role of Speaker unfairly. Thomas responded that he rarely saw the Prime Minister, who had not been to see him for a meal or a drink in Speaker's House since assuming the role. He said he had been friendly with Hughes for 25 years and, like his Conservative predecessor Selwyn Lloyd, saw nothing wrong with keeping old friendships going.

What he didn't tell Atkins was that he felt he had to be on guard with Hughes, whom he knew out of loyalty to the party was telling the Prime Minister about his conversations with Thomas. With the financial crisis getting worse, there was speculation about the possibility of a National government, essentially a coalition of Labour and Tories. The Conservatives confided in Thomas that they wanted such an outcome. He was flattered that they did so. Some leading Labour members thought that if Callaghan pushed for a national unity government, three quarters of the Cabinet would back him, together with around 100 backbenchers, approximately one third of the parliamentary party. Thomas shared the estimate of the extent of support for such a move. As things turned out, the Labour government carried on and the prospect of a National government disappeared.

Demonstrating that he was not, in fact, averse to descending into the political fray despite his role as Speaker, Thomas offered advice to a right-wing Labour Cabinet Minister who was planning to resign and denounce the party's left wing. Reg Prentice, the Minister for Overseas Development, had been talking to a small group of Tories about quitting the Cabinet for some weeks. He was involved in a battle against de-selection by left wingers in his local party at Newham North East. Thomas advised him to stand as an Independent at the next general election, and if elected – as Thomas expected – to apply quickly for readmission to the Labour Party.

During their conversation, Prentice agreed with Thomas that the prospect of 'moderates' from all parties joining together to form a new group had receded. Despite their agreement on this point, however, Thomas was unimpressed by Prentice, who quit Labour and joined the Conservatives before the next general election. Thomas later stated: 'The more I talked with Prentice, the more I marvelled that Harold Wilson, still more Jim Callaghan, included him in their team. There were so many other people with higher ability on the back benches waiting for promotion. Prentice went on to become a Conservative and a junior minister in Mrs. Thatcher's first government, which I found equally surprising.' In March 1977, having lost its majority following a number of by-election defeats, and facing a motion of no confidence from Margaret Thatcher's Conservatives, Labour negotiated a deal with Liberal leader David Steel. The Lib-Lab pact allowed the Labour government to limp on for another two years.

13

Open House

George Thomas was very proud of living in Speaker's House. When the actor Stanley Baker visited him there, they looked out over the Thames. Baker pointed out a large building and said: "That's mine, George", going on to point out that as two boys from the Rhondda they had not done badly. Thomas replied: "No, but you have done better. I am only a tenant here."

Before Thomas, Speaker's House was little known to the public. Shortly before he stepped down from the role, Thomas' predecessor Selwyn Lloyd agreed that a TV film about the work of the Speaker could be made. But Thomas himself had taken over by the time the film came to be produced.

Presented by Leslie Timmins, a Methodist minister – although that isn't made clear – the programme, *Mr. Speaker*, gives an idealised portrait of Thomas, and, with hindsight, the viewer is left extremely uneasy by his over-familiarity with children and young people who fleetingly appear.

Within two minutes of the programme starting, four elements of Thomas' life are depicted. It starts with footage of a Royal horse-drawn carriage procession through Westminster – an entirely suitable beginning for a documentary about a politician who was besotted with the Royal Family and the outdated trappings of the monarchy.

The scene then switches to a juvenile jazz band playing kazoos as they march along a street in Cyncoed, Cardiff, to a garden fete, immediately after which Thomas is seen outside a church hall, ruffling the hair, pinching the cheek and holding the chin of a boy aged around nine. He is seen preaching a sermon in the Forest of Dean and we hear a radio clip of him announcing the result of a vote in the House of Commons (Parliament was not yet televised).

The extract from his sermon shows him using the rhetorical style of a revivalist preacher to get his message across to a congregation in awe of him. With demonstrative hand gestures, pregnant pauses, a voice with exaggerated enunciation and raised almost to the level of shouting, not omitting the melodramatic removal of his spectacles, Thomas declared from the pulpit: "Our sturdy fathers believed that Jesus Christ was the Son of God who claimed EVERY man, EVERY baby born ... for God Almighty. They knew in their heart that the handicapped and the underprivileged, the strong and the powerful, all alike were made to walk alike with God himself ... This is the belief on which we have established our way of life."

Before Thomas became Speaker, most MPs' knowledge of Speaker's House was restricted to an annual tea party which like many of his colleagues he didn't like because he considered it to serve no useful purpose and which most MPs only attended out of a sense of duty. He decided to adopt a more open and friendly approach, inviting small groups of MPs to dine with him or take tea after Prime Minister's Questions when he left the chair until the evening.

He also entertained a wide cross-section of visitors, ranging from the Archbishop of Canterbury to Israeli Prime Minister Menachem Begin, President Richard Nixon, Chairman Hua of China, actress Penelope Keith and Saudi Arabian Oil Minister Sheikh Yamani. There was also a sprinkling of trade union leaders.

Clearly relishing the material benefits of living in Speaker's House, he wrote: '[The] table was splendid, particularly when set with the Speaker's state silver. Speakers now receive a parliamentary pension, but until the end of the 18th Century, the Speaker took the state silver for himself as if it was considered a perk of the job.'

In his first month he gave a dinner for all the church leaders in the country, delighted that they 'dressed for a state occasion' in their various robes and cassocks of different colours. Thomas saw himself as '[giving] a lead in cementing the relationship between Church and State'.

Shortly afterwards he gave a dinner for the Commons' eight party leaders which went well, with Wilson and Thatcher teasing each other good-humouredly.

After he called the proceedings to a halt at 9.20pm so he could resume the chair in the Commons chamber, Liberal leader Jeremy Thorpe said: "Mr. Speaker, this is an historic night for we have all met happily in this neutral place and we thank you for underlining the fact that although we are each seeking power for our respective parties, we can still respect each other personally." Such flattery made Thomas 'glow inside' that he could preside over a chamber which showed such respect for democracy.

He also felt proud when he was able to establish a rapport with Nicolae Ceausescu, the tyrannical and murderous dictator of Romania. According to Thomas, Ceausescu felt uncomfortable staying in Buckingham Palace during a state visit. He was also supposedly overwhelmed by the grandiose atmosphere of Speaker's House, until Thomas confided that he was the son of a miner. In reality, Ceausescu was well used to a life of opulence, living in a palace of his own and having up to a billion dollars stashed in overseas bank accounts.

Thomas was also proud of playing host to 28 visiting Speakers when they came for a meeting of the Commonwealth Speakers' Association. It was 'a tremendous experience' for him to meet colleagues from around the world and realise how much respect they had for Westminster. Characteristically going over the top, he wrote: 'I sometimes feel that [Westminster's] history and traditions are better known throughout the Commonwealth than they are by our own people.' For him, being free of party restrictions because of his role as Speaker made others willing to enter 'more open friendships' with him. Never in his life before, he claimed, had he had a better opportunity of listening to both sides of a question put so eloquently.

Thomas came to know Sheikh Yamani, the Saudi Oil Minister and Secretary General of OPEC, to whom he was introduced by his friend Sir Julian Hodge. Yamani became a frequent visitor to Speaker's House, and Thomas couldn't resist the temptation to write of him in flattering terms: 'He is my idea of a sheikh, very cultured, courteous and possessed of great natural dignity. He is a deeply religious man, but not in the fanatical, cruel sense of Ayatollah Khomeini, and like me he is a firm believer in the golden rule: do unto others as you would have them do unto you.' Thomas and Hodge visited Yamani at his summer home in the mountains at Taif in Saudi Arabia, where they mingled with members of the Saudi royal family. Thomas wrote: 'It gave me the opportunity to meet the oil ministers who represented countries that were traditionally our friends but which we were in danger of offending.'

He didn't go on to explain how he felt 'we' were in danger of offending countries that were our oil-producing friends, although the fact is that they resented the West's support for Israel. That was by far the major factor which had led to the massive increase in oil prices imposed by OPEC countries following the Yom Kippur war in 1973.

Nevertheless, Thomas does provide us with some insight

about the future dangers threatening Saudi Arabia, doubtless gleaned from his convivial talks round the dining table with Saudi princes: 'Saudi will not fall to the communists; the real danger could come from the extremists on the far right.'

Having a friend like Sheikh Yamani didn't conflict with Thomas' love for Israel, which he had fostered since his early years when he studied the Old Testament. He also greatly admired the way Israelis had in relatively few years 'made the desert bloom'. Meeting Menachem Begin, the hard-line Israeli Prime Minister, Thomas thought the only thing he might have in common with him would be their love of Israel. It was Thomas' turn to be flattered when Begin – who had been a member of the Irgun guerrilla force that killed British soldiers during the Palestinian Mandate period after the Second World War – said at the steps of Speaker's House: "Mr. Speaker, Sir, to think that I have come to the Speaker's House of the Mother of Parliaments to whom the world owes so much."

Visiting Israel at Easter 1978, Thomas broke down in tears as he was being shown round Yad Veshem, the memorial to the Holocaust. The memory of his post-war trip to Auschwitz had come flooding back.

Controversially, Thomas agreed to welcome the disgraced US President Nixon when he came to London. The request had come from Tory MP Jonathan Aitken, who years later was disgraced himself when he was jailed for perjury after denying during a libel case that a bill from the Ritz Hotel Paris had been paid for him by an Arab businessman, in breach of parliamentary rules. Although it was made clear that Nixon would not be welcomed in Downing Street, Thomas took a different view, writing: 'I believe there is always room for compassion, so when Jonathan Aitken ... asked me if I would receive ex-President Nixon in 1978, I had no hesitation in agreeing. There was a general air of disapproval but I have always believed that if anybody has done wrong and been punished for it – as President Nixon undoubtedly had been – it was not for me to say that the punishment must continue. Sitting in judgement on other people is a very risky business.'

By opening up Speaker's House in the way he did, Thomas made it more of a part of Parliament than it had ever been before. He gave farewell dinners for the likes of Lord Denning, who was retiring as Master of the Rolls. He also had a tendency to invite people he met on official or unofficial business to tea or dinner at Speaker's House, and they invariably accepted. Children could also be heard in Speaker's House regularly – a deliberate policy on Thomas' part, who invited MPs' families as well as themselves to tea. He also allowed use of rooms in the house for wedding and christening parties.

It comes as no surprise to discover that, for George Thomas, the most memorable visitor to Speaker's House – and the one deserving of the greatest sycophancy – was the Queen. In his memoirs, he embarks on a lengthy description of his preparations for the great day, which coincided with a ceremony commemorating the Queen's Silver Jubilee in 1977. He tells how he wore his heavy gold state robes at a rehearsal in Westminster Hall, and how because he was relatively short he caught his foot in the hem as he practised going down on one knee in front of the Queen, then standing up and walking three paces backwards. He horrified his staff by suggesting a lump of the robe would have to be cut off.

On the morning of the ceremony, Thomas got up early and said his prayers 'with deep feeling'. He then spent some more time practising kneeling before the Queen before he discovered that by throwing part of his gown backwards as he rose, he could avoid stumbling.

Arriving at Westminster Hall, he felt a mixture of excitement, pride and humility as an attendant shouted out: "Make way for

Mr. Speaker!" He revelled in describing the scene years later: 'As we processed through the hall, the Serjeant at Arms carried the mace before me and then placed it in front of me in the great hall, where I waited for the Lord Chancellor. The audience of ministers, Members of Parliament, judges, ambassadors and people representative of our national life all remained standing with me until the Lord Chancellor came. We bowed to each other and took our seats.'

The dinner at Speaker's House that followed was attended by every living former Prime Minister, as well as the current office holder Jim Callaghan. Callaghan had only come after Thomas frantically called him to say that all the former PMs would be in attendance, together with the current leaders of every other party.

Thomas wrote that the Queen was 'relaxed and gracious', and he believed she had thoroughly enjoyed herself. So far as he was concerned, the night was probably one of the most glittering in the history of Speaker's House, and Thomas was glad it had happened in his time.

Weeks later he thoroughly enjoyed himself when he rode in the Speaker's coach to St. Paul's Cathedral for a commemorative service. His enjoyment was heightened by the knowledge that, because he had used the coach, his own coat of arms depicting a miner's lamp and an open Bible would be inscribed on its door.

The one sour note for Thomas during the Queen's Jubilee celebrations was when he was told by the Lord Chamberlain – the senior officer of the royal household – that it would not be appropriate for him to wear the same state robes when the Queen paid her official visit to Wales. He claimed the idea for him to wear the robes was not his, but that of 'the people in Wales'. He speculated that the Government had told the royal household behind the scenes that it should object to his wearing the robes, but he wasn't able to substantiate that and had to abide by the Lord Chamberlain's ruling.

Convinced that he was fighting a battle on behalf of the people of Wales rather than giving expression to his own love of Ruritanian excess, he concluded: 'There are people who will say that I should not have paid so much attention to tradition and pomp, but again I think it is the politicians who are out of step with what the people like.'

14

Hating Labour

Relations between George Thomas and his erstwhile Labour colleagues did not improve. While he maintained that his rulings on procedural matters were based on sound advice, the minority Labour government increasingly saw him as an ally of the Conservative opposition.

Robin Maxwell-Hyslop, the Tory MP for Tiverton who had advised him concerning the handling of the Aircraft and Shipbuilding Industries Bill, came up with a way of delaying Bills that had not been used for centuries. He persuaded Thomas and his advisers that it was possible for the Opposition to challenge a motion setting up a committee to draft the reasons why Lords amendments had been rejected. Invariably such a motion had previously gone through unopposed.

Thomas was visited by Michael Foot, Leader of the House, and Michael Cocks, Labour's Chief Whip. He wrote: 'Michael Foot was in a belligerent mood, which was becoming increasingly common, and asked me outright what my ruling was going to be. As he was responsible for arranging government business in the House, I told him I would rule in favour of the Opposition, at which he flared up and said such a thing had never happened before. I replied quietly that if it had not happened before, it was only because no-one had discovered the loophole before.'

According to Thomas, Foot's attitude was so aggressive that he also began to speak sharply, saying to him: "You are not to come here to try to twist my arm. I am not going to be pushed around by anyone in this House. If the House does not like my ruling, they know what to do and you know what to do, but my ruling will be that the motion cannot be discussed if there is opposition to it." Foot, by Thomas' account, gave a vigorous response and Thomas suggested the Clerk of the House should be called in. When the Clerk arrived, Foot asked how the Government could deal with the situation. The Clerk told him the Government could propose a motion to ensure that all business motions for the rest of the session would be covered by the guillotine. Foot asked Thomas whether he would regard such a motion as a challenge to his ruling. Thomas responded that it would not be right for Foot to tell the House that he'd received advice from the Speaker because it would give the impression that they had been colluding. Thomas wrote: 'He clearly resented this and, from then to the end of the session 16 months later, relations between us were always strained.'

Asked what had alienated Thomas from the Labour Party, Patrick Cormack said: "I think it was probably cumulative. I think quite a lot of the left in the Labour Party didn't really approve of what they saw as George consorting with the Establishment. But George became part of the Establishment. He felt he'd grown up, as it were, and they resented the fact he now was a real figure in the land.

"And because he was the Speaker at the time when Parliament was first broadcast – on radio, not televised – his 'Order Order' became a household phrase. There were those in the Labour Party with whom he continued to get on well, but others not. He really fell out with Michael Foot in a big way [over the Shipbuilding Bill] when George decreed it was a hybrid Bill.

"Michael Foot tried to put pressure on George. I remember one night going up and having a whisky with him. He was absolutely seething. He said: 'That man is trying to influence me. I am the Speaker and I will not be influenced. I've taken advice from the clerk and I have been advised that my ruling is the right one.' And indeed it was the right one. George was very punctilious, and he had a very good relationship with the Clerk of the House.

"Clifford Boulton was a very good Clerk of the House. He always said George was a very meticulous Speaker. He took advice, but the decision had to be his. I know this, because when I was chairman of various committees, you always sought advice from the clerk, and you always listen to what they say, as I did when I was chairman of the select committee. At the end of the day it is the chairman who takes the decision. George felt he made the decision, but he made it having gone to some considerable trouble to take advice. He sometimes had to take a second opinion, but when the decision was made, it was his. He wasn't going to be browbeaten or bamboozled – words that he used – by anybody."

When Thomas' memoirs were published years later, Michael Foot strongly objected to the passages dealing with behind-the-scenes rows involving the Speaker's rulings. In his book *Loyalists and Loners*, Foot devoted a chapter to Thomas, largely concentrating on the issue of whether it was appropriate for a Speaker to disclose details of confidential discussions that took place with Ministers and parliamentary party managers.

Foot wrote: 'I did not believe that any Speaker of the House of Commons would do what George Thomas had done ... it certainly never crossed my mind that George, the immaculate upholder of convention and custom in all other aspects of the Speaker's duties, would be the first to break the most important convention of all.'

After serialised extracts of Thomas' book were published in *The Sunday Times*, Foot wrote to Thomas, stating: 'I am surprised to read, in *The Sunday Times*, extracts from a book of yours in which you report confidential conversations and exchanges which took place when you were Speaker. I cannot see how this can assist the present Speaker or future Speakers who may wish to have similar confidential conversations. It seems to me that their publication is a breach of trust and can only do injury to Parliament.'

In the letter, Foot went on to describe some of Thomas' reports in the book extracts as giving 'a highly biased account of events'. Thomas responded, stating: 'The whole purpose of me writing this book is because, like you, I am a believer in open government. I believe that the nation has a right to know that the most difficult part of the Speaker's job is by no means sitting in the Chair presiding over debates, but rather the pressures to which he is subject behind the scenes. The intention of the book is to make life easier in this regard, both for my successor and for all subsequent Speakers.'

Foot wrote back, saying: 'I am sorry you have not attempted to deal with the main point of my letter – the breach of faith involved in reporting confidential conversations. I do not for a moment imagine that the present Speaker regards your precedent as an assistance to him; indeed, I imagine that he takes the exact opposite view."

At the time Thomas' book was published, the controversial decision to prosecute senior Ministry of Defence civil servant Clive Ponting had come under criticism. Ponting was charged and stood trial for breaking the Official Secrets Act after leaking, to Labour MP Tam Dalyell, documents relating to the sinking of the Argentine naval warship General Belgrano during the Falklands War. The documents showed that the ship, contrary to government claims, was sailing away from an exclusion zone imposed by the British when she was attacked and sunk.

Foot told *The Times*: "George might be covered by the Official Secrets Act. There's a better case against him than against

Ponting. I am glad to see that the present Speaker is doing his best to restore the necessary confidential authority of his office."

Thomas' successor as Speaker, Bernard Weatherill, had made it clear that he would not be writing his memoirs.

The controversy continued in *The Times*, with Foot extending his attack on Thomas' memoirs to include a further questioning of its accuracy, writing: '[Page] after page in Viscount Tonypandy's book is grotesquely misleading in the impression it seeks to give, and this is a view that has been expressed to me by several Members of Parliament who have now had a chance of reading the passages which refer to themselves.'

Sir Barnett Cocks, a previous Clerk to the House of Commons, wrote a letter to *The Times* in which he stated: 'I remember the controversy over the Aircraft and Shipbuilding Industries Bill, in which the Speaker preferred to take his opinion from Robin Maxwell-Hyslop rather than from better informed authorities. It puzzles me that he now claims, 'I had to keep to the rules of the House' ... I have in front of me, as I write, books written by Lord Tonypandy's immediate predecessors, Lord Selwyn Lloyd and Lord Maybray-King. Neither of these former Speakers departed from the normal practice of respecting private representations by Members.'

Foot concluded that Thomas' memoirs revealed a malicious side of the former Speaker's character that had not previously been evident to his colleagues: 'His good nature and comradeship were just a trifle too effusive and often seemingly overflowing in too many directions. That was indeed my experience all through the years when I had special dealings with him as Leader of the House or Leader of the Party. I could remember no occasion when he accused me of belligerence or ill manners towards him or his office ... Nothing so severe as a critical word seemed to come to his lips naturally, and Jim Callaghan, it seems, during that same period had the same experience. All the more amazing were the charges of turpitude, moral and political, proclaimed in those memoirs.'

Foot wrote: 'I had not known until I read this volume how fierce was [Thomas'] hostility towards those who favoured almost any form of devolution for Wales and how some of this antagonism brushed off on Cledwyn Hughes, at that time MP for Anglesey, when George was supposed to be serving him as Secretary of State for Wales ... He even implied – quite monstrously – that Cledwyn showed less sympathy and understanding than George himself after the terrible Aberfan disaster.'

Writing generally about Thomas' political position, Foot stated: 'Most of us assumed that while his Methodism was certainly the strongest strand in his political character, his sympathies, deriving from his upbringing in the Welsh Valleys, were certainly on the left of the party ... However, the memoirs uncover deeper predilections and animosities. All too often personal whims and pique seem to have played a larger part. The pacifist sympathies are allowed to run into the sand; even a fairly early and ostentatious support of the United Nations is not considered worthy of mention. The boast is made that 'in a way I helped to form' the Campaign for Nuclear Disarmament, but on the next page the suggestion is properly qualified.'

Foot also chided Thomas for his rare but disparaging references to his political hero, Nye Bevan: '[Considering] the foremost part which Aneurin Bevan played in the politics of those times and the knowledge which any Welsh MP could have of his true mettle, the few scraps and sneers about him which figure in these memoirs leave a sour taste indeed.'

Setting out his approach to what was considered acceptable language in the House, Thomas said that as well as always coming down heavily on MPs who accused each other of lying, he also considered blasphemy to be unparliamentary, disapproving of the Labour MP Eric Ogden's use of the word 'Christ'.

Thomas was appalled when the Labour backbencher Reg Race became the first MP ever to use the word 'fuck' in the Commons Chamber. He did so when referring to advertisements for prostitutes reading out "phone them and fuck them" in the Chamber. Thomas had not been presiding at the time, and wrote: 'When I read Hansard the next morning I was horrified and told the Deputy Speaker I was not prepared to allow that word to be inserted in Hansard or accepted just because it was quoted. If we had accepted it, there could be all sorts of filth repeated in the House under the guise that it was being quoted.' He made a statement to the House ruling accordingly.

Illustrating his instinct to sympathise with MPs he considered part of his circle even when they had clearly behaved badly, Thomas expressed support for two Tories caught up in the Poulson corruption scandal. John Poulson, an architect and property developer from Pontefract in Yorkshire, was jailed for five years, later increased to seven, after being convicted of bribing politicians and officials to win building contracts.

When news of a police investigation into his activities broke in 1972, the Home Secretary Reginald Maudling resigned. Back in the 1960s Maudling had been anxious to build up income from business interests, while Poulson needed an influential and well-known name to front one of his companies, Construction Promotion. The MP accepted a salary of £5,000 to chair the firm. Also, Maudling's son Martin went to work for another of Poulson's companies after leaving university without a degree. In addition Poulson donated large sums to a charity patronised by Reginald Maudling's wife, Beryl.

In return, Maudling brought pressure on the Maltese government to award a £1.5m building contract for a new hospital in the island of Gozo to a Poulson company. Maudling also argued strongly against defence cuts that would have impacted on Malta, and succeeded in changing Conservative Party policy so that overseas aid to the country was allocated on the basis of 75% grant and 25% loan, as opposed to the existing 50%-50% split.

John Cordle, the backbench Tory MP for Bournemouth East, was paid £1,000 per year by Poulson to be a consultant in West Africa, where he had extensive contacts. Nevertheless, his approaches to the governments of Nigeria, Gambia and Libya on behalf of Poulson did not bear fruit. He wrote a letter to Poulson asking for the £1,000 payment, outlining precisely what he had done for him, and it wrecked his parliamentary career.

The damning sentence that exposed him as dishonest read: 'It was largely for the benefit of Constructional Promotion [a Poulson company] that I took part in a Commons debate on the Gambia and pressed HMG [Her Majesty's Government] to award Constructional contracts.'

Although the two MPs themselves were not charged with criminal offences because of a legal loophole, a Select Committee inquiry into their association with Poulson concluded that Maudling and Cordle, together with Labour MP Albert Roberts, had engaged in 'conduct inconsistent with the standards which the House is entitled to expect from its Members'.

Cordle resigned from Parliament, while Maudling and Roberts remained as MPs. The Select Committee recommended that they should be reprimanded by the House of Commons as a whole. Thomas wrote: 'I felt very unhappy at the way [the House] dealt with John Cordle ... and Reggie Maudling ... I was feeling terrible because it would be me who would actually reprimand Reggie, whom I had always looked upon as a friend ... I was so upset that when I came to call Reggie Maudling to speak, I called him Mr. Reginald Amery, as Julian Amery was sitting in front of him.'

Thomas expressed delight that Maudling was saved by a 'magnificent' speech by Ted Heath, who ended his praise for Maudling with the statement: "Mr. Speaker, Sir, my right honourable friend is a right honourable gentleman".

MPs voted to note the report rather than endorse it. Thomas wrote that Cordle should not have resigned, adding: 'The House can be cruel and I think it was unjust for John Cordle, who had merely made an adjournment debate speech about a building project in Nigeria without declaring an interest ... I felt at the time, and I have felt since, that this was one of the occasions when the House was unworthy of itself.'

Thomas' stance demonstrated solidarity with MPs who had broken the rules – a clear sign of his absorption by the Establishment. His own tendency to sanctimoniousness may also have endeared Cordle to him. A bastion of the Church of England, Cordle had a penchant for sounding off in colourful terms about issues of sexual morality. In a wholly typical statement, he said: "Priests who indulge in the abominable and intolerable practices of buggery and homosexual genital sex should be expelled from the Church."

At the time of the Profumo Affair in 1963, when Secretary of State for War John Profumo resigned after lying to the House of Commons about his sexual relationship with Christine Keeler, a 'showgirl' who was dating a Soviet diplomat at the same time, Cordle was at his most shrill, saying: "Men who choose to live in adultery ought not to be appointed to serve our Queen and country ... I was appalled to hear that our beloved Queen should be so wrongly advised as to give an audience to a minister who has proved himself so untrustworthy ... It is an affront to the Christian conscience of our nation."

Commentators were not slow to quote his censorious words back at him when his own wrongdoing was exposed.

Another reason why Thomas would have sought to excuse Cordle was doubtless the latter's strong association with the Royal Family. He was a Gold Staff Officer at the Queen's coronation, a friend of Princess Margaret and an usher at her wedding.

In the last period of Callaghan's government, Thomas became even more jaundiced in his relationship with his fellow Cardiff MP and with Michael Foot, the Leader of the Commons. Referring to Callaghan's controversial and much criticised decision to appoint his son-in-law Peter Jay as British Ambassador to the United States, Thomas wrote: 'Jim was clearly under considerable strain throughout 1977 and it may have been this that led him to the very strange decision in May to appoint Peter Jay ... If the Tories had tried something similar, there would have been uproar in the House. It was bad enough that the post was going to somebody without any experience in Parliament, let alone any diplomatic background. That he was the Prime Minister's son-in-law added injury to the insult caused to our ambassadors and diplomats across the world.'

Thomas couldn't resist the opportunity to take things a stage further in making common cause with those who were critical of Callaghan over the appointment, by suggesting he may have been suffering some mental aberration as a result of political problems afflicting his government.

When Home Secretary Merlyn Rees proposed deporting the American former CIA agent Philip Agee and journalist Mark Hosenball as security threats – Agee had written a book, *Inside the Company*, about CIA dirty tricks in Latin America, while Hosenball had written exposes about GCHQ in Cheltenham – former Labour Home Office Minister Alex Lyon called for an emergency Commons debate. Agee had enraged the US administration by revealing shocking activities of the CIA that it didn't want to see in the public domain, while Hosenball's disclosures about GCHQ 's eavesdropping activities in association with the United States were perceived as equally damaging. From Thomas' point of view, however, the issue was simply a matter of parliamentary protocol, with him as the Speaker having total discretion over whether an emergency debate should take place or not. Describing Lyon as a 'difficult' man, he said: 'I explained that I never gave reasons for rejecting an application for an emergency debate, but I reminded him of what usually happened when national security was involved.'

The following day, Lyon renewed his application and pointed out that Thomas had only granted four emergency debates in his year as Speaker – all at the request of the Tories. The implication that he was biased appalled Thomas.

Thomas also resented Michael Foot's refusal to use government time for an emergency debate on the Agee and Hosenball deportations, and especially his advice to MPs that they should keep pressing Thomas for one. The matter was resolved when Foot changed his mind and allowed a debate in government time after some left-wing Labour MPs had threatened to jeopardise devolution legislation by not supporting a guillotine (restricting the length of a debate) unless it was granted.

Using his change of mind over the debate as an opportunity to launch a general attack on Foot, Thomas wrote: 'Throughout my experience of Michael Foot, his ability as a political acrobat never ceased to surprise me. He could stand on his head with the greatest of ease and reverse his firmly announced decisions within 24 hours. It always astonishes me that he survived for so long at the top of the Labour Party.'

Personalising it further, Thomas concluded his attack: 'One thing was very clear. If he felt that he could escape from any difficulty by planting his responsibilities on to me, he never hesitated to do so.'

Thomas defended his decision to grant the Conservatives an emergency debate about a toolmakers' strike at British Leyland on no better grounds than that they wanted one. After receiving a request for a debate from Hal Miller, the Tory MP for Bromsgrove and Redditch, Thomas initially said no, but changed his mind after confirming that the Conservatives were 'very serious' about wanting a debate.

After stating that he was minded to grant a debate, he received a visit from Foot and government Chief Whip Michael Cocks, urging him not to do so on the grounds that it could imperil the chances of a settlement of the dispute. Thomas wrote: 'This had caused me deep anxiety, but since there appeared to be no prospect of a settlement, I felt that the House of Commons had a right to discuss what was an important issue.' He claimed there was a precedent for acceding to the request for a debate: when Labour had been in opposition, they had been granted an emergency debate about a nurses' strike.

When he announced to the House his decision to grant an emergency debate, Callaghan slammed his papers down and said, as he passed the Speaker's chair, "Bad, bad". The Prime Minister wrote Thomas a note telling him 'in rough language' that he had made a bad decision.

Insisting on his right to grant emergency debates as he saw fit, Thomas acknowledged that every time he did so he hurt the Government, but claimed the country was 'on the brink of anarchy' and said he passionately believed MPs had the right to discuss the issues he considered most important, like the firemen's strike which – rather implausibly – had him imagining Britain's cities being engulfed by fire.

After granting another emergency debate to the Tory opposition following the loss of £212m by the Crown Agents,

Thomas had a conversation about the issue with Callaghan before a dinner in London hosted by Israeli Prime Minister Menachem Begin. Thomas wrote: 'I was not a bit surprised by his attitude because I have not met a Prime Minister yet who liked an emergency debate, which will inevitably criticise the Government. When things are going well or calmly, nobody wants an emergency debate; it is only when things go wrong, as they did for Labour, that they are demanded. I remember very clearly saying to him: "You want to be a good Prime Minister, I presume. I want to be a good Speaker. History will judge who did best, but my job is to look after the interests of this House, not the Government".'

Callaghan was concerned there would be pressure to have a public inquiry into the Crown Estates losses – something he didn't want because 'innocent people' could be damaged. According to Thomas, Callaghan said to him sharply: "You should use your influence ... This is not a party political matter, it is merely one to protect the innocent people who serve us in public life."

Thomas told him the Government was likely to be defeated in a vote, because there was strong feeling in favour of a public inquiry rather than the private inquiry favoured by the Government. When the vote took place, Thomas felt vindicated when there was a majority of more than 30 in favour of a public inquiry. He was self-righteous in his victory, writing: 'I felt that I had fulfilled my historic role as Speaker in upholding the rights of the House against the will of the executive, who would have preferred silence from the Members of Parliament. Once again it had been made clear that the Commons is indeed the guardian of public standards as well as of public liberties.'

More trouble arose over the passage of Bills providing for Scottish and Welsh devolution. Initially the Government intended to create Scottish and Welsh assemblies without referendums. But Leo Abse, the wily anti-devolution MP for Pontypool, conspired with Thomas in his role as the Speaker to ensure referendums were part of the deal – thus delaying for 20 years the establishment of a Welsh Assembly.

In his book – *Margaret, Daughter of Beatrice: A Politician's Psycho-Biography of Margaret Thatcher* – Abse revealed how he had engineered the change. He did so by tabling a 'reasoned amendment' to the Bill requiring referendums in the two countries on whether Assemblies should be established or not. Normally, reasoned amendments proposed by a backbencher to a Bill of major significance would have practically no chance of being called for debate by the Speaker. On this occasion, however, Thomas made it known that he would do so if there was sufficient support from both sides of the House.

Several years before, claimed Abse, he had used his expertise as a solicitor to help the Burnley MP Dan Jones avoid prosecution in a local corruption scandal. Now was the time to call in his debt. He tasked Jones, who originated in the Rhondda, with raising as many signatures as he could in support of the reasoned amendment. Government whips realised that Thomas, whose antipathy towards Callaghan and Labour generally was apparent, would be prepared to accept the amendment for debate. If the Government were defeated on the amendment or failed to get the Bill passed, it would fall and there would be a general election. While Abse was by no means certain that Labour MPs would have backed him when the consequences of doing so became clear, the Government blinked first and accepted the referendum as part of the Bill.

By making it known that he would permit Abse's amendment to be debated, therefore, Thomas played a crucial role in blocking devolution at that time.

Prior to that, Michael Foot precipitated stormy scenes in the House when he announced that the Scottish and Welsh Bills would only get one day's debate each for their second readings – a limit Thomas subsequently described as 'ridiculously short'. So far as Thomas was concerned, Commons exchanges between Foot and Francis Pym, his Tory Shadow Minister, over the duration of the debates were won hands-down by Pym.

Revealing his implacably anti-devolution stance, Thomas later told how for the first time he felt frustrated that he could not join in a debate over which he was presiding. He wrote: 'I was fearful for the future of the United Kingdom and felt I ought to join the battle.' The Government won its second reading after an enormous amount of 'arm-twisting' and 'brutal tactics', according to Thomas.

There was another setback for pro-devolutionists at the report stage of the Scottish Bill when Islington South Labour MP George Cunningham (later to defect to the SDP – Social Democratic Party) made an effective speech in which he backed an amendment that meant for an Assembly to be set up, 40% of the electorate and not just a simple majority would have to vote Yes in a referendum.

Thomas was jubilant, saying that Cunningham's speech had killed Scottish devolution. While there were more Yes votes than No in the Scottish referendum – 51.62% to 48.38% – the 40% threshold was not achieved. In Wales, there was a four-to-one vote against setting up an Assembly.

The referendum defeats led directly to the defeat of the Government in a confidence motion, precipitated a general election which ushered in 18 years of Conservative rule.

Thomas' relationship with the incoming government under Margaret Thatcher would be far more cordial than the one he had enjoyed with its Labour predecessor.

15

Adoring Thatcher

On October 14, 1982, Thomas wrote a gushing letter on Speaker's House notepaper to Margaret Thatcher which read: 'My dear Margaret, In my travels during the recess I have constantly been asked to convey to you affectionate greetings from overseas admirers. From Houston, Texas, there comes a torrent of praise! In the Netherlands the Prime Minister asked me to give you his warm good wishes. I feel deeply privileged to have served as Speaker during your Prime Ministership. You <u>know</u> [underlined twice] how much I appreciate your friendship and your unfailing support. Words are inadequate to express my gratitude.

'When the House resumes we shall begin a fairly long run up to the general election. You probably feel that it will be in your interest and that of the House, for the Speaker who will contest the next election to preside over the Queen's Speech and get well run in. If this is your feeling I should announce next week that I shall retire on October 28. It was my hope to complete seven years in the chair, but I realise that the above course may be better from your point of view, and I have always told you that I would try to behave honourably in my departure. Because I love the House and all that it stands for, I am naturally upset at the thought of leaving. I know you will understand such a feeling.

'Margaret, <u>no-one at all</u> knows that I have sent you this letter.

I have let them all guess that my departure will be nearer next summer, so the element of surprise should be complete. You have become a very dear friend of mine, and I wish you well with all my heart. Your strength and courage are a blessing for our country. May you be guided and inspired in the long years of service you have yet to give.'

The unctuous tone is matched by the manipulative way in which Thomas makes it clear to Thatcher that he wants to stay on in the Speaker's role so he can get in his full seven years' service. It's hardly surprising that Thatcher was happy for Thomas to stay on as Speaker until Parliament was dissolved for a general election the following spring.

The sycophancy displayed in a private letter to the Prime Minister disgraces the office of Speaker and shows Thomas to be a lapdog of the executive. It also puts a different light on Thomas' repeated assertions that he upheld vigorously the independence of the Speaker's role.

His offer to stand down as Speaker wasn't the first he had made to Thatcher. Immediately after she had been elected Prime Minister he offered to quit, but she wouldn't even discuss the matter, saying that she and the new Cabinet wanted him to continue.

Thomas quickly decided that this would be his last term, although he didn't want to make an early announcement. He soon became aware, however, that Cardiff West Conservatives wanted to field a candidate against him at the next general election, on the assumption that he would be standing again. He was told by Edward du Cann, chairman of the Tory backbench 1922 committee, that Tory Party chairman Lord Thorneycroft was sympathetic to the Cardiff West Conservatives' wish to adopt a candidate. In the event, Thomas decided to announce – in March 1982 – his intention to stand down at the next election, reasoning that if the Tories wanted to choose a candidate, Labour should be given ample time to pick one too. Tellingly, it seems that while he had direct communication with the Conservatives about his future intentions, he didn't with Labour. It was a further mark of how far he had travelled from his political roots.

His description of the new parliamentary landscape from his point of view is also very revealing. He wrote: 'I was pleased the air was now clear and that I could leave the Chair in my own time and I really began to enjoy myself as my experience grew. The pressures of the minority government were no longer present, although the Labour left were no less active in the House, clearly believing that noise would win the battle they had lost at the ballot box. There was also a noticeable change of style under the Conservative government and, strangely, I met with far more courtesy from Mrs. Thatcher, who had for so long been my political opponent, than I had from Jim Callaghan, whom I had known and worked with for 35 years.'

In portraying the contrast between how he saw himself treated by his former Labour colleagues and by his new Conservative friends, Thomas comes across as an unashamed attention and status seeker. He related how when Labour was in government it was the practice for the Prime Minister to read the Queen's Speech to invited party guests at a 'very informal' reception in 10 Downing Street on the evening before the State Opening of Parliament. All the guests were away by 8pm. The Tories, however, were very formal, with male guests wearing black ties and eating dinner after the speech was read. Thomas told with pride: 'Every member of the Government would be present and I always sat on the right hand of the Prime Minister with Willie Whitelaw on the other.'

He recalled how Harold Wilson, as Prime Minister, tended on such occasions to look in the direction of people whose Bills were being introduced – a favour bestowed on Thomas when

Wilson announced: "A measure of leasehold reform would be introduced".

But while Wilson and Callaghan did not see fit to consult Thomas as Speaker about proposed legislation, he revealed how he was asked by Mrs. Thatcher how he thought various measures would be received.

Speakers are supposed to act with political neutrality. When elected, they sever their links with the party they are likely to have represented for many years. Yet he contemplated channelling money to a right-wing Labour group called Campaign for Labour Victory (CLV) via David Owen, subsequently one of the founders of the SDP. Owen wrote to Thomas on March 4, 1980, stating: 'As promised I enclose some copies of recent CLV literature and copies of the financial appeal. Anyone who wished could send money to the CLV current account ... or alternatively I would be happy to arrange any payment myself and this could come through my own account and therefore be completely confidential. I will keep you in touch with progress. I greatly enjoyed our talk and your advice.'

With Owen's letter came a CLV briefing paper entitled *Militant: Why We Must Defend the Party*. The paper accused Labour's NEC of hypocrisy for advocating open government while suppressing debate about the Militant problem. There is no record as to whether Thomas made a financial contribution to the cause or not.

Ten months later, when Owen, Roy Jenkins, Shirley Williams and William Rodgers announced their resignations from Labour and the formation of the Council for Social Democracy (later to become the SDP), Thomas kept a copy of the press release for his archives.

Perhaps rather oddly, Thomas kept in his private papers a press release from the East German (GDR) Embassy hailing the meeting between East Germany's communist leader Erich

Honecker and West German Chancellor Helmut Schmidt as 'convincing proof of the vitality of the policy of peaceful co-existence between states with different social systems, the GDR's party and state leadership'.

Thomas was a late convert to the merits of broadcasting parliamentary proceedings – a slightly surprising fact, given that his trademark cry of "Order, Order" became so deeply associated with the early years of Commons radio coverage. The two words got Thomas known throughout Britain and the English-speaking world. He took pleasure at parents coming up to him as he travelled round to tell him that their young sons or daughters imitated his utterance of "Order, Order" with his Welsh accent. He wrote: 'Some of the examples I listened to were enough to make me cringe and I had visions of a whole generation of English children growing up with a Welsh accent.'

From a self-interested perspective, Thomas was flattered that broadcasting raised the profile of the Speaker, with people realising the crucial role played by the office-holder in ensuring parliamentary business proceeded smoothly.

He also attributed an increase in visitor numbers at the Palace of Westminster to the advent of broadcasting. In his memoirs, he didn't pass up the opportunity to refer yet again to the ceremonial aspects of his role: '[There] would always be about 400 or 500 people milling about in the central lobby waiting to see the Speaker's procession pass – a very simple procession with one of the attendants walking in his white tie and tails in front with the measured step and bearing of a guardsman, followed by the Serjeant at Arms carrying the mace on his shoulder, his sword at his side, followed by the Speaker in wig and gown and the train-bearer behind holding up the gown, followed by the Speaker's chaplain and secretary walking together.' And so on, and so on.

His love for abasing himself before the ceremonial aspects of his role could be interpreted as a form of narcissism. He wrote: 'As the procession enters the Chamber, the Speaker stands at the Bar of the House and bows, then he walks forward with the Serjeant at Arms at his side and bows to the Chair from the table. When he is at the steps leading to the Chair he bows again before kneeling for prayers. There was inevitably a tiny handful of members who did not believe in acknowledging the authority of the Chair by bowing, but I told them I used to bow to the Chair three times a day and I did not think I lost any dignity by it.'

One of Thomas' least favourite MPs was the Labour left winger Dennis Skinner, who had absolutely no truck with parliamentary ritual. Thomas was appalled by Skinner's 'unparliamentary' behaviour, taking particular exception to his heckling of the likes of the Liberal leader David Steel and the SDP founders Roy Jenkins and David Owen. Thomas wrote: 'In the old days, Skinner's behaviour would not have achieved anything, yet he was elected to the national executive of the Labour Party, and that staggers me, as he seems to have become known more for his rudeness than for fighting for the people he represents in the House.'

In one altercation with Skinner, when the Labour MP was interrupting Employment Secretary Jim Prior and 'shouting abuse at the Prime Minister', Thomas ordered him to resume his seat. When he ignored the instruction, Thomas called for the Serjeant at Arms to remove him from the Chamber – the first time such a request had been made for 100 years. Skinner walked out when the Serjeant at Arms was within one yard of him.

According to Thomas, Skinner was shaken, his nerve cracked and he walked out docilely. Skinner's recollection of the incident in his memoirs – *Sailing Close to The Wind* – published in 2014 was considerably different. He wrote: 'In

1980 ... it was pathetic that I was shown a red card for calling Jim Prior the Minister of Unemployment. Dole queues were lengthening rapidly under Maggie Thatcher and on their way to three million, yet the Tories howled. Speaker George Thomas called "Order, Order" and demanded I withdraw. Minister of Unemployment was deemed unparliamentary language. Today nobody would bat an eyelid. I thought, I'm going to stand my ground here. I refused to leave. Prior jumped up and down. The Speaker ordered the Serjeant at Arms, in his tights with sword dangling at his side, to remove me. As he approached, I snarled, "Geroff, I don't need you to escort me. What do you know about unemployment?" The Serjeant looked startled. I don't think he knew what had hit him. Wisely, he didn't make a grab for my arm. Rather he took a step back. I knew I was on my way. I got to my feet and walked out under my own steam.'

When the Falklands War was being debated on May 26, 1982, Thomas refused to allow the Labour MP Andrew Faulds to speak, even though he had been sacked from the Labour Shadow Cabinet because of his outright opposition to sending a military taskforce to recapture the islands from the Argentinian invaders.

Thomas had refused to allow Faulds to speak in an earlier debate on the war, and felt that if he allowed him to take part in a later debate he would be giving in to bullying – a precedent he was not prepared to allow. Thomas wrote: 'When he got up that day, he was most abusive, asking if I was aware that he had stood in the three debates and he had not been called in any of them. I pointed out that he was not alone as at least 100 members had also been standing without being called in either debate. He would not stop shouting so I ordered him to leave the Chamber for the rest of the day's sitting.'

Thomas went on to point out that the debate was being broadcast around the world, and claimed that Faulds, an actor by profession, was overcome by the drama of the occasion. Thomas wrote: 'He turned round and started to wave his hands and shout at me.' Thomas 'named' Faulds, meaning he was ordering him out of the Chamber for the rest of the day. But the move to exclude Faulds was not backed by the Labour opposition, and for the only time during Thomas' Speakership a division was necessary. Most Labour MPs abstained and the motion to exclude Faulds was passed by a big majority, with 27 MPs plus two tellers opposing the exclusion. The 29 consisted of 28 Labour MPs and Plaid Cymru's Dafydd Elis-Thomas. Thomas said Labour leader Michael Foot had 'very mixed feelings' about sacking Faulds from the Shadow Cabinet, and for that reason had not backed his exclusion from the Commons.

The Hansard record of the debate shows that shortly before Faulds complained about not being able to speak, the right-wing Tory Sir John Biggs-Davison called for Argentina to be put on warning that military strikes would be launched against it if necessary. This was regarded as perfectly acceptable.

When Faulds was not allowed by Thomas to speak, he said: "You are purposely trying to silence the Opposition to this senseless operation. You will not accept Members who are opposed to this lunatic operation." It was those words that led Thomas to 'name' Faulds. At the time, Faulds wrote to Thomas saying: 'I think if you bother to examine your conscience in Christian honesty, you may have to agree that my accusation that you were trying to silence the voices of dissent in the Falklands Debates and Statements had some validity. Of course, you called members of the 'Loony Left' because their opinions are dismissable. But with moderates such as Tony Meyer, David Crouch, Tam Dalyell and myself, you were less generous. And I should not need to remind you of your duty to protect, not government policy, but the interests of backbenchers.'

In the cases of both Skinner and Faulds, Thomas claimed to be maintaining the order of the House, but the fact is that he intervened to silence criticism of the Conservative government's positions on unemployment and the Falklands War. He was deluding himself – or hoping to delude others – when he claimed to be impartial.

It was during a banquet for US President Ronald Reagan that Thatcher, for the first time, showed strain associated with the Falklands War. She had been informed of heavy losses in Bluff Cove as Welsh Guardsmen were landed prior to the taking of Port Stanley, but the news had not been released.

In a further display of hyperbolic sycophancy, Thomas wrote: 'I think that had a man been Prime Minister, he would probably have lost his nerve long before. Any man would have gone back to the United Nations to make sure he was not going to be ostracised by the world community, in much the same way as the Opposition were putting themselves in the clear if things went wrong. Britain would have lost all influence in international affairs if Mrs. Thatcher had submitted to the pressures and gone back to the United Nations. It would have meant that never again would Britain take any decisive action to defend her people. The Prime Minister showed remarkable courage and determination throughout the whole of the tragedy, and she knew tragedy was inevitable once the islands had been invaded by Argentina. But by her action she saved the good name of Britain.'

The fact is that Thomas' best friends were by now far more likely to be Conservatives. A letter he wrote to the Tory MP Patrick Cormack in October 1980 is revealing in this respect: 'Words are hopelessly inadequate to express the enormous gratitude I feel for your action in obtaining for me an Honorary Membership of The Athaneum. It seems impossible for me to believe that such a marvellous honour should come my

George and Mam—they were inseparable [National Library]

139 Miskin Road, Trealaw. The Spartan home shared by the young George with his mother and siblings.

201 Trealaw Road, Trealaw, built by Thomas' maternal grandfather. George Thomas lived here with his mother, step-father and siblings. He died in 1997, not 1998.

Marlborough Road primary school in Roath, Cardiff, where Thomas taught in the 1930s.

George enjoyed – and promoted – the ever-present support of Mam throughout his career. [National Library]

As a young man with (far left) James Callaghan MP (Cardiff South), (centre) Aneurin Bevan MP (Ebbw Vale) and (right) S.O. Davies MP (Merthyr Tydfil). [Western Mail]

Campaigning in Cardiff West - the parliamentary seat he held for 38 years. [Western Mail]

In discussions with (left to right): Cledwyn Hughes MP (Anglesey), The Rev. Tecwyn Evans and Tudor Watkins MP (Brecon & Radnorshire) in 1955. [National Library]

On the campaign trail in Cardiff. [Western Mail]

Celebrating St. David's Day in 1955. [National Library]

As a supporter and 'informer' for Prime Minister Harold Wilson, George was rewarded with a Cabinet position - Secretary of State for Wales. [Western Mail]

Undertaking his duties as Welsh Secretary. Visiting a hospital [Western Mail] ...

... And the Urdd National Eisteddfod in Llanrwst, in 1968 [National Library]

October 21, 1966. The Aberfan disaster, when 116 adults and 28 adults were killed. [Western Mail]

George Thomas' decision to put party loyalty and personal career ahead of defending the interests of the valley community has, more than anything else, secured his infamy in Wales. [Western Mail]

62 Ely Street, Tonypandy, where Thomas' family moved in 1932.

George was totally devoted to his mother and was devastated when she died in 1972. [Western Mail]

The aptly located house - on King George V Drive East, Heath, Cardiff - where Thomas lived, firstly with Mam and then alone until his death.

The Investiture of Charles as Prince of Wales was the brainchild of George Thomas, who correctly judged that it would be popular with the Welsh people. [Western Mail]

The Investiture of 1969 combined two of Thomas' obsessions: the pomp and grandeur of royalty and his wish to destroy the growing popularity of Welsh nationalism. [National Library]

George revelled being in the company of royalty, pictured here with the Queen. [Western Mail]

Thomas' 1970 election address, in which he sought voters' backing for the eighth time. [National Library]

George addressing a public meeting. 'He had a prodigious "gift of the gab".'
[Western Mail]

Parliamentary colleagues since 1945 but George always harboured a resentment
towards Jim Callaghan [Western Mail]

Thomas, admiring his portrait as Speaker of the House of Commons: Cardiff Castle, 1978. [Western Mail]

The bust of George Thomas, sculpted by Robert J.R. Thomas in 1979, on display at City Hall, Cardiff. [PMSA]

George and Diana open the George Thomas Scanner Suite at the Princess of Wales Hospital, Bridgend. [Western Mail]

Ysbyty George Thomas in Treorchy, Rhondda. For how long will his name be associated with this cottage hospital?

Launching his book *My Wales* in 1986.

George would have been proud. In June 2016, whilst the rest of Wales was celebrating their football team's exceptional performances at Euro2016 in France, the shop that bore his name in Whitchurch, Cardiff only had eyes for the British royals.

The newly renamed City Hospice in Cardiff. The hospice's excellent care for terminally-ill cancer patients can now continue, without the 'negative connotations' of being associated with George Thomas,

way. You have been a marvellous friend to me ever since we met, and my heart is full of gratitude. I am more excited about this than I have been about most of the Honours that I have been fortunate enough to receive. Bless you all. When I come to dinner on Sunday next I will bring the Athaneum correspondence which I have received.'

Membership of the Athaneum was seen by Thomas as the acme of achievement and success. Thomas subsequently wrote an introduction to Cormack's book *Westminster – Palace and Parliament*.

Just after Christmas 1982 Margaret Thatcher wrote thanking him for his 'very beautiful Christmas gift'. She added: 'You are most generous and kind to us and you take so much care in the perfect choice of gift. This one – and the others you have given us – will help add to the Thatcher family heirloom which Mark and Carol will cherish – especially because they know and admire everything you are and stand for. We all needed a Christmas break and it is wonderful to have a few days at Chequers before taking the decisions of the new year. And 1983 won't be easy for <u>you</u> or for me. But if we got through the last year – the same <u>qualities</u> and beliefs will take us through the next year.' She signed the letter: 'With great affection, Margaret'.

After Thomas had stood down and Thatcher had won a landslide victory in the 1983 general election, the re-elected Prime Minister wrote to him saying: 'My dear George, Forgive me for the delay in writing when there is so much to thank you for. Thank you for your outstanding leadership as the Speaker. You kept the dignity and order of the Commons when it might otherwise have been lost. Thank you for your total integrity – integrity whose strength and purpose could only come from belief in God. Thank you for your humanity, warmth, kindness and generosity. You brought us through difficult years. Democracy needs very strong leadership if it is not to degenerate into a battle for rights between organised and often artificial protest groups. Someone has to be the custodian of the greater qualities. We miss you very much and hope to see you soon.'

Describing Thomas' treatment of Plaid Cymru while Speaker, Dafydd Wigley said: "I'll be honest with you – during his time in office, we couldn't complain at all. He was totally fair with us. Whether or not he intended to be, or whether he was killing us with kindness or whatever, we had no room to complain at all. There'd be numerous times when I'd be sitting, waiting, and perhaps getting agitated or over-excited, and I'd get a note from him saying 'Calm down, Dafydd', and then – incredibly – there'd be a sentence in Welsh. I've got a whole collection of these at home, buried away, because I thought I shouldn't throw them away. He'd know more Welsh than he'd want to admit – that is certainly so – not only in terms of conversational Welsh, but he could write it as well.

"I'd imagine – I take it that his religious beliefs were totally genuine, I wouldn't for a moment challenge those – that being so, and coming from Wales at that period he might well have read some religious texts and phraseology in Welsh; certainly some sermons, and that sort of thing.

"He and Cledwyn had a very interesting relationship. Cledwyn would say all sorts of things – a metaphorical kicking – about George, in private to us. Poor old Cledwyn and George have gone now and I don't think Cledwyn would mind my divulging that. On one occasion George had invited himself to stay with Cledwyn. I'd heard some of Cledwyn's comments about that separately, but at that time George actually came over and called at our home, and had afternoon tea with us. It was a time before our two boys had died [from a congenital disease]. He was very, very sympathetic, and I think that was genuinely so. He had called by for that reason. So, in that context, you have to accept the guy as he was and the way that he behaved. On that particular visit it was I think heartfelt and genuine – and one accepted it.

"Then, of course, as Speaker he created a profile for himself which brought the job of the Speakership of the House of Commons to life for millions of people who would never have had the opportunity of hearing anything live until it started being broadcast. And he was the character who stepped in, on to that particular platform, as the platform was first being unveiled for the general public. The way he developed his 'Order, Order' – it became his signature phrase. In terms of his performance as Speaker, forgetting for a moment what the Labour MPs would have regarded, no doubt, as a betrayal – although they have no right to expect the Speaker to be on their side any more than anybody else has – George had the ability, because he had a sense of humour. Nobody could question that at all and, when the place was boiling up, as it did – with perhaps Dennis Skinner saying something about something or other – George would make a quip, a joke, an aside or whatever and the whole place would fall about laughing, and then they'd forget why they were arguing with each other and get back to work. So he used his humour in a very effective way like that.

"There's a lovely story about Dennis Skinner showing a crowd of schoolchildren from his constituency around the building. He was in the Central Lobby, pointing out what was there, and, by then, George Thomas was in the House of Lords. He said, 'Dennis, how are you, Dennis? Are you not going to introduce me to these nice little boys?' Dennis grunted and scowled in response, and said: 'Kids, Lord Andy Pandy'.

"I didn't find him difficult to deal with. There were times, obviously, when we'd be tearing our hair out and we felt we weren't getting a fair crack of the whip and all the rest. There was a radio broadcasting ban on us at that time – we weren't allowed to have party political broadcasts – so we certainly felt hard done by. I suspect what we got from George was a certain amount of superficial sympathy, but a greater degree of the need to be respectful of the working practices of this great institution – the mother of democracies, and all the rest. I can hear him waxing eloquent about that.

"Gwynfor [Evans] had perhaps an even more difficult time in relation to George. Gwynfor – between 1966 to 1970 – would have been travelling, very frequently and alone, on the train and sometimes the two of them would engage in conversation. It came back to Gwynfor that George had said things about him behind his back while he was being all sweetness and light and sugar candy to his face. He was quite scathing about Gwynfor in his autobiography – he was quite scathing about a lot of people in his autobiography. Because of that, and because of the way in which the Prince of Wales had been used in the run-up to the 1970 election when Gwynfor lost the seat, Gwynfor had very little time indeed for him, and understandably so."

As Speaker, Thomas was supposedly politically neutral, and he quickly distanced himself from the Cardiff West Labour Party. David Seligman told how Thomas was offended by the local party's frustration at no longer having a Labour MP: "I do remember once when he became Speaker – I was still chairman of Cardiff West – we were very concerned that he no longer had this contact, politically, with us. He had to be very careful, so he was no longer the sort of MP you could get involved with. He became very much detached from the constituency. We passed a resolution, which I drafted, saying there should be reform and that when someone was elected Speaker they should sit for the constituency of St Stephen's and their previous constituency should be able to elect a new MP. He took that as a personal attack and wrote me a terrible letter saying 'after all these years how could you do this to me?' I wrote back to him saying it wasn't directed towards him at all, and that we just felt we needed someone to represent us in Parliament as he used to do, and as the Speaker he couldn't. He misconstrued it entirely and thought it was a personal attack upon him, but it never was.

"When he was in his final term as Speaker, he delayed saying he was going to stand down for a long time, and we couldn't have a selection conference for a new candidate until he gave us his decision about whether he was going to leave the Speakership. It was delayed and delayed and delayed and whoever was going to be selected couldn't do any work in the seat. Eventually he made his decision and we had very limited time to get the new candidate known. I was selected, but I lost to the Tory candidate Stefan Terlezki in the 1983 general election. He wrote me a nice letter saying how sorry he was, but he didn't campaign at all. He wouldn't put anything on my election address – I would have liked to have had his endorsement."

16

George Thomas and Christianity

In his autobiography, Thomas included a short chapter in which he described the importance of religion to him. He chose to begin it by launching an attack on Labour MP Geoffrey Edge, who had called for Thomas' resignation after he made a speech saying Christian teaching in schools was "necessary". Edge had accused him of being not impartial.

Thomas heard Edge's call for his resignation on the radio. He was angry, and asked Edge to visit him in the State Rooms of Speaker's House – a signal that the matter was regarded by him as significant and that needed to be dealt with on a purely formal basis.

He wrote: 'I told him that his view seemed to be that I should not express opinions on anything, particularly something with which he disagreed ... I made it plain that neither he nor any other member had bought me body and soul just because I was Speaker, and that I would go on saying those things – maybe even more so. I would keep my mouth shut on party political issues but teaching the scriptures was not a mere party issue, rather one on which I would have thought all parties would have agreed.'

In relating the anecdote, Thomas failed completely to put it in context. On March 19, 1976, he presided over a Commons debate on the motion: 'That this House recognises the need to maintain and improve the opportunities for religious education and an act of worship in schools'. The motion was moved by the Conservative MP Michael Alison, a friend of Thomas who on the next page of his autobiography was introduced as having come to see him with his wife Sylvia to request the setting-up of a Christian wives' group in the Commons.

In questioning whether it was appropriate for Thomas to preside over such a debate after making his views known in a speech, Edge was making an arguable point.

The issue of religious teaching in schools was a controversial one in 1976, and remains so today. Thomas made his speech at a Catholic boarding school near Leicester called Ratcliffe College – in his autobiography he mistakenly referred to it as Radcliffe College.

In his Commons speech proposing the motion, Alison quoted from the Spens report of 1938 that informed the 1944 Education Act which made religious education and a daily act of worship compulsory in schools. The Spens report said: 'No boy or girl can be counted as properly educated unless he or she has been made aware of the existence of a religious interpretation of life.' But Alison went further, quoting from a Church of England leaflet which said: 'No teacher of English would think it enough to teach about poetry. His task is to enable boys and girls to create within themselves that imaginative insight which will make it possible for them to enter into the poetic experience. There is a close parallel here with the task of the teacher of religious education, which is to bring children to the point when they understand what a Christian commitment would mean.' And he asserts: 'The fact and act of worship is an inherent, inseparable and essential part of any attempt to teach religion to children.'

Most of the speakers in the debate supported religious

education. Geoffrey Edge did not participate, but the view to which he subscribed was given voice by Labour MP Bryan Davies, who said: "I believe that schoolchildren should be taught to question, discuss and think for themselves about moral values. Yet daily we are insisting that those faculties be suspended, even among the more mature students, and that they should participate in an act to which many of them do not subscribe." The motion backing religious education was backed by MPs without a recorded vote.

Thomas went on to refer in his autobiography to an occasion later in that Parliament when Edge accompanied a vicar from the Midlands who had undertaken a charity sponsored bike ride to London when he was greeted by the Speaker. Thomas wrote: 'I could not resist saying [to Edge], "Hello, have you been converted then?"' Doubtless with some glee, Thomas concluded the anecdote by stating: 'He lost his seat shortly afterwards.'

Asserting the importance of 'Christian ethics' to him, Thomas wrote: 'People [like Edge] make the mistake of underestimating the strength of the spiritual belief in our country. Not so many people go to church now, but they do want their children to grow up knowing the difference between right and wrong – that at the very least our society has an undercurrent of Christian ethics.'

Thomas hosted regular meetings of the Christian wives' group mooted by Alison, sometimes with guest speakers like the Archbishop of Canterbury. There were times when, accompanied by husbands, there were as many as 120 people crowded into the Speaker's dining room. Some of the wives were under stress, and one told Thomas she had been able to keep her sanity after a terrible bereavement only because of the support she had received from the group.

Speaker's House also saw monthly Christian breakfasts for MPs, typically attended by around 25 politicians from across the political spectrum. After taking communion in St. Margaret's Church, they would eat toast made by the Roman Catholic MPs. According to Thomas, most members of the group did not want to proclaim their Christianity widely, not wishing to be accused of campaigning for the Christian vote. Thomas himself had no such inhibitions.

He gave permission for the House of Commons crypt to be used for a commemorative mass to mark the 500th anniversary of the death of Sir Thomas More. It was the first time a Catholic mass had been held there since the Reformation, and inevitably it was condemned by the Ulster Protestant firebrand, the Rev. Ian Paisley. Paisley went to see Thomas, hitting the table as he said: "This is blasphemy, Mr. Speaker." He said he intended to protest as the Host was raised, the most sacred part of the service. After a discussion, Paisley agreed to make his protest at the start of service and then leave. Amid heavy security, that's what happened, with Paisley standing up to complain as Cardinal Hume, the Archbishop of Westminster, entered the crypt.

Thomas wrote: 'It was more than 500 years since Catholics had been allowed to worship God according to their beliefs in that crypt and I found the service most moving. I believe that God used me on this occasion to provide another step forward in religious freedom in Britain: the bigotry of 500 years ago should not decide the way we behave today.'

"I entered the House of Commons in June 1970," said one of Thomas' closest friends, the Conservative MP Patrick Cormack, a senior lay Anglican, "and one of the first people I met on the Labour side was George Thomas, who was a very ebullient character. He was very nice and welcoming. The first time I really got to know him was about a year later when I was serving on the committee of a local government Bill, which was going through the house, night after night. In those days we didn't really have timetabling, we had the guillotine occasionally, but when a Bill went into the committee stage you would sometimes work on it for a very long time. With this particular Bill, we had 50-something sessions, many of them very late nights and one or two through the night sessions. George was one of the two opposition MPs leading on this Bill, and he was particularly anxious to try and get support for some amendments which affected the boundaries of Glamorgan. In the small hours he would occasionally beckon me out so we would have a coffee together and we would chat. We struck up a parliamentary friendship.

"When George became Deputy Speaker I formed a small group of Christians in Parliament, and our friendship developed further. We used to meet for breakfast, once a month at the Stafford Hotel: it was always bacon and eggs. It wasn't over-pious evangelicalism, but we used to invite people like the Dean of Westminster, who would breakfast with us. There were about a dozen of us in all, with about seven or eight in attendance at any one time. So I got to know him better through that.

"During his time as Deputy Speaker he was going to a banquet in the Guildhall. I think it was for the Queen of Denmark. It was the very first time I had taken my wife to such an event; it was actually the very first time we'd been invited to such an occasion. George Thomas was there and he came and chatted to us and was particularly nice to Mary, my wife, and she thought 'what a lovely chap he is', and our friendship blossomed.

"When he subsequently became Speaker, the group of Christian MPs changed the format of our monthly breakfast and we used to have holy communion in St Margaret's, Westminster and then go across to Speaker's House. It was a very simple affair: never more than toast and marmalade and a cup of coffee. So the friendship developed in a very positive way. I think – well I know – George felt he could completely relax with us because I would never take advantage of the fact that he was Speaker.

"When George celebrated his 70th birthday in Speaker's House, we presented him with a very nice silver salver from his breakfast friends, a gift he eventually to left me in his will, which was very touching. It still has pride of place in my London flat."

To some, though, Thomas' Christianity was a facade. Dafydd Wigley said: "There's no doubt at all that for all his protestations of his Christian faith, he had rancour. I suppose there's a fair number of Christians who also have human vices and shortcomings as well. George was certainly a very, very complex guy."

17

In the House of Lords

Leaving the Speaker's chair was not the end of George Thomas'
political involvement. It's usual for retiring Speakers to be
offered a peerage. What had ceased to be usual was the offer
of a hereditary one.

Margaret Thatcher decided it would be appropriate to offer
Thomas a Viscountcy, and he was very pleased to accept it.
At the same time she conferred a hereditary peerage on her
deputy Willie Whitelaw, who became Leader of the House of
Lords.

For Thatcher, hereditary peerages were a good thing. She had
an ideological adherence to the view that Britain should not
be a 'one generation society', which to her validated the idea
of peers passing on their titles to their children. In Thomas'
case, of course, such considerations didn't apply because he
had no son.

Before the introduction of life peerages in 1958, retiring
Speakers were offered hereditary peerages as a matter of
course. In fact William Morrison, who retired as Speaker in
September 1959, carried on the tradition and accepted the
title Viscount Dunrossil. However his successors as Speaker,
Horace King and Selwyn Lloyd, both became life peers when
they retired in 1971 and 1976 respectively.

Thomas, though, was not offered a life peerage. Instead he
received a phone call from 10 Downing Street while visiting

the home of Tory MP Fergus Montgomery – another secret homosexual – in which he was told of the proposal to offer him a hereditary Viscountcy. He wrote: 'I have to confess that it did not take long for me to decide that I would accept happily, because if you are going to the Lords anyway – and I had made up my mind years before that I would go, if asked – there seemed no reason at all not to accept what had been the traditional honour for retiring Speakers for 200 years.'

He went on to make the point that Parliament had never voted to abolish hereditary peerages, but that Ted Heath had made it his practice not to offer them and that the Labour Prime Ministers Wilson and Callaghan had done the same. According to Thomas, Selwyn Lloyd was disappointed not to have been given a hereditary title, feeling 'quite deeply that he should have had the same honour as his predecessors stretching down through history'. Doubtless Thomas would have felt the same if he hadn't been offered a Viscountcy.

He wrote: 'It was put to me ... by an hereditary peer that it was very reactionary for Mrs. Thatcher to have gone back to hereditary titles in the case of Willie Whitelaw, [former Tory Prime Minister Harold Macmillan] and myself. Neither Willie nor I have a son to inherit the title anyway [and Whitelaw's daughters were ineligible] but surely the answer to that is either to abolish the system entirely or to continue it to introduce new young blood into the House of Lords.'

There was little doubt which side of the argument Thomas was now on. Doing away with the House of Lords would be a 'terrible gamble', he argued. According to him, it gave both the Government and the Opposition the chance to have 'second thoughts' about legislation before it was set in stone. It also prevented legislation being pushed through without proper consideration and, at a time when 'a handful' of MPs wanted to destroy parliamentary democracy by shouting down those they disagreed with, the Commons needed the 'restraint' imposed by the Lords. He wrote: 'In my view these people are the weevils working remorselessly to destroy the fabric of our parliamentary democracy. If ever they gained a majority in the Commons the only safeguard for our people would be a vigilant House of Lords.'

Thomas was convinced – or convinced himself – that the quality of debate in the Lords was much superior to that in the Commons, with Bills being subjected to much closer scrutiny. He wrote: 'There is not the same vested party interest, with people looking for votes. There is an independence of mind and considerable scholarship that serves the nation well.'

Interestingly, his heroine Margaret Thatcher appears to have formed quite the opposite view, according to her biographer Robin Harris, regarding its atmosphere as 'soporific', and its 'ponderous style' offending her taste for argument.

Addressing the undemocratic nature of the House of Lords, Thomas accepted that the Labour Party had been opposed to it all his life and that he had often spoken against it himself. His position had, however, changed, and he wrote: 'There is a great deal wrong with the hereditary system but I have been very impressed by the number and quality of young men in the House of Lords who may be there only because a distant ancestor was rewarded many years ago, but who take their roles in the parliamentary machine very seriously indeed. I hope some way can be found to keep them if the hereditary principle in government is finally abolished.'

He went so far as to argue that, whatever reforms might be introduced in the future, the second chamber should not be an elected chamber. He wrote: 'If it is elected, it would have to be given financial sanctions and that would take away the essential power of the Commons. Both America and Australia provide us with examples of how two elected chambers in one legislature plunge the country into crisis when they disagree.'

For Thomas, the second chamber needed to be an advisory chamber for tidying up legislation. He favoured an arrangement under which it would be appointed in proportion to party strengths in the Commons, and made up of the likes of trade unionists and business people, together with others from universities, the professions, public life and (inevitably) retired politicians.

He had clearly imbibed all the establishment arguments that sought to justify the perpetuation of an unelected second chamber.

For himself, on taking up his new position in the House of Lords, he felt it would be inappropriate to take the Labour whip, despite being urged to do so by some old colleagues in the party. To do so would be unfair on his successor Bernard Weatherill, he argued, because people would assume that his assumption of neutrality was only skin deep. In fact, there were already good grounds for believing that Thomas had moved so far from his roots that he would have felt entirely uncomfortable on the Labour benches.

He decided to sit on the cross-benches – and he made it clear to former Labour colleagues that he would not be prepared to support the party line, even informally.

In expounding his credo, he wrote: 'I have not changed my ideals or my values but I am determined to remain independent. I entered politics as a Christian Socialist, and I went out of the House of Commons with the same belief that there is no unimportant person in this land and that our parliamentary system is devised to help everyone to grow to their full stature.'

He concluded his memoirs thus: '[As] I look back I count my blessings. God has been good to me and I remember those days in Tonypandy when my mother said God would open doors for me. I was not to know that the doors would open to lead me in to the Speaker's Chair at Westminster. I can only say now what I thought as I left Speaker's House for the last time and looked at the portraits of my predecessors: "I hope I didn't let you down".'

On February 1, 1984, Thomas received a letter from the Liberal MP Cyril Smith, later to be exposed as a paedophile. It read: 'Thank you for your typically kind letter. You may be 'old', you are certainly a gentleman, but you are also clearly extremely perceptive! Yes – I have been deeply hurt. I feel honestly George as if I've been badly wounded with malice aforethought – and I just feel as if all I want to do is honour my commitment to my Rochdale people until the next election and then get out of it all. I still feel very close to people. That is why I am so thrilled for you in your new work for the children – wonderful, I envy you in that respect! I am a highly emotional person and so tricks such as [name indecipherable] had done on me (and the press and public don't know one half!) deeply hurt me. I could weep. Well – there we are – like a true Methodist you succeed in getting a [word indecipherable] to pour out his soul. I'd love to come and have coffee – and even a chat – though it would be grossly unfair of me to burden you with my troubles. My best mornings are Wednesday, though I can at a pinch, do Thursdays. Wednesday July 22 would be ideal. Any chance this would be convenient? My best wishes – and if I can help you with your new task in any way – do let me know. I look forward to seeing you soon. Mum sends her love. She is 80 this year.'

It is unclear exactly why Smith felt 'deeply hurt', although it has since emerged that from 1970 he had been the subject of successive police investigations into allegations of child sex abuse. His reference to Thomas' 'new work for children' concerned the former Speaker's role as president of the National Children's Home charity.

Closer to home, and by contrast, Thomas received a letter from the mother of one of four young men who had been acquitted of all charges in a criminal trial. David Burns, of Canton, Cardiff, together with Nicholas Hodges, Adrian Stone and Robert Griffiths had been found not guilty in the Welsh Conspiracy and Explosives Trial after nine months on remand in Cardiff Prison. Burns' mother, Freda Burns, had written to Thomas several times in 1982, when he was still an MP. In a letter to him she stated: 'These young men suffered wrongful arrest and imprisonment, during which time their families also endured considerable stress. Indeed, the father of one (whom you met, together with Mrs. Hodges, Mrs. Stone and myself at one of your surgeries) has died very suddenly in the past fortnight, aged 53. He was a dear friend, deeply concerned with civil and human rights, a Christian who practised his faith in a very real way. We shall miss him very much. In the light of the circumstances surrounding this case and the very questionable behaviour of the police officers involved, I write to appeal to you for your support in the forthcoming inquiry, to be headed by Lord Gifford QC, and due to begin on March 19. It is imperative that all Christian and right-minded people should have these matters very much at heart. I therefore ask you most earnestly, to lend your valuable name and support to this important public inquiry.'

Thomas responded: 'Thank you for your letter. I must say my heart aches for you and the families who have suffered so much when your young people were in prison for so long. You may recall that I have been to see the young men. I have written to Mrs. Jones [he meant Mrs. Hodges] for I believe that that poor woman must be going through an exceedingly difficult time. I did not know there was to be an inquiry, but there is no evidence that I could give to Lord Gifford. to add to an infringement.'

Mrs. Burns wrote again, saying: 'I would beg you to reconsider your decision, since you have been requested simply to give your approval to such an Inquiry taking place – not to give evidence. We feel that in your position, it is reasonable to ask you to 'back' those concerned, otherwise what can possibly be respected in British democracy?'

But Thomas was not to be moved, and wrote back saying: 'Thank you for your further letter. I clearly misunderstood your original letter because I thought that there was to be a public inquiry. I think you mentioned the name of the Queen's Counsel who was to conduct the inquiry. I think that with cruel regularity there are protests in Parliament about the long delay in bringing people to trial when they are held in custody. However, now that I am no longer an elected Member of Parliament, I have to take particular care not to intervene in the Cardiff West constituency affairs. I am in honour bound to let the elected MP act in these matters.'

Thomas passed on a letter to the Jewish Labour MP Greville Janner – also an alleged paedophile – saying: 'I was so pleased to see you in the Harcourt Room the other night. Enclosed please find a distressing letter which I have received. I wonder if it is possible for you to comfort the writer.'

Janner responded: 'Many thanks for sending me this sad letter from the unfortunate Mr. Gadany. I will pass it on to the Jewish Welfare Board who I am sure will do what they can to help him – he does not, alas, appear to be in top mental condition! And I am sorry to hear that you have been burdened – but we'll see that we do what we can to help.'

Tory MP Dr. Keith Hampson was arrested for alleged indecent assault on an undercover police officer in a gay club in Soho. After receiving a letter from Thomas, Hampson wrote saying:

'What a wonderful note you wrote, it was a tonic for both of us, and <u>deeply</u> appreciated. The warmth and support so readily given by many has helped tremendously during this ordeal I've so stupidly landed myself in. Many thanks.'

In October 1984, when Hampson's case went to court, Thomas wrote a character reference stating: 'Dear Mr. Staple (Solicitor G.W. Staple of Clifford Turner) I write to you concerning Dr. Keith Hampson MP, whom I knew exceedingly well throughout my years as Speaker of the House of Commons. Dr. Hampson is a man for whom I held the utmost respect, not only on the grounds of his exceptional ability, but also because I looked upon him as a man of integrity and reliability. The incident for which he is being charged is so totally out of character with the Keith Hampson that I know, that I just cannot understand what happened. In all my experience with Dr. Hampson I found him to be an honourable man who was worthy of the utmost respect and trust. It was therefore a very great sense of shock when I read of the Court case. I can only say that the whole business is entirely out of character with the person whom I know.' Hampson was acquitted.

Thomas was now a considerable celebrity and received huge numbers of invitations to speak, open events and simply visit all kinds of organisation. They were mostly rejected, with a typical response being: 'Thank you for your kind letter. I wish in my heart that I could accept your kind invitation, but unfortunately my diary is hopelessly overcrowded.'

At the beginning of September 1984 Thomas was diagnosed with throat cancer and told to give up making speeches. In his final years he suffered recurrently from the condition. Whenever there was a news item about his illness, he received literally hundreds of goodwill cards and messages, all of which he kept and are now preserved in an archive at the National Library of Wales.

He was not prepared to help the defence case of civil servant Clive Ponting, facing charges under the Official Secrets Act after leaking documents which proved the Argentinian ship Belgrano was steaming away from the Falklands exclusion zone when it was sunk by the British Navy. He wrote to Ponting's solicitor saying: 'Unfortunately I fear that there is no way in which I can help you. There was a ruling about 30 years ago that privilege does not apply to correspondence sent to a Member of Parliament.'

In May 1985 Thomas received a letter from Leonard Rayner, a CBI official who had met him in Singapore at a dinner in the High Commissioner's residence when he was Secretary of State for Wales: 'In the recent Ponting case it seemed to me that he was faced with the same appalling problem that some German civil servants had in the 1930s. The allies at Nuremberg trials after the war took the line that these people could not hide behind the excuse they were only carrying out orders albeit illegal orders. Ponting obviously took the same line and the courts have upheld him. My query is can a public servant, in this situation, decide which political party he will pass information to and arbitrarily decide which member? If Parliament has a right to know that the Government may be misleading it, should not the information be given to the Speaker for him to pass on? It seems to me that the Court decision, which I assume sets a precedent, could have serious consequences. I would be grateful for your views on this point.'

Rayner got a terse response: 'Thank you for your letter concerning the Ponting case. I do not feel able to comment on the questions you raise since I am now out of office myself.'

The contrasting views of Thomas were illustrated by two letters he received within weeks of each other in March 1985. A man from Derby called Andrew Broughton wrote to him and said: 'I would like to tell you that, since reading the whole of your autobiography, I have started going back to church again for the first time in almost 16 years. The last church service that I went to was Sunday School. I can't thank you enough for reaffirming my beliefs on who protects us and whom we must always look up to, when we are down especially.'

The opposite view of Thomas was expressed by Ken Llewellyn of Rhiwbina, in Cardiff: 'Dear Mr. Thomas, I do not think that I would have written to you except for the remarks attributed to you: "I can look the British people in the face and say that I have kept faith ... with the British people." Let me remind you how you were keeping faith with the people of Wales when you were Secretary of State for Wales. A small but significant incident to show how I regard your faith. It was an early Sunday morning meeting in a Cardiff hotel, held in secret (I could never understand why) and there were perhaps eight or ten people there. When you arrived you were introduced to each person and your interest was to ask each one where he came from. Having ascertained that all were local to Cardiff, you proceeded to denigrate the people of north Wales for some minutes. This had nothing whatever to do with the business in hand. This petty and unwarranted outburst from the Secretary of State for Wales! Perhaps the 'for' should have read 'against'.'

The publication of his autobiography led to criticism from some of Thomas' former colleagues, who thought he had unfairly portrayed them and in some cases breached obligations of confidentiality. But Thomas was defiant. He responded to a sympathetic letter from Anthony Bourne-Arton, who had been the Tory MP for Darlington between 1959 and 1964: 'Dear Tony, My heartfelt thanks to you for your overwhelming kindness in sending me such an encouraging letter. You can well imagine that the unfair criticism by some of my former colleagues of my book has distressed me. However, it is part of public life and I have been enormously encouraged by the heavy mail I have received from the general public writing in support.'

His supporters in the Christian community were oblivious to the political controversy stirred up by the autobiography. A Scottish reader wrote to say: 'My Lord, Having concluded reading your autobiography *Mr. Speaker* I felt it incumbent to express appreciation of such an inspiring narrative. Your warmth and feeling for the disadvantaged shines clearly throughout, and in this seemingly acquisitive age, is heart-warming. Your Christian witness throughout, in high places and low is a challenge to all believers, and, as a Salvationist, I share your views. Indeed, through our founder William Booth we are really an offshoot of Methodism, and certainly Charles Wesley's hymns abound in the *Song Book of the Salvation Army*. May God continue to use your powerful influence. With grateful thanks.' Thomas responded: 'Thank you for your most moving letter, I deeply appreciate all that you say. I shall cherish your letter as long as I live.'

When there was a literary lunch at Foyles bookshop in London, to commemorate the publication of his memoirs, Thomas proudly spoke of his political trajectory to the right. After saying that when he was a young man it was the *Daily Herald* and the *Daily Mirror*, he added: "Now, Mr. Chairman, it is the *Daily Telegraph* – they call it the hardening of the arteries."

In March 1985 Thomas decided to give up his flat in Cardigan Street, which he rented from the Prince of Wales' estate, and instead live while in London at the Travellers' Club in Pall Mall. He received a letter from Ian Gow, a former Tory Minister who had been Thatcher's parliamentary private secretary, which said: 'I am sure that you have made the right decision about the flat in Cardigan Street. The Club will be much more easier [sic] for you, and you will be extremely well looked after there. Jane and I were so relieved to hear of your <u>excellent</u> prognosis from your doctor. I hope that you will have a restful Easter and that we will see you back in London before the month is out.'

Although a firm Methodist, Thomas was no teetotaller. In January 1986 he received a note from a fellow peer saying: 'Dear George, Drinking again! I have my spies everywhere.'

The one serious campaign issue he was prepared to take up at this time was that against allowing shops to trade on Sundays. Many people from across the UK praised him for his interventions against Sunday trading. He made an impassioned speech in the Lords during the second reading of the Shops Bill. This brought him many letters from Christians and others who shared his views. He wrote to one: 'I share your feeling of betrayal and disgust at the Government's attempt to destroy our Sunday. I fear the only way to fight this is to continue to put pressure on our local MPs and the newspapers.' Later he was made Patron of the Keep Sunday Special Campaign in Wales.

He was not, however, prepared to take part in local community campaigns against the closure of public services. When Sister Janet Rogers of Gelli in Rhondda asked him to support a campaign against the closure of the local hospital, Thomas refused to get involved, telling her: 'Thank you for your letter concerning the Pentwyn Hospital, Treorchy. I know this hospital well because before the war my mother was on the Committee for Rhondda Hospitals and she used to visit Treorchy. I usually took her there in my car. I realise what this hospital means to the community. The only reason why I have not joined is that I feel that Bryn Davies, Chairman of the Health Authority, also must be aware of the importance of the hospital in the area, but he has to deal with the realities of spending the money that is available. I notice that Allan Rogers MP is supporting your campaign and I presume therefore that he will have been in touch with Bryn Davies. I honestly believe that it would be wrong for me to intervene, although the Rhondda is my home valley, this is one of those occasions when I have to acknowledge that the sitting MP is the best person to champion the cause of the valley.'

In February 1986 Thomas received a letter from Ian Gow telling him he was 'a real hero' for visiting Gow and his family at Eastbourne the previous weekend. Gow wrote: 'We did, indeed, hear 'the rustle of the wings of greatness about us'; you have a unique capacity to deliver a vitally important moral message, because of your own humility and sense of humour.'

At this time, however, Thomas was 'with regret' turning down a range of invitations to be interviewed by journalists, and attend dinners and charity receptions etc.

He was also declining the opportunity to take up issues affecting school teachers – the group of professionals he had most affinity with. In February 1986 he received a letter from a maths teacher living in Buckinghamshire called Paul Luckraft. It said: 'I have chosen to write to you as I believe that you were once a schoolmaster, and I know that with your career as an MP and your Christian faith you must have a concern and some influence ... Sufficient to say that current government policy is damaging education, and frustrating and alienating teachers and parents to an alarming extent. There is a complete breakdown in respect and trust in the DES [Department of Education and Science] and especially Sir Keith Joseph. Morale is rock bottom and many teachers have to take on other jobs to help keep their families, or even contemplate leaving the profession. Prospects are not encouraging.'

Luckraft expressed extra concern about the introduction of new GCSE exams: 'All teachers, including headteachers, agree on this. There is not enough time, money or training to introduce them successfully this September. The situation is desperate and it is very disturbing when all we get from Sir

Keith is that they will go ahead 'come hell or high water'. I hope that pressure from the Lords might get through to the top in a way that we have not been able to do. I will be grateful for your support.'

Thomas responded: 'Like you, I am deeply concerned about the appalling educational scene but I fear that I cannot see any way in which I can help. I wish that I could.'

Thomas wrote to a man researching the Thomas family roots in Carmarthenshire, saying: 'I am afraid that I have no details at all of my Carmarthenshire links. I have often wished that I had been able to make enquiries but such has not been the case. It was kind of you to let me see your wife's family tree in Carmarthenshire and I return it to you in case you need it.'

In June 1986 Thomas received a rather strange letter from Sir William van Straubenzee, the Tory MP for Wokingham and a former Minister. He was also a member of the General Synod of the Church of England. The letter read: 'I am quite certain that you will not let it slip your mind, but I hope perhaps you will kindly put on your 'thinking cap' about a good medical practitioner in Cardiff to whom I might refer two young friends whose marraige (sic), regrettably, is going on the rocks. Any help you could give would be enormously appreciated.'

Thomas' response is not contained in his files. The most likely explanation for the letter is that it was a cryptic request for help with a sexually transmitted disease contracted by van Straubenzee, another closet homosexual.

On February 4, 2015, Home Secretary Theresa May issued a written ministerial statement in which she referred to a number of files relating to allegations of child sexual abuse that had been found in Home Office archives. One, referred to as Prime Minister's Office File, related to van Straubenzee and covered the period between April 2, 1982 and February 9, 1987. It included material relating to the notorious Kincora

Boys' Home in Northern Ireland, where child sexual abuse is said to have been covered up by MI5 so its own intelligence gathering could proceed. Thomas stayed with Tory MP Sir Michael Latham and his family in their home at Gretton, Northamptonshire, preaching at their local church on the Sunday. After his departure, Latham wrote: 'My Dear George, I cannot begin to tell you how much Caroline and I appreciated your kindness in coming to Gretton last weekend. Indeed, Caroline is deliberately delaying her letter to you for a couple of days because her heart is just too full to write until then. The children were absolutely desolate when their Uncle George left them. Poor little Richard sobbed in a heart rending manner and even James, after being very brave for several hours, broke down as well at bed time. I don't mind confessing that there were some moist adult eyes as well. And both of us felt utterly drained at such a deeply moving and spiritual experience – not just the service, wonderful though it was, but the whole weekend. People will never forget it – everyone is talking about it. God bless you, and again thank you for a wonderful weekend. With much love from us all.'

In July 1986 he declined to lend his name to an Emergency Declaration circulated by the Anti Apartheid Movement calling for mandatory sanctions on *apartheid* South Africa.

He remained on very good terms with John Cordle, who had resigned from the Commons in disgrace because of his dealings with the corrupt architect John Poulson. In September 1986, responding to a letter from Cordle, who had arranged for him to be guest of honour at a grand event in Salisbury for a spire appeal to raise £6.5m, he wrote: 'My dear John, Thank you for your very welcome letter. I am looking forward with immense pleasure to being with you, and of course I will gladly accept your advice about my greetings. Enclosed is a suggested brief message for the programme, but of course I realise that I must speak for about seven or eight minutes during the evening itself. Bless you, dear John. I am looking forward to staying in your home overnight. With love to you all.'

When Conservative Party deputy chairman Jeffrey Archer resigned after being exposed as having paid £2,000 'hush money' to a prostitute, Thomas wrote to commiserate with him. Perhaps the circumstances were too close to home for the former Speaker. Archer responded: 'Dear George, Thank you so much for taking the trouble to write. Mary and I have been shattered by the events of the past few days and we have both been much comforted by the kind words of many friends Yours Jeffrey.' Archer added a handwritten note, which said: 'I doubt if I have had a kinder letter in my life. You are truely [sic] a good friend and a fine man.'

With exquisite bad timing, Thomas nominated Archer for a Sheaffer Award for politics. He complained to the *Evening Standard* after he was mocked in the paper's diary column and claimed he had chosen Archer 'for his writing, not his political career'.

On November 4, 1987, Thomas wrote to Jenny Leith of Broad Lawn, Eltham, London saying: 'I am thrilled to know that your son, Alistair will be reading English and Drama at Aberystwyth. I am sure he will fall in love with our little Wales. Please warn him not to fall victim to the extremists of the Nationalist Party who have plenty of charm in talking to English people but whose real attitude towards them is not something I like.'

Thomas went on a month-long speaking tour of the United States, returning on October 19, 1988.
In December he told Daisy Heaton, his pen friend in Toronto, that he had taken on too much in America and had ended up with a stomach ulcer.

He appeared slightly irritated when the chairman of Cardiff

Castle Committee, Councillor Mike Flynn, wanted items he had promised for display in the castle as soon as possible. He wrote to Flynn saying: 'Thank you for your letter concerning the items which I have promised for display in Cardiff Castle. I hope you realise that a very great proportion are to be left to you in my Will, if they all went now my home would look bare. I will get in touch with you after Christmas to make more firm arrangements.'

Thomas spent six weeks in South Africa in early 2008, returning in late February before going with Julian Hodge to Cyprus. People who wrote to him were told he was not expected back until spring.

Thomas wrote to Robert Purnell, a boarder at The Oratory School near Reading, saying: 'I was thrilled to hear from you and so glad that you remember you were my little Prince. I think that when I come back home on April 7 we ought to have a long chat about your future career. My own instinct is that you first go ahead and qualify as a lawyer, that is a good basis for all sorts of professions. You need a good degree whether you go into politics or no. I wonder if you will be home from your boarding school when I return home on April 7. If you are, I would love to have a long chat with you. You are a fortunate boy to be at such a good boarding school. Bless you, Robert. If you are half as good as your father and your grandfather you will be excellent.'

In 1988 the BBC journalist Patrick Hannan wrote to Thomas after being refused permission to use extracts from two of the politician's broadcasts in an anthology called *Wales on the Wireless*. Hannan told Thomas he had spoken to his agent but wanted to approach him personally. He said the book was a 'modest and frugal production' and he could not offer any significant increase in the copyright fees being offered. He asked

Thomas to reconsider. When the book appeared, Thomas' two broadcasts duly appeared.

In the early months of 1989 Thomas underwent chemotherapy treatment. He wrote to a well-wisher: 'My chemotherapy treatment keeps me in an up and down situation so that I cannot guarantee from one day to the next that I shall be able to fulfil the commitments into which I have entered. However, I do the best I can.'

By July he was recovering. A friend wrote to him saying: 'I can't tell you how elated I was when I left your house on Friday. It was so marvellous to see that you had put on weight, grown your hair and were clearly returning to health in a way that no one thought probably a month ago! I can understand that you are indeed happy in King George V Drive; you have so many comforts there, memories of your mother and family and tokens of the esteem in which you are held by the highest in the land.'

When Margaret Thatcher was challenged by Michael Heseltine for the Tory leadership, Thomas sent her flowers. She responded in a note which said, 'It was so thoughtful of you to send me the beautiful flowers. At times like this it is such a comfort to hear from friends and I really did appreciate your kind message of support. With grateful thanks and all good wishes, Yours ever, Margaret.'

But when a week later John Major won the contest to succeed her after she had failed to defeat Heseltine sufficiently convincingly, Thomas wrote to congratulate the new Prime Minister. Major responded: 'Dear George, It was so kind of you to write offering your congratulations and I am sorry it has taken so long for me to respond. Norma and I have been overwhelmed by the many kind messages that we have received and it gives me enormous encouragement to hear from so many friends within the Palace of Westminster.' A handwritten addition said: 'Yours ever, John. How lovely to hear from you!'

On October 29, 1991, Roger Ordish of the BBC wrote to Thomas on *Jim'll Fix It* letterheaded notepaper saying: 'Last week Cathryn Milowsky telephoned you from this office and asked you if I might write to you on the subject of an item from the *Jim'll Fix It* programme concerning the House of Lords, which unfortunately had to be abandoned last year in somewhat unexplained circumstances. I should be most grateful if you were able to throw any light on what actually happened to cause our plans to fall through. In 1990 eight-year-old Anna Kaufman from North London wrote to Jimmy Savile and asked him if he could fix it for her to be a member of the House of Lords for a day. As producer of the programme I wrote originally to Lord Belstead, then Leader of the House. He replied non-committally but not unfavourably. I heard next from his private secretary, Douglas Slater, with whom I had a meeting at the House. We discussed a plan in some detail of what young Anna might be able to do. On this occasion we happened to request informally to meet 'Black Rod', who was informed of our request although not in any detail.'

Ordish went on to say that he thought the Leader of the House was in favour but someone (Black Rod?) had blocked the whole thing. They weren't allowed to film in the Chamber and were offered an alternative location within the Palace of Westminster, but as no other area looks like the Chamber, it wasn't going to work. He asked Thomas to find out what happened. His response is not recorded.

18

Final Acts

In his final years Thomas became consumed by the case against what is now known as the European Union.

He kept the summer 1991 edition of the members' newsletter of the Campaign for an Independent Britain, which consisted of a rant about the EU and against the Brussels-inspired Euro Festival Week.

An article in the newsletter complained of 'the likely loss of half a million jobs owing to the effect of joining the Exchange Rate Mechanism of the European Monetary System; the forthcoming loss of control over the export of live horses for slaughter; the loss of frontier controls after 1992, making the Single European Act into a drug barons' charter; the step-by-step destruction of the self-governing powers of our own Parliament, if economic, monetary and political union are imposed upon us.' Calling on readers to resist European integration, it said: 'Above all, ridicule the very idea of celebrating Britain's greatest peace-time disaster – membership of the European Community.'

Thomas remained on warm terms with Jeremy Thorpe, who wrote to him in October 1994 saying: 'My dear George, I hope all goes well with you. I have just finished hanging you – or to be more precise your photograph – in my study. You are next door to a cartoon of my father who is also wearing a full bottomed wig! Can I at some stage seek your advice? I could call on you at the House of Lords if most convenient and needless to say Marian and I would be overjoyed if you were able to come here for lunch or dinner. I was so delighted that Winston successfully persuaded you to stay on as Patron of NBFA (National Benevolent Fund for the Aged).'

Thomas did, however, step down as president of National Children's Home at the end of 1994. He sent a message to the organisation which said: 'It has been both a privilege and a joy to serve NCH Action for Children for you represent the social conscience of Methodism. I am profoundly grateful to you and your colleagues and to a veritable army of voluntary workers for the kindness that has surrounded me throughout the years that I have been linked with NCH Action for Children.'

Thomas kept a record of a parliamentary question asked in the Lords by Lord Pearson of Rannoch, a future leader of UKIP [United Kingdom Independence Party], on April 28, 1995: 'To ask HMG what are the implications of Article N of the Treaty of Maastricht (whereby any alterations to the Treaty may only be made with the unanimous consent of the signatories) for the Government's negotiating position at the forthcoming InterGovernmental conference.' Pearson went on to suggest that 'this Article means that we need not simply have opted out of the Social Chapter at Maastricht; we could have prevented the other countries from having it unless they set up an entirely separate bureaucracy etc outside the Community institutions'.

Although increasingly frail, Thomas went to Harold Wilson's funeral in the Scilly Isles in June 1995, where he gave the eulogy. He was thanked by Wilson's son Robin.

Thomas made a speech against the EU in the Lords on April 15, 1996, which reads like something from the Leave campaign in the 2016 referendum on EU membership. He began the substantive part of his argument by quoting a former Tory Chancellor. He said: "In his book *Sovereign Britain*,

Norman Lamont states: 'I cannot pinpoint a single concrete advantage that unambiguously comes to this country because of our membership of the European Union'. That we are in pursuit of continental integration is regularly denied in this House, but none the less the policy seems to be relentlessly pursued. Propaganda to convince us that we are incapable of survival as an independent nation has poured upon us. It is emphasised that we need European crutches to be mobile. Facts and figures are more impressive than propaganda. I look to the impeccable source of the Treasury red books for my evidence. The results of European membership are very different from what we are encouraged to believe ... The total financial cost to Britain of membership of the European Union—and mark my words; these are not my figures but the Treasury's—is now a colossal £108 billion. This results from our cumulative visible balance of payments deficit with the EU since 1973 amounting to £87 billion. In addition, our net contributions to the Community budget amounted to £21 billion. Those are mind-boggling figures. No wonder the Government have been so shy about bringing them to our attention. In addition, there has been a serious effect on the cost of living in the United Kingdom. When we entered the European Union, we ended the cheap food supply from Australia, New Zealand and the Americas in favour of the highly expensive food regime in Europe.

"Membership of the European Union is ferocious for us. It has severely weakened our balance of payments. It has reduced our political and economic rights to a pale shadow of what they were. Another place [the House of Commons] has already been diminished beyond measure compared with what it was as recently as when I presided in the Speaker's Chair. When this Parliament passed an Act preventing Spanish fishermen from sailing under our flag and stealing the quota of fish allotted to us, the European Court of Justice in Luxembourg declared the Act illegal—an Act passed by the British Parliament!—and told us we had no business to do so. If any foreign court had tried to overrule the sovereign rights of our Parliament as late as the 1970s it would have been told to jump in the river. What has happened to our self-respect in the meantime? What has happened to us that we now submit to overruling by foreign courts with a docility that is a disgrace to the 'bulldog breed'?'

With characteristic hyperbole, Julian Hodge wrote to Dr. Adrian Timothy of St. Thomas Hospital, where Thomas was receiving treatment again, to say: 'I am enclosing a copy of the famous speech make by Viscount Tonypandy in the House of Lords. There can be no doubt that this amazing event startled many politicians into waking up and taking fresh stock of the position. What they found mystified many of them, especially those who had been lulled into a false sense of security by the misleading statements of so many high politicians, who clearly had not taken the time, or the trouble, to ascertain the truth for themselves. Viscount Tonypandy's remarkable speech will go down in history as something to be cherished by all those who love the freedom of our way of life. And you may have noticed that, almost without exception, our newspapers have been quick to align themselves with what he had to say. Only a Churchill could have done it!'

On July 3, 1996, during a House of Lords debate on the British Constitution, Thomas set out his opposition to the creation of a Welsh Assembly, which was to be the subject of a further referendum if Labour won the general election. He said: "If an assembly were to take powers from the Secretary of State, it would mean disaster for Wales ... The strengths of the Secretary of State for Wales in the Cabinet depend upon his being able to say, 'I am speaking for Wales'. How can people gain access to an assembly, or to quangos? How can they challenge those, as we can challenge Ministers in the Welsh Office and bring them to account? To weaken the Welsh Office would be a disastrous loss for the people of Wales. I hope they hear my voice as I say it. They know that the Welsh Office has made an enormous difference to the quality of our life ... If the assembly is as anaemic as it appears it will be, this House may be assured that it will have a voracious appetite. It will want more power and more influence – of course it will. The agitation will begin. First, people will say, 'What has happened in Scotland? Are we second-rate? We must have the same: a Parliament with tax-raising powers'. It is idle to say that there is not a danger to the Union, because every political assembly by its nature always seeks more power for itself. That is the history of another place. It began in a small way. Within four years it was claiming the right to control expenditure in the United Kingdom, and that is a quality of local government that has not changed. Naturally, the assembly in Wales will want more power. Of course it will strengthen the nationalists. I am not here to argue about Labour, Liberal or Welsh nationalists, but it would not be difficult for noble Lords to guess my feelings and opinions. I say this: rather than take the risk of a process that would lead to us having racial parliaments in Scotland, Wales and England, we should say 'No' now, and that will be my advice to the people of Wales.'

Former Tory Minister Jonathan Aitken, who was subsequently jailed for perjury, sought Thomas' help in the fateful libel action he was bringing against *The Guardian*. In a letter dated September 2, 1996, Aitken wrote: 'Dear George, Many months ago you said, with your characteristic kindness and generosity of spirit, that you might be willing to give a witness statement on my character as a parliamentarian for the purposes of my libel action against *The Guardian* and Granada's *World in Action* programme. I am therefore writing to follow up your kind offer, as we have reached the stage in the case at which witness statements are being prepared. In confidence I can tell you that there are some encouraging signs that my adversaries may be going to offer an apology and an out-of-court settlement. However, we cannot rely on these preliminary signals, so I have to prepare my case thoroughly by collecting witness statements now.'

Aitken went on to say: 'In their pleadings, publications and broadcasts *The Guardian* and *World in Action* have made two offensive suggestions about me which I will summarise as follows: 1: Concealed from Parliament, colleagues and constituents his business connections with the Arab world. [Aitken claimed these dealings were known]. 2 His business connections 'compromised my ability to act independently in the interests of my constituents and the electorate generally'.'

Aitken concluded there was no evidence for this and said he was contacting six or seven witnesses along with Thomas to support him. He enclosed, in strictest confidence, witness statements from former Speaker Jack Weatherill, former Tory MP Julian Amery and Labour MP Stuart Bell. His legal team had already drafted out some of the statement for Thomas, and Aitken asked that Thomas add to it and give it a personal touch.

Thomas complied with Aitken's request, getting a further note dated September 12, 1996, which said: 'Dear George, Thank you so much for your kindness in signing the witness statement and for sending it back so promptly. My legal team are delighted and I am eternally grateful to you. Thank you again and God bless you.'

Lord Pearson wrote to Thomas again, on September 6, 1996, stating: 'Dear George, I see that you very wisely sent a copy of [Tory MP] David Heathcoat Amory's recent masterpiece on the single currency to Sir Julian Hodge, with the result that he has offered to pay for re-printing several thousand more copies. I have been talking to David, who is keen to write another booklet which would take a serious look at what life might really be like outside the EU. As I told you, the IEA [the right-wing think tank the Institute of Economic Affairs] is making a bold stab at this with a publication entitled *Better Off Out?*, which they plan to launch on Friday October 4 in the City (your invitation will reach you shortly). I received the draft of this today, but have not yet been able to absorb it fully. However, I suspect that more detailed research is needed if David is going to convince the world that we would be Better Off Out! Do you think Sir Julian might help with finance for such research? I don't think it would be very expensive – perhaps a couple of researchers for six months or so.'

In the run-up to the 1997 general election, Thomas agreed to provide a filmed message for Sir James Goldsmith's anti-EU Referendum Party's conference.

A dying man, his appearance drew on the pro-monarchist, pro-Establishment love of imperial Britain that had come to mean so much to him. But the content of his address to the camera for the October 1996 conference pushed him into the camp of half-crazed obsessives who write letters in green ink to newspapers, complete with heavy underlining and unnecessary capital letters.

With a backdrop of cartoons of former Speakers, and a patriotic orchestral dirge playing in the background, he said: "My support for Sir James' initiative is natural, for I am in harmony with the sturdy defence of our British Parliament advanced by my predecessors in the Speaker's chair in the House of Commons. For me to remain silent now would be an act of treason, for such cowardice would betray the noble heritage handed on to me by former Speakers of the House of Commons."

Now apparently addressing Goldsmith himself, Thomas said: "God bless your efforts as you battle for Britain. I wish you well." Turning back to the TV audience, he concluded: "This election is the last chance you will ever have to make your voice heard."

A letter from Lord Pearson dated October 21, 1996, said: 'Dear George, Thank you very much for sending me your really excellent speech to the Referendum Party's conference in Brighton on Saturday. Christopher Booker, who was there and spoke about fishing rang me last night, mostly to tell me what a great speech you made via the video screen. He said it was extremely effective and beautifully done. So bravo! Bravissimo! I look forward to seeing you soon. (Please don't overdo things!)'

Also on October 21, 1996, James Goldsmith wrote to him saying: 'Dear Lord Tonypandy, As you can imagine, the room, which was jam packed with about 5000 people, was moved to tears by your speech. On behalf of all of them, many thanks.'

But, according to Patrick Cormack: "That was a terrible mistake towards the end, it was a terrible mistake. And I did tell George. I said 'George you really shouldn't do that.' I said 'You are no longer a party politician of any sort and you should not give any support to any political party.' I said, 'your views on devolution are a different matter entirely because you've got people in a referendum from all parties on different sides, and for you to make your views known on that is entirely proper. But for you to back the Referendum Party, that's just not what you should do.'

"He did rather equivocate. It was the last serious political conversation that I had with him. I said, 'You're very naughty George, you shouldn't do that. It's quite wrong,' and he was very silly to do that [a filmed statement for the Referendum Party's conference]. Look – he was approaching 90. He died at the age of 88. Very few of us are wholly and absolutely – at

88 – what we would have been at 58, and he was an old man. He was a sick old man. He'd had his cancer from 1984. Until he died in 1997, he was battling with that illness, that disease, and it took its toll. And towards the end it took a particular toll. It was wrong of people to exploit a name when a man was not any more what he had been. "

In a handwritten letter to Thomas, Margaret Thatcher wrote on December 12, 1996: 'Dear George, I was <u>delighted</u> to read your letter in today's *Daily Telegraph* and then to read your kind note. I feel exactly the same way as you do. The question before us is not only about a single currency (which I would <u>never</u> agree to on principle but about the whole issue of Parliamentary, Legal and Financial Sovereignty. But the language our opponents use carefully conceals their real purpose. It is not only that <u>we</u> are 'Euro-sceptic' – much more important is that we are passionately <u>pro-British</u>: we stand for all the good and great things our country has done. Your letter may have changed the whole course of history.'

On January 28, 1997, Thatcher wrote again to Thomas, saying: 'Thank you for your very kind letter. I was delighted to read that you are making the most of the summer climate in the Cape. I have also read the newspaper reports about the coming House of Lords Debate on Friday next. Malcolm Pearson told me some time ago about his Bill [which if passed could have led to the UK leaving the EU] and I did agree to attend the debate. Unfortunately the reports were somewhat inaccurate in that, as I am sure you will appreciate, I do not feel able to speak at this time. With the election so close, I fear that even sensible and serious discussion of this subject would be manipulated by the media for purely party political purposes. However, I shall listen with the greatest interest to all that is said, even though I shall not be able to stay for the vote – I have a constituency engagement in the country that evening. And as you know, my views on the EU are not 'wait and see' but 'No, No, No'.'

On February 3, 1997, after the debate, Margaret Thatcher wrote Thomas a handwritten letter which said: 'Dear George, Thank you for your letter ... alas I was not able to speak in the Lords debate because I should have been accused of disloyalty to the PM. But I sat in my seat for three hours nodding vigorously at all the right things. I had to leave before the end as I had an engagement to speak at Newbury. The quality of the speeches was outstanding. The case <u>our</u> colleagues made was unanswerable. And the news that we had won the division by one vote (51 to 50) gave us all new hope. My dear George – the people are overwhelmingly of our view, so we must and will carry on the fight.'

On April 7, 1997, Jonathan Aithen wrote to Thomas saying he might be required to give evidence in the libel case against *The Guardian* and Granada TV.

On May, 10, 1997, days after Labour's landslide victory in the general election, Lord Pearson wrote to Thomas saying: 'In the wake of the massive Labour victory I think we all feel we should keep a slightly lower profile until we see how Labour gets on in Brussels. I fear of course that they will make too many concessions in their attempt to improve the atmosphere. Margaret also feels that it is now not yet the right moment to tell the world that she was misled. Do please look after yourself: you are our great hero. We need you in the fray but don't get up too early. With love, Malcolm.'

Thomas then turned his attention to the upcoming referendum on whether a Welsh Assembly should be established. On July 25 Thomas wrote to the editor of the *Western Mail* saying: 'The clear mandate given to the Labour Party to use a referendum to find out the will of the people resident in Wales concerning the establishment of a National

Assembly is being shamefully misused. Unscrupulous pressures are being exerted on members of quangos and on members of county councils to declare support for an assembly to which they are privately opposed. Members of quangos (whether set up by Labour or by Conservative administrations) are in an especially vulnerable position. Many are due to be reappointed or to be dropped within the next two years. To invite such people to express public support for an Assembly is disgustingly close to blackmail. My advice to recipients of such letters is to photocopy the original document and send copies to the media, both press and television, and radio. Fear of defeat seems to have distorted the judgement of those in charge of the Yes! Campaign. I have never sought to hide my hostility to the proposed Assembly, because I am convinced that a strong Welsh Office team combined with equally strong local government is our best guarantee of a sound economy in Wales. Another expensive tier of bureaucrats interfering in industry and in commerce in Wales will have a devastating and destructive influence on our small businesses. An Assembly that weakens the influence of the Secretary of State for Wales in the Cabinet is bad for Wales and will undermine the United Kingdom. The referendum should not be subject to arm twisting or to bullying tactics. Heaven protect us from those who pretend that party political loyalties are involved in this matter. It is not a question of Labour, Liberal, Conservative, or Welsh Nationalist Party policies: it is a non party question whether Wales wants another tier of government or not. My vote will be cast with the 'Noes'.'

Thomas died of cancer on September 22, 1997, four days after the people of Wales voted narrowly in favour of establishing a National Assembly. Patrick Cormack, who had a phone conversation with him the day before he died, said Thomas had been very dispirited by the result.

"Without being malicious in any way," said Dafydd Wigley, "I was glad he lived to see the result."

Obituaries were generally positive. *The Independent*, for example, opened its with the statement: 'George Thomas was the first Speaker of the House of Commons to be known by the whole nation; known, and loved too. In 1978, two years after his appointment, the BBC began broadcasting *Today in Parliament* and its opening call 'Order! Order!', declaimed in Thomas' rolling Rhondda accent, became a national catchphrase.'

Swansea poet Nigel Jenkins took a diametrically opposed view, describing Thomas – in an anti-eulogy – as 'The Lord of Lickspit'.

Richard Watson, who chaired Cardiff West Constituency Labour Party, asked members of the general committee to observe a minute's silence out of respect to the seat's long-serving former MP. They did so, although some complained afterwards about having to commemorate someone who had done nothing to help his successor as the Labour candidate get elected.

Thomas' final Will was signed by him on September 4, 1997, less than three weeks before his death. After allocating a series of cash legacies totalling £44,000 to surviving family members, friends and assorted good causes, as well as bequeathing mementoes to friends, bodies and clubs he had been associated with, he left the remainder of his estate in trust for two charities: The George Thomas Memorial Trust and The Friends of Ysbyty George Thomas of Treorchy, Rhondda.

The net value of his estate, as certified bilingually by the Probate Registry of Wales, was £233,225. An earlier draft of the Will dated August 25, 1984, had given the Jane Hodge Foundation first refusal on buying Thomas' bungalow, presumably with a view to its being converted into a shrine museum, as advocated at one time by Julian Hodge. He also planned to leave the leather-bound Oxford University Press Bible presented to him by the House of Commons to Margaret Thatcher, for whom he expressed his 'deep admiration and respect for her moral courage and her superb national leadership'.

He had also originally planned to leave an equestrian statue given to him by the Austrian government to 'our gracious and honourable Queen Mother'. Patrick Cormack delivered the address at Thomas' memorial service in Westminster Abbey: "I had been Warden of St Margaret's at Westminster for 14 years from 1987 to 1991, so I knew quite a bit about memorial services. Of course, George had no immediate family to do that sort of thing for him. He had some relations, but he wasn't all that close to them. So Jim [Callaghan] said 'I think we can rely on you to get this together', which I did, with close consultation. I said to Jim, 'You do the address', to which he said 'No'. Taken a little aback, I replied, 'you've known him longer and he was very close to you'. But Jim was adamant: 'I can't. I don't want to do it. It's been such a relationship, it's had its ups and downs – I'm genuinely very fond of him – but you should do it. I'm getting old.'

"So anyway I did and Jim was very kind about it. He was there, obviously, as was Prime Minister Blair, the Leader of the Opposition, the Prince of Wales and everybody else."

In his speech at Thomas' 80th birthday celebration, Julian Hodge had spoken of turning his bungalow into a museum. Asked why the idea hadn't come off, Lord Cormack said: "Well I suppose ... I knew the bungalow quite well. He had an extension with an extra bathroom on. We were the first to christen it. We stayed there certainly on two if not three occasions. We visited when we went over. Of course we could drive over for lunch. It was a long drive, but because of the M4 we could do it. He had an extraordinary accumulation of things. Of course many are in the castle at Cardiff, aren't they? How could you have had a relatively modest, small bungalow as a museum? I don't think that you could easily have done that.

"In America it's almost the done thing for a major figure, political or otherwise, to have a museum but, of course, the other thing one has to recognise is that we all have our contemporary heroes who we admire who don't always stand the test of time. It doesn't in any way diminish the affection in which George was held while he was alive, if that doesn't continue for long after his death. Take Ted Heath; they've had a complete failure with his house, Arundels, as a museum. It's still open to the public, but has lost money hand over fist. I often go there.

"A group of us who had been friends of George's in various ways, for about five or six years after he died, used to meet for dinner in the House of Commons as near as possible to the anniversary of his birthday. Then it sort of rather petered out."

19

George and Julian

Mam aside, the most intense emotional relationship of George Thomas' life was with the controversial businessman and banker Julian Hodge.

Both had huge egos, the capacity to be vain and the belief that enemies were seeking to do them down. Where they differed is that while Thomas was comfortable gaining advancement through his sycophantic approach to the establishment, Hodge liked to portray himself as one battling against the (banking) establishment to overcome its prejudice against him.

Nevertheless, they provided each other with mutual support – speaking to each other on the phone every day at an allotted time – and Hodge eventually invited Thomas to join him as a director of the bank he founded, which he wanted to call the Bank of Wales but which the industry's regulator opposed on the grounds that the name gave the misleading impression that the bank was a public sector institution.

The bank did, however, attract support from diverse quarters. A young Dafydd Wigley invested, he thinks, £100 in it: "I didn't particularly believe in Julian Hodge, but I believed in the need to have institutions like a Bank of Wales where there was the possibility, hopefully, of getting people to save money in Wales-based institutions. Instead of it all being invested in the City of London and disappearing like water into the sand, it could re-circulate in the Welsh economy."

Although by his own account he was already a friend of Hodge's for 15 years, the first reference to the businessman in Thomas' papers appears on March 21, 1968. Thomas – at the time Minister of State for Commonwealth Affairs at the Foreign Office – wrote a cryptic letter to Cledwyn Hughes, the Secretary of State for Wales, saying: 'I enclose a letter and a copy of the printed accounts of the Anglo Auto Finance Company Ltd [one of Hodge's companies]. I would be glad if you could do something to help.'

The letter didn't specify what kind of help was being sought and, not unnaturally, Hughes' secretary, Betty O'Keefe, was puzzled. She wrote a note to her boss: 'We received a copy of these accounts which was acknowledged as attached – nothing more seemed to be called for. Do you think there is anything behind this letter from George Thomas or do you think that his secretary has perhaps mistaken the situation? Advice please!!'

Hughes wrote to Thomas: 'Thank you so much for your letter of March 21, enclosing this letter and report from Julian Hodge – in which you said that you would be glad if I could do something to help. Julian wrote to me in similar terms, but it did not seem to me that he was asking for any help. However, I may have missed the point – and in any case, you undoubtedly know the background better than I do. If, therefore, there is anything specific that you think I might be able to do, please do not hesitate to let me know.'

In fact, Hodge had enlisted the support of Thomas to help him secure a knighthood. Letting politicians know about the success of his businesses was, he thought, a necessary part of the campaign.

The *Financial Times* reported two weeks later that Anglo Auto had merged with the Julian Hodge Group the previous October. Hodge posted the *Financial Times* press clipping to Thomas. It made one reference to government policy: 'The immediate prospects [of the merged company] are over-shadowed by impending government measures to restrict consumer spending.'

In January 1969 a preliminary announcement to the City showed that Anglo Auto's profits had risen to £841,000 from £647,000 in the previous year.

Two days later Hodge sent Thomas a Merchant Bank Diary for the year and told him: 'I do hope you will be able to use [it], if only to remind you from time to time of the first bank in Wales for over 100 years. Aren't I naughty? But the truth of the matter is that my own little merchant bank gives me more pleasure than this would dream of – and it is not so little either.' He concluded the letter: 'May we send our love to Mam, please?'

Shortly afterwards Hodge sent accounts of another of his firms – the Reliant Motor Group, which specialised in cars at the lower end of the market – to Thomas. Hodge wrote: 'Unfortunately, we are not selling many three-wheelers at the moment, as over 90% of these are actually sold under hire purchase to working class users and the new restrictions hit them hard, whereas only about 25% of all other new vehicles are sold under hire purchase.' Thomas simply wrote back thanking Hodge for the documents and suggesting they might meet the next weekend.

The hire purchase agreements made between Hodge's companies and 'working class users' in fact became extremely controversial because of the high rates of interest charged. Hodge was dubbed the 'Usurer of the Valleys' by the Welsh radical magazine *Rebecca*, and by *Private Eye*.

London-born, Hodge was brought up in Pontllanfraith, then in Monmouthshire. He launched his first business in 1946 with £1,000 and over the following decades built up his Hodge Group into a £265m empire to become the largest private employer in Wales. Apart from banking, car and instalment credit firms, there were 10 'check trading' companies from which people bought clothes on a weekly payment plan. There were also three money-lending firms in the group.

Hodge was also into the highly lucrative second mortgage business in a big way. Shrewdly, he covered his tracks by using a network of self-employed brokers to sign up people for loans. Many of the clients came from immigrant communities in the West Midlands and South London, some of them dreaming of returning to their homelands. A significant proportion got into financial difficulties, couldn't afford the repayments and ended up having their homes repossessed.

The other side of Hodge was his generosity in endowing UWIST (University of Wales Institute of Science and Technology), which later was merged into Cardiff University. On March 5, 1969, Thomas wrote to him, saying: 'My warmest congratulations and thanks to you on the establishment of a Chair in Banking and Finance. Your generosity has once again put Wales in your debt. I was delighted to see what a splendid Press you received. Bless you Julian.'

In the run-up to the Investiture of Prince Charles as Prince of Wales, both Thomas and Jim Callaghan – who was Home Secretary at the time – pleaded with Prime Minister Harold Wilson to give Hodge a knighthood. Two weeks before the ceremony, Callaghan wrote to Wilson saying that three new knighthoods in the Investiture Honours List were not enough. He wanted to 'reinforce the pleas George Thomas has made' requesting that Julian Hodge gets a knighthood. Callaghan added: 'If you could increase the number by one I would press very strongly, as George Thomas has already done, the claims of Julian Hodge. George Thomas has, I am sure, told you of his benefactions and other claims to recognition.'

As things turned out, Hodge had to wait another year for

his knighthood. This delay gave him the opportunity to give vent to his feeling of personal injustice in a letter to Callaghan that he asked to be passed on to Thomas. Hodge wrote: 'I have indeed been persecuted because of my political convictions and also the fact that I dared to encroach upon the City's preserves in my efforts to build a financial centre in Wales. You may not know but the hostility really started with the London Stock Exchange years ago, when they bitterly opposed the granting of the dealer's licence in the first instance – the first in Wales. I don't think I have ever told you that story. And they seemed to go quite frantic when we started up our Unit Trusts. Things would have been very different had I agreed to join them. It is true too that in the process (almost by accident) I have made a fortune. But at least I have quietly given away a little more than £3m of it to charities, the full details of which are only known to our auditors ... But all this I have done because I have wanted to do it. It has been as much part of me as my religion. I have never asked for any special recognition, nor perhaps been fully conscious of the value it might have been to me and my work for Wales. But to have the chance of a prize you never expected to receive, and then apparently have it snatched away at the last moment is perhaps the most unkindest cut of all.'

Responding to a further letter in which Hodge recounted how he had told the author, fundraiser and soon-to-be Tory MP Jeffrey Archer over a drink in the Carlton Club that he had donated £3m to charities – and committed a further £257,000 – Thomas told Hodge: 'I think you have an outstanding record of service to charitable causes; I marvel that you have been so generous and I think you really must put a brake on your generosity.'

Like Thomas, Hodge had a tendency to cite his religious faith as an inspiration – in his case, helping him cope with whatever his opponents threw at him. In a letter to Sir Archie

Lush, chairman of the Welsh Hospital Board and former political agent and friend to Nye Bevan, Hodge wrote: '[There] is wonderful help and comfort to be found in making a real effort to recapture the faith of our fathers and live with it. Quite frankly, without it, in my own case, I do not think I could have survived the vicissitudes, financial and otherwise, with which I have had to contend over the years. Not only have I had the whole of the Establishment arrayed against me, determined to try and bring me down, but I have not always found unanimous support nearer home in Wales, so strongly is opinion influenced by the insidious power of the press. But my religion gave me strength and it helped to remain unshaken my conviction in my own honesty of purpose, so that I never wavered. It gave me courage at all times to continue cheerfully and unafraid, especially unafraid.' Religiosity of this kind was music to the ears of Thomas, to whom Hodge sent a copy of his letter to Lush.

In a typical expression of his feelings towards Thomas, Hodge wrote to him in January 1970 in these terms: 'My dear George, What a great pleasure it gave me to be with you on Saturday evening, because as I have told you before, you always have a profound effect upon me. As a matter of fact, I always think you bring out the best in everybody, and you make one feel that life is really worthwhile.'

As well as a personal friendship it was, however, a business relationship, in which Jim Callaghan was also involved. At a time when Hodge was having difficulty persuading the UK Government to let him call his bank the Bank of Wales, Callaghan wrote to Thomas saying: 'I have heard from Julian Hodge that the latest proposed title for the Bank of Wales is The National Bank of Wales. I really think the Board of Trade are now getting to the stage of splitting hairs. There is, to the *cognoscenti*, a difference between having the Bank of Wales and having the National Bank of Wales, and I really think we should stick out for the straight simple title without prefix or suffix. I thought you would like to know my views.'

Further correspondence shows how the three men were involved in trying to get the partnership of a joint stock bank to help them move the Bank of Wales project forward.

When Hodge's knighthood was finally confirmed in June 1970, he wrote to Thomas saying: 'I don't think I thanked you properly for your lovely greetings telegram, if at all, because there were so many other things we had to talk about. But I do want you to know that both Moira and I are deeply grateful to you for taking the time to send your congratulations, in spite of your many other preoccupations. I would also like you to know that we are deeply conscious that we owe this splendid honour to the fact that you sponsored it, in spite of all the problems involved. We also want you to know that we will regard the honour as conferred on us in acknowledgment of the importance of the work of all of us for the Welsh Economy. We regard it in that sense too as almost an official recognition of our endeavours to set up a financial centre in Wales. And we will never relax in our efforts to do what we can to further the good of the people of Wales, as far as it lies in our power. But above all, at all times we will be deeply conscious of the great confidence you have had in us, and do everything possible to continue to justify it. We are also deeply conscious of your very great friendship, which has its own very special place in our hearts. We send our love to you and Mam and with it go our hopes for the future.'

Thomas was involved in other business schemes with Hodge, including a bizarre proposal to get Labour Party volunteers to sell car insurance door-to-door in south Wales and elsewhere on behalf of Hodge Group Insurance Brokers, with the party receiving commission payments. Agents from other insurance firms were not happy and the scheme was mocked in the *Daily Mail*: 'Perhaps we will soon see our leaders cashing in on TV advertising. Imagine Harold pushing St. Bruno, Callaghan Super Gillette and Barbara Castle a bubble bath. Their opportunities are unlimited.'

Hodge wrote to Thomas saying: 'Unfortunately, it would seem that someone from Transport House has leaked this information to the Tory press, to the embarrassment of us all, as no doubt it was intended.'

Both family and political sources have confirmed that the two men would, if at all possible, phone each other every day. Thomas was also known as 'Uncle George' to Hodge's sons, and was a generous giver of presents – as he was to other friends' sons. According to David Seligman, Hodge also contributed towards Thomas' election expenses.

But Thomas' association with Hodge did not go down well with everyone. A constituent called Charles, who lived in Canton, Cardiff, wrote to the MP saying: 'As a very close friend and a socialist, it is with great reluctance I find myself having to write to you on reading the very sad news in tonight's paper on your acceptance of a directorship on the so-called 'Bank of Wales'. I regret that I cannot let this incident go unnoticed. I cannot believe that you of all people would commit the party and yourself to what I consider to be political suicide. George, I can understand Jim Callaghan, but you, it's beyond words, my heart is like a lump of lead. Having made my feelings plain, as a party member, I must give notice that I cannot let the disappointment of the day be forgotten within the West division. I only hope that our personal friendship will remain intact. This is one day I would wish to come to an end quickly but I see no relief in sight. Why did you do it George? I hope I can remain a friend in the years ahead.'

After the general election in February 1974, when Labour

returned to power with Harold Wilson in 10 Downing Street once more, Thomas expected to be appointed Secretary of State for Wales again. Had he got the appointment he expected, he would have had to resign his directorship at what had ultimately been named the Commercial Bank of Wales. Much to his disappointment, however, he was appointed Chairman of Ways and Means (Deputy Speaker) instead. He asked Wilson whether he needed to resign his directorship, and got this reply: 'As far as I know, there is no formal necessity for you to do so. But I do not think that is something on which the Government can advise you, and I think you had better discuss the matter with the Speaker. If you want to have a word with Ted Short [Leader of the House of Commons] before you do so, I know that he would be very ready that you should do so.' Thomas kept his association with the Commercial Bank of Wales for many years after.

In summer 1977, Hodge, his wife Moira and Thomas went to Saudi Arabia, where they had some kind of religious experience with Sheikh Ahmed Zaki Yamani, the Saudi oil minister, who had become a friend.

The following Easter, Hodge wrote a letter to Thomas in which he expressed his feelings about what had happened, and specifically what Thomas meant to him. In the letter Hodge also referred to a recent conversation he'd had in Downing Street with Jim Callaghan, who had taken over from Wilson as Prime Minister. Hodge wrote: 'I was deeply moved by all the kindly thought and consideration that must have prompted your lovely handwritten letter of March 20. This came as a delightful surprise. It had such a soothing effect on me that I stopped to reflect and consider what had been really troubling me. This self analysis took me back to my earlier misgivings which are now completely removed. But they were, very simply: 1. I was troubled in case Jim thought I had used my friendship with you to try and further my own advancement and possibly that I was personally pressing for some promotion. 2. I was equally worried that Jim might think me ungrateful or unmindful of all that he has done for me already. In my anxiety to reassure him I also thought I had said too much at 10 Downing Street (in your presence) almost to the extent that it sounded boastful. At which thought, I didn't like myself at all.

"Perhaps the unexpected shock of the rather dramatic private chat with Jim at Number 10 caught me off balance and I did not dream for one moment that he had ever seriously contemplated elevating me. [It seems from this statement that Callaghan was considering offering Hodge a peerage]. I found myself bewildered by all that had been said and it seemed to me in retrospect that the attempts I made to justify myself to my two friends only served to make matters worse. Here I was further worried that in mentioning the matter to you at the Mansion House I had not explained myself adequately and so upset you too, which was the very last thing I would ever want to do in this world. I was in that mixed up depressed state of mind when your letter reached me like a breath of sweet fresh air, sweeping away all my doubts and misgivings. The simple cause of all my concern, of course, is that I do value, beyond price, all the great things that you and Jim have done for me. I do value your friendship beyond all others and I do strive ceaselessly to be really worthy of the confidence and affection of you both ... If Moira knew of this letter, she would say that I was very wrong to burden you with it, but in the process I have unburdened myself; and who better than with the friend with whom Moira and I shared such a sublime and unique religious experience as we all had with Zaki in Saudi last summer. So it is, dear George, you have seen into my soul. It is not something I show to the world, or indeed to anyone else. But I think I can fairly claim that after a long, difficult and arduous life it is at

peace. And knowing you has contributed much to its serenity.'
Hodge finished the letter saying: 'Much love and gratitude for
all that you are to me, Julian.'

Five years later Thomas sent a copy of a book by Hodge
to Yamani, stating: 'The serenity which your faith gives you
conveys itself to me every time we meet, and I must say that
during these past few hectic days I have been counting my
blessings that you came to see me once again. I think you do
not know how much you mean to me. You are always in my
prayers and I wish you every blessing for all your family.'

When a gala musical evening took place at St. David's Hall
in Cardiff in 1983 to commemorate Thomas' retirement as
Speaker, it was Hodge who gave the most fulsome praise. He
wrote in the programme printed for the event: 'Certainly one
of the best-known voices in the whole wide world since 1976
has been that of the Rt. Hon George Thomas of Tonypandy in
the Palace of Westminster, where for seven years until recently
he was the very distinguished 137th Speaker of the Mother of
Parliaments. He entered politics in order to put into practice
his fervently held Christian principles. And so he not merely
represented but nurtured, spoke for and lived for his Cardiff
constituency for a grand total of 35 years. During which time
he gave a new lease of life to thousands of tenants in south
Wales. And as the most outstanding Speaker of this 'Home of
Democracy' in all its long history of over 606 years, he is not
only highly respected, but universally loved and admired by
people of all shades of political opinion regardless of race or
religion, for George Thomas is blessed with the divine gift of
ennobling every task he undertakes.'

In the summer of 1983 Hodge and Thomas went on the
first of a number of holidays they spent together in Paphos,
Cyprus, as guests at a hotel owned by Thomas' friend Alecos
Michaelides, who had been Speaker of the Cyprus House of

Representatives. In a letter to Michaelides and his wife Yolanda, Hodge said that until he had met them he thought Thomas had mixed them up with his knowledge of Greek mythology, 'such is his admiration'. Hodge wrote that it was 'the happiest week's holiday I have ever spent', saying he had told his wife all about their trip to some monasteries.

Michaelides wrote to Thomas saying: 'Your brief stay with us has been the highlight of our summer. We are grateful to you because being with us, we have had the most enjoyable week of our holidays. Julian is a remarkable person and extremely interesting to talk with. It is amazing that a person of his wealth is not only so humble but he has maintained a keen interest in religion. We look forward to seeing more of him.'

Concerned at Thomas' failing health, Hodge wrote to Thomas in November 1983 telling him he and his wife were very worried about him: 'You are in such demand from the highest to the lowest in the land that you are chasing around like a scalded cat, which is a most offensive remark for which I hope you will forgive me. But you did promise us that you would look at your diary and cancel the bulk of your appointments for 1984, and that you would get those letters off before Christmas. If you go on like you are at the present time you will kill yourself, which worries me terribly as you are the only real friend I have left, and then what would I do?'

Hodge arranged for the Commercial Bank of Wales to provide Thomas with administrative assistance. The banker also took it upon himself to interfere in the financial arrangements for Thomas' autobiography to be ghost-written, writing him a letter to say: 'Frankly, I am astonished at the figures quoted, which was not at all in accord with what Timothy O'Sullivan told me at the time over the telephone. So in his defence I can only plead that it was Timothy O'Sullivan's agent who was attempting to negotiate this exorbitant figure, and not Timothy

O'Sullivan himself. Alternatively, perhaps he was entirely mistaken on the figures that were involved. But be that as it may, it is really unsatisfactory. So I am glad that you are very pleased with the man who is working with you on the book at the present time, for this is so desperately important.'

It was Hodge who put a group called Care of the Dying in touch with Thomas to set up the charitable hospice that bears his name. Originally it was called the George Thomas Memorial Trust, but the word Memorial was later removed when Thomas pointed out that it was inappropriate while he was still alive. The charity's objects were: 'to relieve sickness and pain among persons who are suffering from any chronic or terminal illness in south Wales irrespective of race colour or creed and to provide moral and spiritual support to the relations of such patients.'

Hodge was predictably delighted with Thomas' autobiography, writing to tell him: 'It is certainly a most beautiful story and beautifully told. It holds one's interest intently throughout the whole book, leaving an indelible impression of absolute loyalty to early convictions and a matchless sense of political timing that seems to emerge out of a deep and abiding religious conviction. It would add lustre to any name, however famous. And the style in which it is written ensures the widest possible appeal at home and overseas. I will not comment on its historical merit, but that would be enormous too with flashes of wit and humour (for which you are world famous) adding their own piquancy to its pages, It is a kind book too. I would not change a word of it. In haste and with much love, Julian.'

When Thomas was taken ill with throat cancer, Hodge wrote to him telling him he could not sleep for worry: 'I suppose the position is worse because of this distance between us, for had you been in Cardiff we would have been available, and on call, at all times. But as it is the whole world is praying for you, with complete confidence that you will soon be restored to your millions of admirers in good health and with renewed energy to take up again the burden you have had to lay down for the moment.'

Hodge told Thomas he wanted to turn his bungalow into a museum: 'You will remember that the idea I advanced was born out of the misgivings we both had as to the ultimate destination, in the years ahead, of your bungalow and its most valuable and irreplaceable contents. So in my discussions with you during that traumatic evening I suggested the Jane Hodge Foundation would purchase the bungalow at the market price at the time, which currently I thought would be worth £85,000 but possibly more later on. Add that to solve the problem of the contents being disbursed as curios and collectors' items under the hammer of an auctioneer that these might be gifted to the Jane Hodge Foundation on the understanding that along with the bungalow they would be preserved for all time as a George Thomas Museum which would attract visitors from all over the world. After all, tens of thousands of people visit the cottage of Ann Hathaway every year, so we could double that figure if we preserved the bungalow and its contents intact for all the world to see. And it is my belief that people from all over the world would beat a path to Cardiff and to Wales to visit that museum which would then take on the nature of a shrine. In short, before you deal with these matters in any other way, I think you should turn over in your mind again the great importance of preserving the bungalow and its contents for posterity. This can be done without costing your Estate anything. I think you owe it to the world and to Wales and your millions of admirers that after your days (and mine), people of many races and creeds will make their own special pilgrimage to Cardiff in acknowledgement of the greatest Welshman of the 20th century and in submission to the Christian faith in which he has so steadfastly believed. I again say that I don't mind what it costs, because I think the idea, born out of the deep feelings and emotion during that evening, contained a touch of inspiration, although I didn't know it then. And now that you are well on the road to recovery I hope you will be able to stop and see that my ideas are not so daft after all. With love from us all.'

However, 'the greatest Welshman of the 20th century' could not see fit to facilitate sponsorship by the Commercial Bank of Wales, which he chaired, of a concert in St. David's Hall, Cardiff associated with the Urdd Eisteddfod. There is a one-word handwritten instruction to Thomas' secretary on the letter from the Rev. Bob Morgan requesting such sponsorship: 'No'. There is much evidence in the correspondence between Hodge and Thomas that the latter was not simply a sleeping director of the bank, but was actively involved in the running of it. When suspicions arose that there may have been financial irregularities in an associated branch, Hodge consulted Thomas about how they should proceed, railing against the auditors who had failed to pick up on the discrepancies. Hodge wrote to Thomas, stating: '... speed is of the very essence, before evidence is possibly destroyed.' He signed off with the usual 'Much love'.

Their communications with each other were littered with religiosity. At one point, Hodge, who was domiciled in Jersey, wrote to Thomas describing how he had arranged for a photograph of the two of them to appear in the bank's half-yearly accounts: 'I could not resist including the photograph of both of us, although this is very much reduced in size. But it does convey to the many depositors in Jersey that the Methodist influence is very strong and, as you know, this is a Methodist island. And in addition to that of course I think perhaps I have some modest following too, so putting us both together again can do no harm, and it did a lot of good on the last occasion."

In September 1987, Thomas wrote a letter to Hodge after reading an article in the *Financial Times* headed The Divided Brotherhood of Islam, which the banker had sent him. Thomas wrote: 'I fear that I am frightened about the aggressive nature which Islam is once again assuming. By the middle of the next century Islam will be very powerful throughout the UK. This is inevitable in view of the large population of immigrants who hold the Islamic faith. Unfortunately, if we even refer to it people accuse us of being racialist.'

Hodge wrote back, saying: 'I was very pleased to get your letter of September 11 and to hear what you have to say because my feelings are precisely the same as yours. It seems to me that Christianity is in retreat everywhere, and that despite the Pope's many journeys to far distant places, the Catholic Church is having its problems too, some of which seem very serious.'

Stating that he had been having difficulty getting hold of Thomas, Hodge stated: 'I know you won't like me saying it but you are possibly the one person in the United Kingdom who could fill any cathedral and/or the Albert Hall at the drop of a hat. That is such a wonderful and unique gift that there is only one purpose in my opinion for which it should be used, and you know what that is.'

In a later letter Hodge said he found himself in sympathy with the Palestinians. Enclosing a circular issued by Labour Friends of Israel, he said: 'I find it difficult to understand why the Israelis, who for centuries wanted a nation of their own right in their own country, should not even encourage the Palestinians to do the same. No doubt I don't understand it.'

At a gala event for Thomas' 80th birthday, Hodge gave further vent to hyperbole, saying: "Now you will all know that 80 years ago on January 29th, 1909, there was born in the Rhondda to Zacharia and Emma Jane Thomas a son who was to do more to change the face of Wales, and south Wales in particular, than any man before him and to establish an understanding throughout the world of all things Welsh in a manner that has never been equalled before let alone surpassed. That son, of course, was 'Our George', and it would be true to say that his charismatic personality has made him probably the best Ambassador that Britain ever had. To illustrate this, I remember an incident in the mountains of Saudi Arabia when George and I were the guests of the Sheikh Yamani. One day a servant came into the drawing room and said to Madame Yamani that there were some people from the British Embassy who wanted to see George. George looked surprised, so Madame Yamani said: 'If you don't want to see them, we will send them away as we always do'. But George invited them in and after being introduced to Sheikh Yamani and Madame Yamani the latter left us to a private discussion, when the First Assistant to the British Ambassador said rather excitedly, 'This is quite extraordinary, as none of us has ever had the opportunity of being invited into the home of any of the important Arabs before'.

"So close had become the friendship between George and Sheikh Yamani that, the next time we went, Sheikh Yamani sent his $20,000,000 private jet to pick us up in Cardiff. There was some little delay, when the Captain explained to us that we had to fly back to Luton to fill up for the long journey to the south of Arabia as unfortunately they would not give him credit in Cardiff. The answer of course was simple. He should have an account with the Bank of Wales.

"The story is told that when George was in the Commonwealth Office he attended a meeting of the Commonwealth Ministers in Africa. The chairman was a Zambian, black as the ace of spades, and when he came to introduce George he said that he had known him for 25 years and that he was a wonderful person. Not getting very much immediate response from his audience, the Chairman said again: 'I have known George for more than 25 years. He really is a wonderful person, and although his skin may be white, his heart is as black as ours'. There is no need to tell you that George got a standing ovation when he addressed the meeting. George and I often speak on the telephone, and I always feel better and uplifted by my chats with him."

Hodge sent Thomas a copy of his speech, stating: 'It was such an emotive evening that you may not have heard all I said. To me, there is an element of the historical record in what I tried to put over and explain and it may be of interest to you. But all that apart, it does help to summarise some of my real feelings towards you.'

In Thomas' last years, Hodge was undoubtedly a significant influence on George's increasing Euroscepticism. In July 1992, as Britain struggled within the European Exchange Rate Mechanism, Hodge wrote to Thomas: 'Everything seems to have gone wrong with our government's financial policy, and Margaret Thatcher was right after all. And may I quote Winston Churchill who said: "We are with Europe but not of it. We are linked but not compromised. We are associated but not absorbed!" Why in the name of goodness did we not adhere to those words of wisdom? Now we are at the mercy of the German monetary authorities!! Heaven help us! Much love, Julian.'

In July 1996 Hodge wrote to Eurosceptic Tory MP Sir Richard Body saying: 'Although I have never previously read *The Sun*, I have taken copies recently in order to enjoy the simple English in which it lambasts any proposal to take us further into Europe, with particular reference to the single currency.'

Hodge told Body he had written to his fellow Tory Eurosceptic

David Heathcoat-Amory suggesting 10,000 copies of his pamphlet *A Single European Currency* should be printed. He suggested that if a good price could not be had, he may 'have a bash in Cardiff with the University Press'. Hodge concluded: 'In the meantime, James Goldsmith seems to be sending out a lot of material, a copy of which I have not yet had, in which he asks on the cover in simple straightforward English, 'Do you want to be governed by Westminster or Brussels'?'

In a further letter to Body, Hodge backed the idea of a pamphlet about the CBI, showing that whenever in the past 25 years it had expressed an opinion, it had been wrong. Hodge wrote: 'The CBI is under the control of [Adair] Turner, who in turn is influenced by some of the big multi-nationals, to the detriment of all other businesses. And you will remember that it is estimated that at least 66% of all the businesses in Europe are in the smaller category. In fact, in his book *Who Governs Britain?* Jim Goldsmith points out that the number of small businesses that have gone bust in Germany rose from 8,800 in 1992 to about 23,000 in 1995 – a staggering degree of destruction.'

Hodge went on to say: 'How can the Eurocrats be so blind? The figures represent terrible personal tragedy. What is more, despising small businessmen is economically idiotic, because 66% of all employment in the European Union comes from small and medium-sized enterprises. And nearly all new jobs created in the EU between 1988 and 1995 came from such businesses. Heartiest congratulations!'

Thomas kept copies of Hodge's letters to Body, and clearly approved of their content.

In Julian Hodge, Thomas had the perfect friend: one who flattered him to excess, but perhaps more importantly joined him in using the cloak of religiosity as a way of covering his more unsavoury activities.

20

Sexual Predator

On July 18, 2014, the *Daily Mirror*'s website published an allegation that George Thomas had raped a boy – aged about nine – in Cardiff. The accusation was made by a man then aged 55 and living in Australia, meaning that the alleged rape would have taken place in around 1968, the year Thomas was appointed Secretary of State for Wales.

The alleged victim, who has not given up his right to anonymity, told the *Mirror*: "I was raped by George Thomas in Cardiff. I was about nine. He spent a lot of time at my house as my [foster] parents were good friends with him. Things started small but then got a lot worse. It has been with me all my life."

He said the alleged abuse was also carried out at another address in the city. The alleged victim said his foster parents were Labour Party supporters, adding: "We went on many campaigns for Harold Wilson, Jim Callaghan and George Thomas."

He said he had to report the rape claim to South Wales Police on two occasions, saying he had been disappointed by the response from officers.

In a statement to the *Mirror*, Assistant Chief Constable Nikki Holland said: "We were made aware of these allegations in April 2013 and have attempted to get in touch with the victim. Unfortunately incorrect contact information was used. As a result we failed to make contact. We have since spoken to the victim, apologised for the delay and are investigating his claims. This delay was unacceptable and we have referred the matter to the Independent Police Complaints Commission."

In June 2015 it emerged that two further allegations of sexual assault against Thomas had recently been made to the police. A statement issued by British Transport Police (BTP) said: 'BTP was made aware, via South Wales Police, of an allegation of inappropriate touching involving the late George Thomas on board a train from London Paddington to Aberystwyth in 1959.' The complainant was said to have been 22 at the time of the alleged incident.

The British Transport Police spokesman went on to say: "I can confirm that a second report has been received, from Gwent Police, involving allegations of a sexual assault during a train journey from Newport to London Paddington between 1964 and 1966. The complainant, who was aged 16 or 17 at the time, did not wish to make a formal statement to police."

In March 2017, South Wales Police confirmed that the three allegations had all been referred to Operation Hydrant, described by the National Police Chiefs' Council as 'a coordination hub established in June 2014 to deliver the national policing response, oversight and coordination of non-recent child abuse investigations concerning persons of public prominence, or in relation to those offences which took place historically within institutional settings'.

But Operation Hydrant does not carry out investigations itself – it merely coordinates information among forces to prevent duplication. The implication of the decision to refer the three cases to Operation Hydrant while no longer actively investigating them was, according to police sources, a recognition that they were 'going nowhere'.

In other recent instances of historic sex abuse allegations - in particular those involving well-known people such as Jimmy

Savile, Rolf Harris and Stuart Hall - the evidence gathered by the Police clearly showed how the perpetrators had used a particular *modus operandi* on multiple occasions with multiple victims. This enabled the Crown Prosecution Service (CPS) to mount prosecutions of offenders who are still alive, and to declare Savile a paedophile posthumously.

During these and other similar cases, the Police have been assisted by the evidence of many additional victims coming forward, whose painful and dark memories had been jogged following the huge amount of sustained publicity generated during the formal charging process and initial court appearances when footage of the accused individuals walking into and out of court were broadcast on rolling 24-hour news, peak-time news programmes and reported widely in the most popular newspapers.

The level of publicity about the child rape allegation made against George Thomas has been minuscule by comparison, largely because he is not a current or recently deceased celebrity, and this lack of very high profile coverage may be a reason why no further allegations have been forthcoming. It may also be, of course, because there are no further allegations because he was innocent and the existing claims are false yet, since the publication of this book was announced, further unsolicited claims have been forthcoming about Thomas' predatory behaviour, and further allegations may yet emerge.

However, according to a senior South Wales Police source, the one very serious allegation of child rape and two allegations of sexual assault on trains remain the only ones formally made to date and, due to the lack of any further evidence, the investigation into George Thomas is no longer active.

While Thomas' alleged rape victim has been reluctant to give further interviews to journalists, he did make online contact with former Plaid Cymru AM Lindsay Whittle, who said: "He told me he remembered me from decades ago, when I was a young activist in Plaid Cymru. I couldn't remember him, but there were a lot of people around at that time who were associated with Plaid. He told me that George Thomas had raped him when he was about nine-years-old. I have no evidence, so I can't make a judgement. I have no reason to disbelieve him."

Whittle has another story about Thomas. A friend of his told him, in around 1978 to 1980, that around 30 years previously he had been touched inappropriately by Thomas on Pontypridd train station: "At the time the incident happened in the late 1940s, my friend was 17. He told me that Thomas started talking to him on the station. He was very friendly, and he invited my friend to have a few pints of beer. Afterwards, at the station, Thomas touched him inappropriately. My friend shoved him backwards and Thomas knocked his head on a girder and fell down. He legged it, terrified that he might have killed Thomas. He hadn't, of course, and had acted in self-defence. He thought Thomas may have been attracted to him because of his blond hair. When he told me what had happened, he had no hair left. My friend didn't report what had happened, and he died quite a few years ago now. He was a really decent guy, and had no reason to make the story up. I totally believe him."

At this point it's worth turning to the account given, by Leo Abse, of a series of crises in Thomas' life arising out of a threat to expose him as a homosexual who used rent boys.

Abse, the Labour MP for Pontypool and then Torfaen from 1958 until 1987, was a friend and ally of Thomas' in the Commons, sharing an antipathy towards devolution. In his book *Tony Blair: The Man Behind the Smile* – originally published in 1996 – Abse described Thomas succinctly as 'a primary schoolmaster lacking gravitas and with seemingly few qualifications', who nevertheless had 'an astonishing and rare charisma which enabled him not only to capture his electorate and the Royal Family, but to seduce a tough House of Commons which yielded to his charm and made him Speaker'.

Abse described how, as a confidant for Thomas, he was able to help him when he was 'endangered' as a consequence of 'barbarous laws and primitive social attitudes' relating to homosexuality. Abse wrote that Thomas was, mostly, able to 'sublimate his inclinations' while doing his political work. Sometimes, however, he was 'overwhelmed' and what Thomas himself regarded as lapses occurred.

According to Abse, the final occasion when he intervened on Thomas' behalf – making it very clear that he had been involved on earlier occasions too – was in 1984, the year after Thomas had retired as Speaker. A sobbing Thomas phoned Abse at 6am one morning, saying: "I'm in terrible, terrible trouble. Come quickly."

Revealingly, Abse wrote: 'I knew I had to dash to him for he was a man who, with the wit and aplomb to keep himself cool and damp down the passions stirred in Commons debates, would, I was well aware, dangerously over-act and panic if there was the slightest sign of a crack in the thin ice upon which he skated all his life'.

The thin ice on which Thomas skated was his homosexuality which, until legislation promoted by Abse was enacted in 1967, left him liable to criminal prosecution for gay sexual activity in private, and after that in public places like public toilets, parks and cinemas. Paying for sex with strangers carried the extra risks of blackmail and exposure.

Some gay men – notably the British civil servant and Soviet spy Guy Burgess – were nonchalant about the risks, but for most the homophobic climate engendered fear of exposure, a potential prison sentence as well as a loss of reputation and a career left in ruins.

A Channel 4 'docudrama' made in 2007 called *A Very British Sex Scandal* provided a compelling insight into gay London in the 1950s, when Thomas was in his 40s. Every year 1,000 men were jailed for homosexual offences, with the maximum sentence for buggery being life imprisonment. Many gay men committed suicide because of the huge social stigma that was attached to being exposed as homosexual. Only in 2014 was the pioneering computer scientist and Enigma code breaker Alan Turing pardoned for the gross indecency conviction which had led to his suicide in 1954.

A Very British Sex Scandal focused on the case of Peter Wildeblood, the *Daily Mail*'s Royal Correspondent, who was jailed for 18 months in 1954 after being convicted for a gay affair he'd had with an RAF serviceman. Letters from Wildbloode to the airman, Edward McNally, were intercepted by the RAF and McNally gave evidence against Wildeblood in return for a guarantee that he would not be prosecuted. During the course of the trial Wildeblood admitted he was gay – a turning point which persuaded the jury of his guilt.

After his release from prison, Wildeblood gave evidence to the Wolfenden Commission, which in 1957 recommended decriminalising homosexual acts between consenting adults in private. However, it took another decade before the law was changed, following an initiative by Abse, during which prosecutions continued.

Abse wrote how it had been inevitable that Thomas would fall victim to blackmail. As a solicitor who had prosecuted and defended criminals from Cardiff's underworld, Abse had a fearsome reputation. On one occasion he claimed to have neutralised a young criminal who was blackmailing Thomas by warning him that he would be jailed for 10 years. The criminal was said to have left Cardiff.

Through the contacts in the gay community he had made during his campaign to liberalise the law on homosexuality, Abse learnt that Thomas was becoming well-known for frequenting a seedy cinema in Westminster where men engaged in sexual activity under the cover of darkness. Thomas was alarmed that Abse had found out about his covert excursions to the cinema and promised Abse that he would desist from going there again.

On another occasion, said Abse, when Thomas was a backbencher, he had asked to borrow £800 from him so he could pay the fare to Australia and resettlement costs of a young man who was extorting money from him. Thomas refused to let Abse 'deal with' the man, and Abse gave Thomas the money. Years later, when his friend was a government minister, Abse said Thomas handed him an envelope containing money and said "Thank you", quickly moving away because he obviously did not wish to discuss the matter further. In fact, Thomas did not repay the full amount but short-changed Abse who, however, was convinced the underpayment was not deliberate.

According to Abse, the slightest tremor of scandal could reduce Thomas to jelly – as also occurred, he says, when, in 1976, journalists wanted to interview him about his role in helping Liberal leader Jeremy Thorpe deal with a sex scandal of his own. Some 12 years before, as a Home Office Minister, Thomas had facilitated a meeting between Home Secretary Sir Frank Soskice and Peter Bessell, a Liberal MP and alleged fraudster who was acting as Thorpe's protector. The suggestion was that in 1960, under a Conservative government, there had been political intervention to stop Thorpe being prosecuted for a homosexual offence against a minor. In 1964, at a time when Thorpe was trying to suppress further gay sex allegations relating to himself, he was concerned that details of the earlier cover-up should not emerge.

Thomas was said by Abse to have been terrified that journalists pursuing the Thorpe cover-up would ask him about his own sex life. Abse wrote: 'It was clear to me that if he submitted to an interrogation by the investigative journalists, he was in danger of betraying himself; he could, with unmatched deftness, control the most noisy of Commons debates but, witnessing his anxiety state now, I doubted if, under pressure, he would successfully control the nascent guilt-ridden self-castigations that were just beneath the surface and forever waiting to be released.'

Thomas had a penchant for referring in sermons to passages from St. Paul's Epistles to the Corinthians, in which the apostle condemned sexual incontinence. Abse stated: 'I wanted not the slightest betraying hint of cleansing repentance to emerge in an encounter with his press tormentors'. Thomas was persuaded not to be interviewed, and the journalists were told it would be inappropriate for the Speaker to discuss with them a matter relating to his time as a minister.

The panic call in 1984 from Thomas to Abse was made not from a police station, as Abse feared, but from a hospital bed. Abse claimed there was a pattern linking Thomas' episodes of sickness with occasions when dangerous threats of exposure were bearing down on him: he cited in particular an 80th birthday party for Thomas held in London's Guildhall when Thomas collapsed in a 'spasm of shame' after having praise heaped on him by those present.

When Abse got to the hospital, he found Thomas 'convulsively sobbing'. Grabbing Abse's hand, he said he was ruined: soon the whole world would know he was suffering from venereal disease.

Abse told him to get a grip of himself and suggested the

reason for his stay in hospital could easily be attributed to 'waterworks'. Thomas calmed down and contacted a friendly journalist to say he had been rushed to hospital with prostrate problems after being unable to urinate. The lie worked – and Thomas' fear of exposure was averted.

Thomas' fear of exposure extend to his actions when his parliamentary colleague moved his landmark Bill to decriminalise homosexuality. Thomas voted for it at the second reading stage but, like most other MPs, was absent in July 1967 for the highly charged debate which culminated in its third reading. While the Bill had secured Government support, Thomas was not prepared to be over-conspicuous in his public backing for a measure that touched on his own behaviour. Perhaps Abse's references to gay men being victims of blackmail under the existing punitive legal regime were too close to home.

Whilst there is no doubt that Thomas was gay, and that he hid his sexuality for his entire life, his extensive archive contains nothing that represents an overt acknowledgement that he was homosexual. What we can say with certainty is that he was on close terms with MPs like Jeremy Thorpe, Cyril Smith and Greville Janner, all of whom were accused – though never convicted – of abusing under-age boys.

A photograph that was published in the *Daily Mail* shows Thomas and Janner bending forward to greet a party of young schoolboys as they visited the House of Commons in 1976. The picture certainly appears disturbing with the retrospective knowledge of what the men have been accused of.

There are a number of references to Thomas as a paedophile on sensationalist websites, sometimes adjacent to implausible allegations relating to living politicians. Usually they refer to the Abse material and to the child rape allegation, invariably without providing any further information. Thomas has not

been named specifically as having been present at the Elm
Guest House in London, where sex parties involving politicians
and young boys are alleged to have taken place. Nor has he
been referred to in relation to flats in Dolphin Square, Pimlico,
where a paedophile ring including politicians was said to have
operated, and where allegations have been made that young
boys were abused and murdered.

One paradox in assessing Thomas' involvement or otherwise
in child sexual abuse is that those who knew him well and
are still around to be interviewed will not countenance it as
a possibility, while many who didn't know him are happy to
assert with confidence that he was, based on hearsay evidence
whose source cannot be traced.

"He got to know our boys," commented Patrick Cormack.
"Our sons were born in 1969 and in 1971, and they were
very young when George became Speaker in 1976. Charles
was seven and Richard was five. That was the first time George
came to our home – and they really took to Uncle George. They
thought he was absolutely the bee's knees and when they went
away to prep school at the age of eight – Cheam, near Newbury
– he went there twice, to preach. Then he would come and stay
with us at our home in the country.

"The boys really did look upon him as an adopted uncle and
he was immensely generous to them. He used to buy them
lovely presents and things like that. They really were very, very,
very fond of him. Charles is now 47 and Richard 45 but they
still talk fondly of George and how, when he went to preach
at Cheam on one occasion, Richard had had a weekend *exeat*
[permission to leave the school] and was going back on the
Sunday night. We went in the Speaker's car and George insisted
that Richard sat in the front seat so that when he got to the
school he got out of a car with a pennant on the front. Little
things like that they still remember and talk about."

Asked what he thought of the allegation of child abuse against Thomas, Lord Cormack said: "I cannot believe that. I mean George clearly never got married – but I cannot believe that George did anything that was damaging to the young. It was a more tactile age. Our boys would sit on his knee while he read them a bedside story. Sometimes he had one on each knee when he was staying with us. And he would tell them stories, make stories up. He would write little things for them about our dog, a yellow Labrador called Shandy: he loved that dog. But I never, for a moment, would have had any doubt about him. I've talked to my boys, and they say of all the people they felt safe with, Uncle George was very much one. Moreover, I know George was fond of my friend Michael Ancram's children, and I know Michael – who is a member of this House – felt the same.

"Whether George ever had any homosexual contact with another man I do not know. I am absolutely sure he wouldn't engage in such activity with children. I find it difficult to believe at all – and I'm very troubled about some of the things that have been coming out recently.

"Another friend of mine – and a great friend of George – was Enoch Powell. I don't have to tell you that I disagreed with Enoch quite a lot on political issues but he was a very good man. He and George were very close. I saw some of the letters that Enoch wrote to George saying what a great Speaker he was and all that sort of thing. Pam, Enoch's widow, still talks fondly of George. Enoch, you see, was 'fingered' quite recently because it was said somebody had made a complaint – one person – and the safeguarding Bishop of the Church of England, the Bishop of Durham – he's not doing that job now – announced that he'd referred this to the police. Well, if he felt he had to refer it that's his judgement but, to announce that he had done so, I was so incensed by that I got in touch with the Bishop of Lichfield and the Archbishop of Canterbury, both of whom

234

made contact with Pam Powell. But you know this has been a bit of an industry, and it does worry me greatly.

"I don't know more details of Abse, because quite honestly when it came out I couldn't be bothered to read it. I knew George. My family knew George and I do not believe that George was free from sin, because nobody is, nobody – not you, not me, nobody. If you're a Christian, you believe and acknowledge that, more than if you're not perhaps. But George, I think, was a good man. If he had weaknesses – we all have weaknesses – if he succumbed to any of those in his youth or early manhood – he may have done, I do not know – I don't really want to know ... The one thing I am utterly, utterly convinced about is that George would never have harmed a child. I'm absolutely convinced of that."

The solicitor David Seligman, who chaired Cardiff West Labour Party while Thomas was the MP, also does not believe Thomas was a child abuser. He said: "I had a lot to do with George. Once a month, on a Sunday morning, he would come to my house. He always gave the kids half a crown. He was a sort of uncle to the two boys. On those Sunday mornings George would always have a glass of sherry, despite being a Methodist and supposed non-drinker. And he smoked. He always used to say, 'Don't tell Mam'. He was very concerned – it was a very strange relationship he had with Mam. He idolised her."

Some of those who knew him very well will not even accept that he was gay, and show distaste when reference is made to Abse's allegations, which those who were his friends profess not to have read. Otherwise intelligent and rational politicians openly wondered whether it was necessary for a biography of Thomas even to mention the allegations made against him.

On the other hand, many others have insisted that Thomas regularly had sex with rent boys on trains between Cardiff and

London, but no direct evidence has ever been forthcoming. It's been suggested that he regularly used to hang around with a suitcase on a platform after getting off a train at Cardiff Central station, waiting for a passing young man to offer to carry it, so he could strike up a conversation.

Referring to Thomas in his book *Closet Queens*, about gay British politicians in the 20th Century, the historian Michael Bloch wrote: 'Thomas was compulsively homosexual; his sexual encounters, usually taking place anonymously in locations such as cinemas, were numerous, furtive and guilt-ridden. Though his proclivities were no great secret at Westminster, where he showed a more than fatherly interest in various young MPs and parliamentary employees.'

It is clear, however, that so far as Thomas' sexuality was concerned, there were those who were in the know, and those who weren't. Growing up as he did in a period when homosexuality was illegal, Thomas, like many others in prominent positions, became adept at concealment. His very public association with the Methodist Church provided another reason why his homosexuality could not be disclosed.

Former First Minister of Wales, Rhodri Morgan, always considered Thomas to be a 'confirmed bachelor' until Leo Abse's revelations were made public, while Dafydd Wigley said of them: "It was quite a shock when that came out. The sort of thing that came out subsequently about other people has been so dramatic that one accepts there were things that were going on way back – you just don't know.

"In some ways I can imagine that George was quite a lonely person. His links to Mam were so great. So far as the allegations about George were concerned, it was something that we came up against. I'll be honest: I was pretty naïve when I came to Westminster. I think a lot of us were when these sorts of things were going on.

"An example of that was fairly early on when I was an MP. There were accusations of things going on – that children were being abused – in a place called Tŷ'r Felin in Bangor, which wasn't actually in my constituency, so I would pass on anything I got to Wyn Roberts [MP for Conwy] and it was a matter for Wyn from then on. There were inquiries but I can't remember the outcome of it. I do remember it was at that time I first came across the word 'paedophile', and I didn't know the meaning of the word. I'd gone through a reasonably good education, a university degree and all the rest and I didn't know the meaning of the word 'paedophile', because it wasn't on our radar then. And therefore there might well have been things that were 'known' down here [in Westminster], and there may well have been 'wink, wink, nudge, nudge' going on, but a lot of it went straight over my head because I wasn't aware what was being said."

David Seligman adds: "I never suspected that he might be gay. There were suggestions that he was close to Julian Hodge's sister. It was a very strong rumour at one time. I don't know if she was his girlfriend, but there was this link that we were aware of. I remember asking my wife Philippa, 'Do you think that George will ever get married?' She thought he was a confirmed bachelor. He never did, did he?"

Gwynoro Jones believes Thomas carefully cultivated the story about a romantic liaison with Hodges' sister as a diversionary tactic: "There were rumours that George had a romantic involvement with Julian Hodge's sister. I can vouch for one thing. That booklet I wrote – *The Record of the Labour Government in Wales 1964-1970* – was funded by Julian Hodge. George managed to get him to pay for the printing. There were rumours about a romantic liaison going on between George and Hodge's sister, but I have difficulty in believing that, because that was not his predilection. The other rumour that was going around concerned the housekeeper, a white-haired woman in her 60s – this was in the period 1968 to 1971 – I can remember her. She was always there, looking after Mam when George was away all week. I can vouch for the fact she was there every time I was there. There was a rumour about her and George, but I reckon those were throwaway things. In the House of Commons we all used to talk about George's housekeeper, with a lifting of the eyebrows. It was convenient for him – throwing us off the scent – it was very clever."

Promiscuous he may have been, but there were some young men he knew well who say he never made a sexual approach towards them.

John Osmond, a young journalist who later became director of the Institute of Welsh Affairs, was on cordial terms with Thomas for a period, finding him a very useful contact, until it became clear to Thomas that Osmond was committed to the cause of Welsh devolution. On no occasion did he give Osmond the impression that he was sexually interested in him and Osmond does not believe that Thomas was a paedophile.

On a number of occasions in the 1990s, Lee Wenham went to Thomas' bungalow to collect articles written for the *Western Mail*. In his late 20s at the time, Wenham was the paper's news editor. One of the photographers repeatedly joked with him that he was fancied by Thomas, but Wenham is clear that nothing untoward ever took place: "He'd invite me into his study and call for his housekeeper Nellie, saying 'Here's Lee from the Rhondda'. I was from the Rhondda like him. In fact we both went to the same school in Tonypandy. He never made me feel uncomfortable, or say or do anything inappropriate. He didn't try to get me to stay with him or offer me a cup of tea. From my experience, he was a sweet old man."

Considering his background, upbringing and position, it is totally understandable why Thomas, like tens of thousands of other gay men, kept his sexuality private after decriminalisation and, prior to 1967, one can only but empathise with all gay men who lived in daily fear of exposure and potential ruin. Looking back, fifty years after Leo Abse's Bill, the state-backed hounding and persecution of homosexuals is simply horrifying.

Thomas' sexuality and his use of rent boys is, therefore, not the aspect of his personal life that is the focus of this chapter, although it is another example - amongst many - of living a double life. However, the allegation of child-rape and the accusations of sexual assault raise the question of whether his sexual behaviour was predatory in nature, and whether he was a paedophile.

There can be no doubt that George Thomas, even into old age, had a sexual attraction to young men and that there were occasions when his sexual advances were made without the consent of the young men concerned. In law, such unwanted sexual contact is deemed as sexual assault and the contrast between the reality of his sexual conduct and the self-righteous Methodist preacher is sufficient to convict him of brazen hypocrisy. From the allegations of sexual assault already made, and with more appearing as victims feel more able to speak out, it would appear that Thomas did indeed have a tendency towards a sexual behaviour that is regarded as criminal. He also, however, had a strong instinct for self-preservation and knew, like other sexual predators, who to approach, where and when, hence the brief encounters with strangers on trains and in railway stations rather than with those - holding influential positions – he knew through his political work and who could destroy him.

Was George Thomas a paedophile? With one allegation of child-rape there is certainly the possibility that he was but, until the Police have reason to re-open the case due to further evidence and additional allegations, the truth is that we may never really know.

21

Freemason

For someone who was gaining a reputation as a supporter of left-wing causes, George Thomas' membership of the Freemasons may seem a little strange.

While the movement emerged from the Enlightenment, it had a reputation as a secretive organisation which helped members gain influence and further their own interests in sometimes unscrupulous ways. At its worst it could be a cover for corruption and other forms of criminality. Against that there is evidence of considerable social good, in the form of charitable work, undertaken by Freemasons and their Lodges.

Records held by the Library and Museum of Freemasonry in London show that Thomas was initiated into the Sapphire Lodge at Penarth on March 15, 1944, at which time he was a school teacher living in Tonypandy. Using Masonic terminology relating to the three stages of the craft, he was 'passed' on September 20, 1944, and 'raised' on April 18, 1945. According to the records, he resigned from Sapphire Lodge on December 6, 1965.

For more than three and a half years he was also a member of the Cambrensis Lodge in Cardiff, joining on May 15, 1950, and resigning on December 21, 1953. Thomas certainly didn't proclaim his membership of the Brotherhood widely, but his archive contains several documents that touch on it.

On April 5, 1946, Herbert Lloyd, Master-Elect of the

Swansea-based Beaufort Lodge, wrote to Thomas confirming his invitation to Lloyd's Installation as Lodge Master and asking him to reply to the Visitors' Toast. Lloyd addressed Thomas as 'Sir and Brother'.

The letter read: 'Dear Sir and Brother, I acknowledge with pleasure your acceptance of invitation to Installation on the 11th inst and enclose herewith complimentary ticket. It will also give added pleasure if you will be good enough to reply to the Visitors' Toast on that day, and I have duly placed your name on the list to do so. With all good wishes and fraternal greetings.'

After renewing his Masonic subscription to the Sapphire Lodge in November 1964, Thomas was written to a month later to be told: 'Your Covenant on behalf of the Masonic Charities expired in May 1962', and he was asked whether he wanted to resume his Covenant.

Several years later one of Thomas' Freemason friends, Lieutenant Colonel Arthur Lennox of Cardiff, was in touch to tell him he was doing a good job as Welsh Secretary: 'My dear George, Having now retired I can at last find time to write to you and offer my congratulations on the manner in which you are conducting things at the Welsh Office,' he wrote. 'We are a great nation George and I hope the position will arrive that you will be able to continue with the good work for a few more years. Like you I am spending a lot of time in London in my appointment as Grand Treasurer. I now have the title of Very Worshipful Brother, always said you should have sent me to the House of Lords. For your confidential information I have enclosed Minutes of a meeting held in London on December 10, 1968. I organised the 1968 Festival here in south Wales, raised some £70,000 – a record figure, so you see George some boys who had to leave school before they were 14 can make the grade. PS Please destroy minutes after reading.'

Thomas responded: 'My dear Arthur, It was pleasant to hear from you again after such a long time. I offer you my warmest congratulations on your appointment as Grand Treasurer and hope that you will enjoy this very much indeed. You have a splendid record of public service and you have every reason to be proud.'

At the time Lennox wrote his letter, Thomas had, according to Freemasonry's official records, been out of the organisation for three years. Yet the Grand Treasurer was prepared to break the rules of confidentiality by sending him minutes that were confidential to members. For whatever reason, Thomas was not entirely candid when asked by a correspondent from Aberystwyth whether he was a Freemason. A P. Duffy wrote to him in the following terms on December 10 1972: 'Dear Mr. Thomas, I am 65 just on and I have been Labour all my life. My father worked 58 years in the mines. I feel there is something wrong and I therefore feel fit not just to accept but now to question. Question 1. Mr. George Thomas, are you a Freemason? Question 2. To your knowledge, are any Labour Members of Parliament Freemasons? These questions are straightforward. I trust they will be answered, for your and my interest. Please acknowledge this letter.'

Four days later Thomas replied: 'Dear Mr. Duffy, Thank you for your letter. The answers to your questions are as follows: I am not a Freemason. I know of no Labour Members of Parliament who are Freemasons.' Clearly Thomas wished to conceal the fact that he had been a Freemason.

Twelve years later, when Thomas was in the House of Lords, he received a reference request from Roger Clarke, Secretary of the Clive Freemasons Lodge in Cardiff. Raj Aggerwal, who later became the Honorary Consul for India in Wales, had applied to join. Thomas responded: 'I have known the above named person for about 10 years, and have always found him to be a thoroughly capable and reliable person. I met him originally through his activities in the Asian Society of Wales. When I was Speaker he visited me in Speaker's House and he brought his family with him. I believe that he would be an asset to your Lodge.'

Despite having apparently resigned as a Freemason many years before, he was still consulted about the worthiness of a prospective member. Oddest of all, however, was an approach made to Thomas by Commander Michael Higham, Grand Secretary of the United Grand Lodge of England. On June 26, 1985, Higham – the most senior administrative Freemason in England and Wales – wrote to Thomas addressing him as 'Brother Lord Tonypandy'. In Freemasonry, the term 'Brother' is used between fellow members.

Higham and his colleagues were concerned that the Methodist Conference was to consider a report which recommended that Methodists should not become Freemasons. The report criticised the secrecy of Freemasonry, saying: 'While officially the secrecy applies only to the recognition signs of the society, and so may appear reasonable, in practice it is applied to most aspects of the society, including avowal of membership. The secret signs enable masons to recognise one another instantly and secretly but it is difficult for non-masons to discover whether or not someone is a Freemason. There are no public lists of Freemasons or Lodges. The society thus encourages suspicion and lays itself open to charges of corrupt practice which can be neither proved nor disproved. For Christians the secrecy practised by Freemasons poses a problem in that secrecy of any kind is destructive of fellowship.'

The report also objected to the 'blood-curdling penalties' for those who break their oaths, Most objectionable from a theological point of view, however, was the name given in Masonic ritual to the Supreme Being: Jahbulon. The report said:

'The name is a composite, as the ritual explicitly states, The explanation given of the name in the ritual is acknowledged to be inaccurate, but is preserved to bring out the traditional meaning for Freemasonry of the word. The best explanation of the derivation of this word seems to be that two of the three parts, Jah and Bul, are the names of gods in different religions, while the third syllable On was thought by the composers of the ritual to be the name of a god in yet another religion; modern scholarship suggests they were wrong. In any case, it is clear that each of the three syllables is intended to be the name of a divinity in a particular religion. The whole word is thus an example of syncretism, an attempt to unite different religions in one, which Christians cannot accept.'

The report concluded: 'It is clear that Freemasonry may compete strongly with Christianity. There is a great danger that the Christian who becomes a Freemason will find himself compromising his Christian beliefs or his allegiance to Christ, perhaps without realising what he is doing.'

Methodists were to be recommended not to become Freemasons, but if they insisted on joining they should consider making their membership known, to allay suspicion. In addition, Masonic meetings should not be held on Methodist premises.

In his letter, Higham told Thomas he was concerned that the report was going to get passed and asked him to intervene, stating: 'I now fear that the Craft will have no advocate at the Conference, and that our case will not be put. If the report is accepted without debate – which seems likely at the moment – we shall be condemned unheard, which would not be allowed in the House over which you so long presided, or in the other place. If only for natural justice, I hope that you would be able to intervene, or organise an intervention in any debate (or even ensure that there is a debate) on the report on Freemasonry.'

A handwritten note on the letter said Thomas had responded to Higham in a phone call. It does not appear that Thomas took any formal and open action at the Methodist Conference to dissuade church leaders from pushing through the recommendations, which were passed. He did, however, write to a Methodist and Freemason in Seattle who had contacted him to express concern. Thomas wrote: 'I share your concern about the attitude of the Methodists in Britain to Freemasons. I know that across the world Methodists are Freemasons. I was myself one until I became a Minister in the Home Office and then I resigned because I wanted to be like Caesar's wife, above criticism. I have nothing but wholesome respect for Freemasons and the work that they do.'

On the same day he wrote to Higham, stating: 'I think that the Methodist Conference took leave of its senses when it adopted the resolution about Freemasonry. When one considers the social evils and sinfulness of which there is abundant evidence in our generation, it staggers me that the conference should have spent its time arguing about Freemasonry.'

Thomas' statement about resigning from Freemasonry when he became a Home Office Minister is not strictly accurate, even according to the official record. Thomas received his ministerial appointment on October 20, 1964 – 10 months before his resignation from Sapphire Lodge.

David Seligman, who knew Thomas for decades, said: "I never knew he was a Freemason. We had debates in the constituency party about Freemasonry, which I do remember. There was a period when it was very prominent, politically. I don't remember him declaring an interest or anything. We had a debate in the council Labour group and decided you shouldn't be a member of a Freemason Lodge and a member of the Labour Party, but it never got anywhere, unfortunately.

At the time there was a lot of comment about Freemasons getting involved in decisions in local authorities.

Thomas continued to receive correspondence and invitations relating to Freemasonry right into his final years. He accepted an invitation to a reception at the House of Lords in October 1987, for the Cardiff Masonic Hall Company Ltd in the Cholmondeley Room and the Terrace. The personal invitation to Thomas said : 'As our colleague Wyn Calvin may have told you, this reception will highlight our new scheme to provide sheltered accommodation for some elderly and widowed folk here in Cardiff.'

Then in 1990 Higham invited him to attend a touring exhibition in Cardiff Masonic Hall put on by the Association of Methodist Freemasons, formed with the object of changing the Methodist Conference's decision.

After receiving details of Thomas' membership of the two Lodges from the Library and Museum of Freemasonry, the author wrote with a further enquiry. Given that such a senior Freemason as the Secretary of the United Grand Lodge of England had addressed him as 'Brother' and asked him to intercede in a dispute with the Methodist Church 20 years after he had supposedly left the Brotherhood, was there a possibility that he could have joined a higher degree of Freemasonry that did not provide details of its members? There was no reply.

22

Embedded Royalist

There are royalists who admire from afar and those who become embedded with their heroes. George Thomas fell into the latter category.

He had developed a rapport with Prince Charles at the time of the Investiture, and they stayed in touch afterwards. It's clear from the tone of letters written to Thomas by the Prince that they formed a genuine friendship.

After his wedding to Diana in 1981, Charles wrote to Thomas to thank him for reading the lesson. He said: 'It was wonderfully reassuring and moving to hear those famous Welsh tones fill the vastness of St Paul's!'

In early 1983, when he was still Speaker, Charles wanted Thomas to become Lord Warden of the Duchy of Cornwall, chairing the council that runs the vast estate of the heir to the throne. Thomas declined, saying accepting the post would create political difficulties. Charles wrote to him: 'Thank you so much for your letter telling me of the awkward problems you have been having. Although I am extremely sad to hear that you feel you cannot become Lord Warden, I want you to know that I totally understand the difficult position you have been placed in by the party leaders and you may rest assured that I most certainly do <u>not</u> consider you to be unreliable ... All I can say is that your wisdom, experience and humanity will be much missed in the Duchy of Cornwall, as well as your unique ability to get on with people. I, personally, was greatly looking forward to the chance of working more closely with you and of benefiting from your advice – as well as the laughter and jokes we would have had!'

Thomas did, however, occupy a flat in Cardigan Street, Lambeth owned by the Prince of Wales' estate. He signed a tenancy agreement on June 13, 1983.

Thomas socialised regularly with other members of the Royal Family. He was on very friendly terms with Lady Prue Penn, whose husband Sir Eric was the Comptroller of the Lord Chamberlain's Office and a trusted presence in Buckingham Palace. Members of the Royal Family were frequent visitors to the Penns' home, Sternfield House, near Saxmundham in Suffolk. Writing to Lady Penn, Thomas said: 'Forgive me having this letter typed, but it is the only way to get a speedy reply to you. I have not stopped chuckling about your picture on the front page of *The Times* with another lovely mink coat. I could have sworn it came from Russia! We had a marvellous weekend together down at the Royal Lodge. The Queen Mother certainly knows how to make her guests happy. It is kind of you to invite me down to Saxmundham after I have finished my book. That is a pleasure to which I shall look forward to enormously.'

In November 1984, Charles wrote to George, thanking him for sending him flowers on his birthday, as was his custom: 'My dear George, what a hero you are to think of me on my birthday!'

Charles told him that Diana took 'endless trouble' to make sure he was thoroughly spoiled and William was in seventh heaven tearing open all his presents. Diana took him to an Italian restaurant where he had trouble persuading the staff not to sing *Happy Birthday* to him. Charles stated: 'We continue to have a very special place for you in our thoughts and prayers – please know that.'

Charles regarded George as a confidant. In February 1986, he wrote to him about an article that had appeared in a 'thoroughly unreliable newspaper' which suggested he was going to make a speech critical of the Government. Charles wrote: 'I am not <u>that</u> stupid! I fear that all this speculation etc has arisen from the reports in October that I had said I was worried about inheriting a divided nation of 'haves and have-nots' when I become King. What annoyed me so much about these reports, which came out on the eve of a debate on the inner cities in October, was that I had never expressed any of these remarks. Can you really imagine that I would be so pompous as to say such a thing as 'when I become King', let alone such a blatantly political cliché as 'haves and have-nots'... These reports were concocted out of the fertile political imagination of the *Manchester Evening News*.'

Charles ended the letter hoping they could meet and signed off: 'Yours ever, and with affectionate admiration.'

In March 1986 Thomas sat at the table of the Queen Mother during the annual meeting of Queen Mary's London Needlework Guild. The formal invitation said: 'Her Majesty is so pleased you are able to speak for us at the AGM on March 19. I am writing to say Queen Elizabeth would like you to sit at her table for tea after the meeting.'

Patrick Cormack recalls a later occasion when the Queen Mother displayed her affection towards Thomas. It happened on the day Geoffrey Howe gave his resignation speech in the Commons, an act which directly led to Margaret Thatcher's downfall: "I wasn't in the Chamber then because I had raised the money for the statue at Chartwell, of Churchill and Clementine by Oscar Nemon, which now stands by the lake. I raised the money for this and I got the Queen Mother to unveil it. And I invited George. Of course George and the Queen Mother were very close and half way through the lunch she leaned across: there were roses in the middle of the table, George was there and she was there, and she presented them to George.

"He used to absolutely adore the Queen Mother. He thought she was quite magnificent, which, of course, she was. She entertained George at Clarence House and he gave at least two dinners for her at Speaker's House – and he gave one for the Queen."

Organising a private dinner party at the Athaneum Club at which Princess Margaret was the guest of honour, Thomas wrote to the club's reservations secretary saying: 'I promised to let you know what wine I would like to have when H.R.H. Princess Margaret comes to my private dinner party. I gather that the Princess has two distinct choices: Robinsons Barley Water with some Malvern Water, or (as is most likely in the evening) Grouse Whisky. She does not drink wine. Therefore I think I will let you choose a reasonably priced white and a reasonably priced red wine because I would like to serve both.'

Demonstrating that an event like the Investiture could inspire eccentric responses, a Singapore lawyer wrote to Thomas suggesting a 20th anniversary celebration of it in Windsor Great Park with a 'colloquium' convened by the Prince of Wales including Ronald Reagan, George Bush, Mikhail Gorbachev, Deng Xioping, Pope John Paul II, Suharto, Sultan of Brunei, Lee Kuan Yew, Sir Laurens van der Post, Sonny Ramphal, Mother Theresa, Isaac Stern, Sir Richard Attenborough, Armand Hammer, Dr. Andrei Sakharov and Henry Kissinger. The guest list would be headed by the Queen and the Duke of Edinburgh, followed by Margaret Thatcher and Geoffrey Howe.

In a letter to Thomas, the lawyer wrote: 'You, my Lord, were the admirable companion, in high moral courage, of His Royal Highness on that day in 1969, almost 20 years ago, which I now respectfully seek royal consent to commemorate by way of celebrations in the company of creative artists: the investiture of a great prince and an outstanding human being.'

Needless to say, nothing came of it.

A handwritten letter to Thomas dated April 27, 1990, from Martin Charteris, the Queen Mother's Private Secretary at Clarence House, thanked him for looking after her during a visit to Cardiff. Charteris wrote: 'My Dear George, It was splendid to learn from Queen Elizabeth how well you were and what a warm welcome you gave to Her Majesty. The visit to Cardiff was obviously a great success the more so as you were able to be present which made the whole difference to the happiness of the visit, I was sad that I could not be with you all but I hope we shall meet before too long. It is splendid to know that you are fit and well – and I send you my very affectionate good wishes for many more years of activity and happiness.'

Thomas was also on close terms with Princess Diana. After writing to her in June 1991 to express his concern when both Charles and William were unwell, she wrote to Thomas saying: 'Dearest George, A very special thank you for your lovely letter concerning the health of the two men in my life! It made all the difference to know that we are in your thoughts and prayers.'

This was followed by a letter from Charles, who wrote: 'Dear George, Your prayers have been answered! My back is considerably better, thank goodness – even though I am prematurely decrepit! Bless you for being so typically thoughtful to me. I hope you are well in yourself. We think of you often.'

In January 1992, Charles wrote to Thomas talking about 'time racing by before you know it', adding: 'I am so thrilled that you are able to dash about the world again, bringing happiness and laughter to all whom you meet. You have an enviable gift, and the world would be a poorer place without it.'

In June of that year, when Thomas was unable to attend a reception for National Children's Home, the charity he had chaired, at Charles' country home Highgrove. The Prince wrote to him saying: 'We shall miss you dreadfully at the reception for NCH at Highgrove. The trouble is I only agreed to give the reception because I thought it would provide me with a chance of seeing <u>you</u>! Please don't worry for a moment – I <u>quite</u> understand your predicament!'

Thomas remained on friendly terms with Diana after her separation from Charles. In December 1993, she responded to a letter from Thomas who had written sympathising with her decision to cut down on her public appearances. She wrote: 'Dearest George, I was enormously touched by your support and concern expressed from the heart in your letter. Thank you for writing to me about my decision to cut down my public life. It's taken five difficult years to come to this plateau, but I do feel that under the circumstances...'

And in July 1996, at the time Charles and Diana's divorce was going through, she wrote to him saying: 'Thank you for your wonderful letter, so full of love and support and <u>so</u> typical of you. The recent months have been very difficult for all of us but hopefully we can look forward to the future. I was devastated having to make decisions over my charities – it was heartbreaking but nevertheless it had to be done with the change of status.'

Weeks before he died, Charles sent Thomas an unidentified present, accompanied by a letter which ended: 'You are very much in my thoughts and prayers and I wanted to send you this very small token of affection and esteem, together with every possible healing wish.'

23

Patronage

There are repeated instances in Thomas' papers of people lobbying for honours to be bestowed on them. The earliest example concerns Walter Lloyd Pierce, a Labour county councillor from Llanfair Caereinion in Montgomeryshire, who wrote to Thomas saying: 'Dear George, Herewith please find particulars of my activities in the public life of this neighbourhood, of the county and of Wales. At Newtown, I told you of my desire to get recognition of my services to Education and Public Life. You very kindly said you would help and see the Chief Whip. I am the only Socialist public man in this county and have kept the flag flying under great difficulties in this very rural area. Age 75. Son of Wesleyan Minister. On Executive of NUT for 15 years. Magistrate. Local preacher with Methodist Church for 48 years. Headmaster of Evening School Crwys Road, Cardiff. Head of Caereinion Council School for 39 years."

Shortly after being appointed Secretary of State for Wales, T.L. Charlton, Church Secretary of the United Church of Zambia wrote to him saying: 'I am venturing to write to you as a fellow Methodist and fellow Socialist of long standing. I am ... writing to request for Church Council in connection with the return to Britain at the end of this year of our Minister, the Rev. Colin Morris, President of the United Church of Zambia: after what must be the most distinguished missionary career in modern times ... You will understand Mr. Morris himself knows nothing of this letter and its contents.'

Charlton went on at length to request Morris' inclusion in the Honours List. Thomas replied that he was very pleased to do so as he was very pleased to have known Morris, and on the same day sent a letter endorsing his nomination for an Honour to Sir Morris James, a senior official at the Commonwealth Office.

Around the same time, Archie Lush, who had been Aneurin Bevan's best man and was one of his closest friends, wrote to Thomas complaining in a facetious way that he had been left out of the Queen's Birthday Honours List while an undeserving individual had been included. Lush wrote: 'As the Chairman of the Welsh Hospital Board I was anxious that a certain person should be recognised. It was a mistake! His only qualifications were:

a) Staunch SWMF [South Wales Mining Federation] and late NUM [National Union of Mineworkers];
b) Medical and Society stalwart;
c) Years of service to Hospital Management Committee;
d) A powerful advocate with the makers of the National Health Act ('our Act' as he called it).

'Now I found amongst the Honours List the most anti-nationalised industry man I have ever met with the golden handshake he left the nationalised industry but the Labour Party honours him.'

Thomas replied: 'My dear Archie, Thank you for your letter concerning the Honours List. I share your feeling on this matter but, as I believe I told you when I saw you, this year's Honours List was an inheritance so far as I was concerned.'

Liberal leader Jeremy Thorpe wrote an affectionate letter

to Thomas asking him to recommend a DBE for party activist Olwen Carey Evans. The third child of David Lloyd George, she was involved in organising the Investiture. Thomas responded, saying: 'My dear Jeremy, I hope that all is well concerning Olwen. I believe that it will be so.'

He remained indulgent towards Labour people who wrote requesting honours for themselves. Llewellyn ap Gwynn of Welshpool wrote to him saying people from other parties were getting honours and that diminished Labour: 'It would give the small but still solid core of our party workers considerable encouragement were Ben Watkins and I to be considered for inclusion in honours. This is unblushing canvassing – and Ben knows nothing of it – I being some 14 years his senior, soon to retire from local government, would be able to do more for our party if I were more widely known or 'better labelled'.'

Thomas responded: 'My warmest thanks for your letter. I fully appreciate the importance of Honours in an area like yours and will gladly see that consideration is given to your letter at the appropriate time. I know that you will appreciate I cannot make any promises in advance.'

Another Honours supplicant was not so fortunate. A month later, Alec McKinty of the *South Wales Echo* wrote to Thomas asking if a Mrs. Eva Walters Matthews could be recognised in the Honours List for her musical contribution of conducting choirs in south Wales. Thomas wrote back to say there were two other choir masters in Cardiff who had conducted choirs for over 50 years and it was unlikely Mrs. Matthews would be honoured.

Despite the increasing antagonism that existed between Thomas and senior Labour Ministers, he was highly thought of by the staff who served him. The Clerk to the House, Sir Richard Barlas, sought his support in getting an Honour for Anthony Birley, the Clerk of Public Bills. He wrote to Thomas, stating:

'We parted yesterday evening before I was able to thank you sufficiently for your help over an honour for Anthony Birley. I am really most grateful that you should have intervened personally – especially with all the many calls upon your time. I think you know the score. You often say some very kind things about me; but I wouldn't be able to give – or to start to give – you such help as I can without the willing help and cooperation of a loyal staff. And it's not really a question of loyalty to me only – it is a matter of putting in a little extra to be certain they won't let down a Speaker whom they respect and are fond of. And I may add that the clerks have not invariably taken the attitude to <u>all</u> Speakers. They have always done their job, but it's the pressed down and running over bit that one wants. My staff generally would like to see Anthony get his CB [Companion of the Order of Bath]. You have done all you can. I only hope your efforts succeed as I am sure they will in view of the indications you gave me. I am addressing this privately to you at Cardiff.'

Thomas made the recommendation to Prime Minister Callaghan – throwing in another Honours recommendation at the same time. Callaghan responded: 'Dear George, Thank you for your letter of 27 January about honours. I will of course bear in mind what you say about Mr. Birley when I am considering the recommendations for the Birthday Honours List. I am glad to have your suggestion about Miss. Elsie Beaton and will certainly see that it is considered fully and carefully.'

There were occasions when Thomas' attempts to get Honours or other recognition for supplicants did not prove successful. Having made representations on behalf of the Conservative Shadow Sports Minister, Sir Hector Monro, Callaghan decided he did not merit a medal. Callaghan wrote: 'Thank you for your letter of 19 January about Hector Monro who is disappointed not to have received the Queen's Silver Jubilee Medal. As my secretary explained in his letter of 3 January to Noel Short, the distribution of medals on this occasion was much more limited than for the 1935 Jubilee or the 1953 Coronation. The Members of Parliament who were recommended to the Queen for the Silver Jubilee Medal were those who entered the House of Commons before the Queen's accession, together with some national politicians who did not fall into this category. Mr. Monro entered the House of Commons in 1964 and, thus, I am afraid, did not qualify.'

Monro thanked Thomas for his efforts, writing: 'Dear Mr. Speaker, Thank you for your letter and for the tremendous effort you made on my behalf. I am most grateful. I am afraid the Prime Minister or his advisers really have failed to see our points either relating to official duties in the House or in regard to the activities of MPs outside the House, upon which the Prime Minister effectively placed a veto where the award of a medal might have taken place. Sad indeed, but you could not have done more. Hector.'

Callaghan also rejected a suggestion that he should recommend an Honour for the recently bereaved former Lord Mayor of Cardiff, David Purnell: 'Dear George, Many thanks for your letter about David Purnell. I had heard this tragic news when I was back in Cardiff at the weekend, and have written a short note to him. I appreciate the kind thought behind Michael Roberts' suggestion, but apart from any other considerations, I am afraid it is now too late for his name to be included. As I am sure you will also appreciate, much as I like David, it would be awkward for me to include his name in the List, when the previous Chairman, Hugh Ferguson Jones, did not receive a decoration during or at the end of his term of office. Yours sincerely, Jim Callaghan.'

Another grievance related to Callaghan's refusal to nominate Thomas' Deputy Speakers for Honours. Thomas wrote to

Margaret Thatcher: 'Ref: Mr. Bryant Godman Irvine and Mr. Bernard Weatherill. I hesitate to trouble you when I know you are surrounded with heavy burdens but it is on my conscience that I should write to you concerning my above named two Deputy Speakers. Bryant Godman Irvine was the only one of the team who served in the last House and received no recognition for his services. I thought that it was unkind and that he should have appeared in the Dissolution Honours List. I had given a strong representation that he should have been given a Knighthood. If it is possible for you to consider his name for the January Honours List, I shall be deeply grateful. He is a good and loyal servant of the House; he never spares himself. It has been the normal practice ever since I have been in the House for the Chairman of Ways and Means, the First Deputy Speaker, to be made Privy Counsellor. If it is possible for Jack Weatherill to be considered for this Honour, I shall be more than grateful. I thought you looked pale in the Abbey this morning, and I hope that you are taking care of yourself. Every blessing to you.' The Honours requested by Thomas were bestowed.

Equally Margaret Thatcher overruled officials who said it was inappropriate for two members of the Speaker's staff to be recommended for MBEs in the same Birthday Honours List. She wrote to him saying: 'Despite the factors which point the other way, I am ready, in the light of your very strong personal support for Mr. Canter, to include his name in my recommendations for the 1982 Birthday Honours List.'

Even after stepping down as Speaker, he was still clearly seen as someone who could fix honours. A letter dated April 18, 1984, from the wife of former Labour MP Percy Browne, who had served in Parliament from 1959 to 1964, sought his intervention. He responded: 'Dear Mrs. Browne, Thank you for your very kind letter concerning Percy, whom I like to look upon as a friend. Like you, I cannot understand why his public service has not been recognised before this date, and I will certainly do all I can to help. I fear that I do not have much influence now in connection with the Honours List, but I will have a word with friends who may have influence.'

Days later he received a letter from Sir Peter Mills MP which said: 'Thank you very much for your letter about Percy Browne. I do agree with you and have really done my best to help get an honour for him. I wrote a couple of weeks ago and had an acknowledgement from No 10. I must be quite frank, however, and say that for Mrs. Browne to 'lobby' people on behalf of her husband (including an approach direct to No 10!) is not the way to go about it. It may be counterproductive! I return her letter.'

Mrs. Browne wrote to Thomas: 'Thank you so very much for your kind letter which I enormously appreciated. My machinations are now 'in the open' as I saw John Wakeham on Monday in the House – I had ostensibly gone to London to see a senior surgeon about the cartilage in my right knee which is dislocated. Percy nearly had a seizure when I returned home and told him what I'd been up to!'

Another request for Honours preferment came from an administrator at Luton Industrial College, to whom Thomas replied: "Dear Mr. Nevels, Thank you for your kind letter concerning recognition in the Honours List for the long and faithful service of the Principal of Luton Industrial College. I entirely agree that his outstanding service should in some way be recognised. It is always exceedingly difficult to get recognition for a man of the Cloth because there are so many who give a life of dedicated service, but I have asked the Rt Hon. Ernest Armstrong MP, a former vice president of [the Methodist] Conference if he will pursue the matter for me. Since I no longer belong to the House of Commons, any influence I ever had in this field has disappeared, but I know that Ernest Armstrong will do his best to help.' Thomas sent a letter to Armstrong, saying: 'If there is anything you can do in this regard, I know you will.'

In August 1984, Thomas received a letter from Trade Secretary Paul Channon responding to one he had sent about another potential Honour: 'Dear George, Thank you for your letter of 1 August to Norman Tebbit recommending an honour for Derek Crouch. Since the principal business of Mr. Crouch's company is opencast coal mining, responsibility for sponsorship rests with the Department of Energy, and I am arranging for your letter to be forwarded to Peter Walker's office.' Responding to a letter from a Mr. T Kelly from Llanishen, Cardiff, Thomas said on May 3, 1985: 'Thank you for your letter concerning John Williams being recognised in the Honours List. He has a fantastic record and certainly should have his work recognised. Unfortunately, I no longer have any influence with regard to the Honours List but I think you should send the details to the Rt. Hon. Nicholas Edwards MP Secretary State for Wales.'

Again showing Thomas' inconsistency over requests to lobby for Honours, he responded positively to a letter from a senior figure at King's College London which said: 'For some time it has seemed to me that [the cardiologist] Prof. Jack Shillingford ought to receive some public recognition of his extraordinarily distinguished services to medicine'. The writer pointed out that the distinguished physician and geneticist Sir Cyril Clarke was backing the cause and asked Thomas to support it too. Thomas replies that he would do so after finding the name of the new Private Secretary to the Prime Minister.

However, in September 1987 he refused to write to Margaret Thatcher requesting an honour for Tom White, past president of the Association of Directors of Social Services. He wrote: 'I have given the most careful consideration to the letter which you sent me concerning a public honour. The more I think about it the more I realise how impossible it is for me to forward it on to the PM. I would be greatly relieved if you could ask Ernie Armstrong to write. As I think he mentioned to you I had recently broken my rule and written to the PM about an Honour for an MP. In that letter I drew her attention to the fact that I do not normally write to her about the Honours List. I am quite sure it would be counter-productive if I were to send another letter hard on the heels of another one.'

In the same month he wrote to a woman in Ystrad Rhondda explaining he had no influence over the Honours List.

18 Nov 1987, Thomas wrote to Ernest Armstrong: 'Enclosed please find a most encouraging letter which I have received from Neil Kinnock. I think this is pretty well an assurance that you will join us in the Lords in the future. I certainly hope that will be the case.'

Frank Bayliss, past president of the National Association of Toastmasters, wrote to Thomas in November 1988 stating: 'My colleague Bryn Williams [a well known Toastmaster in London] sends you his kind regards. I am still awaiting news re his nomination for civil honours. Everyone I have contacted, from every walk of life and including yourself, have been and continue to be most helpful. In due time I hope to inform you of a successful conclusion for a man who, like yourself, is loved and respected by so many.'

Thomas responded: 'It is too late for any action in connection with the New Year's Honour's List because the decision will have been taken in September last. The best thing is to write in January just before the consideration of the names for the June Honours List. I wish in my heart we could get Bryn's outstanding contribution recognised.'

People soliciting Honours continued to write to Thomas. He responded to one saying: 'Thank you for your letter concerning

Mr. Charles William Jacob MBE. Now that I have retired I have a firm rule that I do not make any recommendations whatsoever for the Honours List. It is exceedingly difficult for me to intervene however worthy the cause because there are so many good names that keep being sent to me. Believe me, your best course of action would be to write to one of the Methodist MPs and ask him to pursue the matter for you.'

Jacob had been the Investment Manager of the Central Finance Board of the Methodist Church. He had received an MBE in 1988, but there had been no mention in the citation of the Methodist Church and it was felt he should have had a higher honour.

Whatever he said, Thomas' rule wasn't as firm as he claimed. As late as 1996, Secretary of State for Wales William Hague wrote to Thomas to say that Captain Norman Lloyd-Edwards, the Lord Lieutenant of South Glamorgan, had recently written to the Honours' Secretary about an award for Ivor Cassam of Rhiwbina and was also in receipt of Thomas' accompanying letter of support.

Asked what he knew about Thomas' interventions to secure honours, Patrick Cormack said: "Every MP gets that. I had that a bit. George didn't countenance it. We discussed it on one occasion, when I'd had a request. He'd had a lot of them. He said, 'never support somebody who is self-promoting'. I never did, and I used to say if someone came to me, 'look I don't want to talk any more about this, but if others approach me to say what a wonderful person you are and what marvellous work you've done, I would listen.' But I'm afraid I do not support people who self-promote. And I think that was George's general line."

Another element of Thomas' use of patronage was that he was sometimes willing to help young men, in particular, find work. He received a letter from the future academic, broadcaster and sports consultant Russell Holden, saying: 'I would be exceedingly grateful if you could spare me some of your much sought after time, in order to discuss my continuing dilemma – my inability after five months of concentrated effort to find suitable employment. I look forward to hearing from you again soon.'

Thomas responded, saying: 'Dear Russell Holden. Thank you for your letter. I am deeply sorry to know that you are still searching to get suitable employment. The best thing for you to do will be for you to come to see me at my home at 3.30pm on Friday afternoon of this week.'

Six weeks later Holden wrote to Thomas again, saying: 'This is just to inform you that I have accepted the position of Executive Officer (Personal Assistant to the Director) at the Welsh Centre for International Affairs. I am absolutely delighted about this and would like to thank you very much for your efforts on my behalf in this connection. I trust that your book is now running to schedule and that we meet again before long.'

Thomas responded: 'My dear Russell, My heartfelt congratulations on your appointment. I am thrilled beyond measure that you will be working for the Welsh Centre for International Affairs, for I know that this work will suit you down to the ground. It is marvellous how things have worked out for you and I rejoice with you.'

Further evidence of Thomas' role as someone who helped people get jobs comes in a letter exchange involving St. Thomas Hospital. Writing to the head of the Department of Medicine at the hospital, he said: 'Dear Professor Cranston, During my holiday in Cyprus I was asked by E.N. Pilavachi, the Cypriot Ambassador to the Council of Europe, if I would help his niece to complete her specialist medical training in the UK. I promised him that I would seek your advice. The young lady

<u>seems</u> to be a gifted person. If there is any way in which you can help, I will be profoundly grateful.'

The young woman's CV was written on Paphos Beach Hotel stationery.

In September 1984, Thomas wrote to Dr. Neil Tanner, tutor for admissions at Hertford College, providing a glowing character reference and recommending Thanos Michaelides, son of his friend Alecos Michaelides, who had been Speaker of the Cyprus Parliament and whose hotel at Paphos he stayed at on several occasions.

Thomas said the would-be student had 'absolute integrity' and was 'a wholesome young man in every way'. He added: "I am quite satisfied that the young Thanos Michaelides will one day play a major part in the life of Cyprus'.

The college agreed to interview Michaelides, but his visit to Hertford was not a runaway success. Tanner wrote to Thomas stating: 'I am writing to report on the recent visit of Thanos Michaelides to this College. He is, as you say, a thoroughly pleasant and sincere young man, but on the evidence before us it seems unlikely that he could cope with the PPE course at Oxford. It is difficult for us to interpret the marks awarded for the Cyprus Leaving Certificate, but the grades for the three 'O' Levels he has taken are not encouraging, and the interview at the beginning of this month revealed little knowledge of the 'A' Level Mathematics and Economics which he is currently studying. It is doubtful whether he could do at all well in those 'A' Levels. This is all a bit puzzling as he is well supported by his school and we wonder whether his lack of fluency in English and the demands of the National Service are making life impossibly difficult for him. As things stand, it would be extremely hazardous to take him on for the PPE as it could end up with a humiliating failure in the Preliminary Examination after two terms. I am sorry to report in this manner, but would like to thank you for taking an interest in Thanos.'

In May 1987, Thomas wrote to Sir Geoffrey Warnock, the Principal of Hertford College, Oxford: 'Re Alexander Luce. The above-named young man (who is the son of Richard Luce, Minister for the Arts) has obtained a BA grade 2:1 at Buckingham University. He is anxious to pursue his studies with a view to obtaining a doctorate. His honours degree is in English and History. I wonder if it is possible for him to gain admission to Hertford with a view to research leading to his PhD? I hate to trouble you like this but if your College could look into this for me I would be very grateful.'

Thomas even helped out with the marketing of the Michaelides' new hotel at Paphos. He wrote to Terry Wogan inviting him and his wife for a week-long free holiday to coincide with its opening: 'Dear Mr. Wogan, Although we have not yet met, like your army of admirers I feel that I know you. I write about an unusual invitation which I hope you will feel able to accept. In Paphos, Cyprus, I have a dear friend, Alecos Michaelides. He is a former speaker of the Cyprus National Assembly and former acting President of the state. During the Turkish invasion of Northern Cyprus in 1974, Mr. Michaelides and his family had to flee from Famagusta leaving all their possessions. Since that catastrophic experience, Mr. Michaelides has shown enormous courage and skill in building up a highly successful hotel business in Paphos. On July 22 this year, I am due to open his five star luxury hotel, the Annabelle – named after his daughter. I write to invite you and Mrs. Wogan – if you are free – to come for the opening ceremony and to stay a week as honoured guests. This would add to the prestige of the occasion and give enormous pleasure to your followers in Cyprus. My involvement is solely that of friendship with Yolanda and Alecos Michaelides. I have tremendous admiration for their achievements and I would like to help them. If you feel able to join us for this very special occasion, it will give much happiness in Cyprus. I <u>hope</u> you can.'

Other celebrities were also contacted, including Dame Anna Neagle, Penelope Keith, Beryl Reid, June Whitfield and Julia Mackenzie.

One of the invited guests was successfully reeled in. Thomas wrote to Alecos Michaelides to tell him: 'I am writing to confirm that Penelope Keith and her husband (their name is Mr. and Mrs. Robbie Timpson) will be able to come to Cyprus on July 17, that is the Wednesday, and then they will leave on Wednesday July 24. I have not been able to get hold of a journalist who is free to come out for the opening and this vexes me a great deal. It will not be long now before I see you all and I am looking forward with enormous joy to being with you.'

On April 30, 1991, the Earl of Stockton wrote to Thomas about a young man named Charalambos Parayiotou. He stated: 'Thank you for your letter of April 22. I must apologise for not having replied to it earlier, but I have only recently come back from abroad. I have passed on your request to support the studies of this young man to my brother Adam, who is the Chairman of the Harold Macmillan Trust, and I hope that he and his colleagues will be able to do something. The problem may be that the terms of the trust are fairly tightly drawn and do concentrate on supporting teachers in third world countries to develop local materials and local curricula for their own education systems. Have you thought of approaching some of the wealthy Greek family trusts? Apart from the Onassis Foundation and the Niarchos Trust, the Mavroleon family have been in this country for a long time, and I am sure that Basil might be persuadable for such a patently good cause."

He went on to explain that he couldn't do anything personally because he had lost a lot of money in his recent divorce.

24

Why Understanding George Thomas is Important

A friend whose opinion I respect asked me why I was writing a biography of George Thomas, saying there are more major Welsh politicians to write about. That may be so, but my view is that Thomas represents a kind of politics that persists to this day and should be consigned to history.

Some have dismissed him as a kind of one-off pantomime villain whose significance doesn't merit further study. Such an approach is, I believe, misguided. His legacy lives on in the Brexit vote and the rise of the populist Right. Understanding George Thomas, and the appeal he had for many people, helps us understand why achieving a fairer, more equal society remains so difficult to this day.

Much is made of the poverty of his upbringing in Tonypandy, and he was certainly not averse to mentioning it himself throughout his career. But his circumstances were more complicated than the norm. His maternal grandfather had migrated to south Wales from the west of England, and made a reasonable living from his building business. It was the dissolute behaviour of his father that made life for the family tougher than it need have been.

He saw his mother mistreated by his father, a Welsh speaker from west Wales. It is difficult to avoid the conclusion that the troubles of his childhood not only led him to idolise his Mam, but bred a suspicion of the Welsh language and the kind of Welshness associated with it that he could never shake off.

His love for his mother made him into a loyal member of both the Methodist Church and the Labour Party, but the Church's opposition to alcohol, let alone homosexuality, forced him to dissemble, and concealment became an essential part of his make-up. He had the capacity to be a charming companion, but he also had a malicious side and bore grudges.

Having flirted with pacifism, he probably came to the conclusion that becoming a conscientious objector while Britain was fighting Hitler would not assist him in a political career. He nevertheless managed to avoid military service thanks, he claimed, to an unspecified and unexplained medical problem. There is a strong suspicion that strings were pulled behind the scenes to keep him out of the British Army.

Intent on becoming an MP once the war was over, he harboured a secret resentment towards Jim Callaghan, over many decades, for the way the future Prime Minister breezed into the safe Cardiff seat he was ambitious to represent. The resentment took hold even though he had no difficulty getting selected for the seat next door.

Once in Parliament he gravitated to the left of the party. He went on a hazardous fact-finding mission to Greece under the auspices of a communist front organisation and became involved with a group of MPs who were manipulated by the Soviet Union and its satellite countries in Eastern Europe. Both at the time and years later when he was writing about these experiences, he sought to give the impression that he had been no more than naïve. Yet there is evidence in Thomas' archive which shows he was wholly aware of the group's links with Warsaw Pact embassies, from which he also received copious quantities of propaganda that he kept.

It is also fanciful to imagine that Stalin would have been prepared to fly a number of Labour MPs from Moscow to meet him at a Black Sea resort for no more than a casual chat. Thomas only distanced himself from the group after receiving warnings from senior parliamentary colleagues that his career would be damaged if he carried on.

During the long years of opposition after Labour lost the general election in 1951, he concentrated on building up his reputation as a good parliamentary performer. He gained respect for the dogged way he pursued the cause of leasehold reform, an issue which caused much hardship and stress to leaseholders across south Wales when their leases expired and they had to choose between paying large sums of money to the freeholder or giving up their home. Eventually his patience was rewarded when greater statutory protection was afforded to leaseholders, but the victory took more than 20 years to secure.

In terms of social reform, the fellow MP who rescued him when he got into scrapes because of his sexual behaviour – Leo Abse – was in a different league, as the backbencher who steered divorce and homosexual law reform through the Commons.

By the time Thomas became a Minister when Labour returned to power in 1964, his credentials as a left-winger were somewhat ragged. He'd attended meetings with fellow MPs about the creation of what became the Campaign for Nuclear Disarmament, but when the body was launched didn't actually join it. There was no coherent explanation offered as to why not.

The Aberfan disaster in 1966 was a testing moment for him, and he let the community down badly at its time of need. Putting to one side his wholly inappropriate slavering over the Royal Family, into which he tried to draw a grieving mother, his acceptance of the Government line that the benefit fund for the village should pay towards the cost of removing the tip was grossly insensitive and unjust.

He should have put up stronger resistance when Harold Wilson, the Prime Minister, argued in favour of a contribution from the fund, but his loyalty to Wilson, to whom he owed his career advancement, was for Thomas the more important factor.

For many Welsh nationalists, Thomas' ultimate sin was his involvement with the Investiture of Prince Charles as Prince of Wales in 1969, when he was Secretary of State for Wales. Yet while he enthusiastically embraced the Investiture, and the opportunity it provided to celebrate the Union at a time when Plaid Cymru had recently had its first MP elected, it was not his idea. He inherited the concept from Cledwyn Hughes, whom he succeeded as Secretary of State for Wales the previous year.

What is undeniable is that a large majority of the people of Wales supported both the monarchy as an institution and the Investiture as a ceremony. As well as opinion polls from the time showing around three quarters of the population backed the Investiture – although almost a half were concerned about the expense – many people wrote personal letters to Thomas in which they expressed their support for it.

There was also very strong opposition to the bombing incidents undertaken by fringe nationalists that led to an RAF warrant officer and a 10-year-old schoolboy suffering life-changing injuries. While Thomas himself did not accuse Plaid Cymru of involvement in this criminal activity, some of those who wrote to him tarred all nationalists with the same brush.

His period as Secretary of State for Wales was defined by the Investiture, and after the Conservatives unexpectedly won the

1970 general election, Thomas never held government office again.

When Labour bounced back in February 1974, he was bitterly disappointed when his sponsor, Harold Wilson, failed to reappoint him as Secretary of State. Wilson had been persuaded that Thomas' perceived anti-Welsh stance was losing the party support and seats.

Thomas was furious, believing Wilson had misread the political runes and the huge defeat of the pro-devolutionists in the first referendum to establish a Welsh Assembly five years later suggests that Thomas was perhaps more attuned to the mood of the nation as a whole than his Labour colleagues.

He was unforgiving towards the party that had given him his political career. During his time as Speaker, Thomas was antagonistic towards Labour, as well as becoming a cloying admirer of Margaret Thatcher. He was comfortable to join the ranks of the Establishment and cosy up further to the Royal Family, several of whose members he had got to know at the time of the Investiture.

His acceptance of an hereditary peerage at the time of his retirement as Speaker represented a new low for those on the left who had watched his political trajectory to the right with dismay. For Thomas, however, it was an honour that enabled him to live the myth of a poor boy who was able to attain high rank by working hard. We know from the patronage he extended to those wanting recognition in the Honours List, and to young men whose causes he took up, that reality was different from the myth.

In his final years he became a strange thing for a Welshman – a Little Englander whose simultaneous hatred for the European Union and Welsh devolution became almost pathological.

At the same time he was happy to extend helping hands to the likes of the soon-to-be-disgraced Tory MP Jonathan Aitken, while turning down pleas to assist more deserving campaigners in his home city of Cardiff.

A politician who began his career with radical credentials, Thomas eventually became an apologist for reactionary views wrapped up in the Union Jack.

If the narrow victory of the Yes campaign in the second devolution referendum in 1997 prompted Thomas to die, as his friends believe, the vote for Brexit in June 2016 gave him some posthumous vindication.

Our society continues to have too much cap-doffing to our perceived 'betters' and a craving to ingratiate ourselves with them for social and career advancement. There remain, to this day, too many politicians like George Thomas who combine a self-seeking ambition with the readiness to pretend that Britain persists in being a great power built on the remnants of an empire that makes it superior to all other European countries. It's a populist tactic which works, and which prolongs an unrealistic view of the world among so many of our fellow citizens.

However, publicity associated with the 50th anniversary of the Aberfan disaster exposed his betrayal of the community to a younger generation that is not so deferential as its predecessors.

Even more damaging is that in an age which has woken up to the evils of predatory sexual behaviour towards the young, Thomas' carefully cultivated image of an upstanding Christian of strong moral rectitude can be seen as a sham. Restrained by his fear of exposure, he may not have been the most prolific of sexual predators but he was certainly one of the most hypocritical.

George Thomas may have been dead since 1997, but his legacy – as a sycophant supreme – has yet to be extinguished. His personal reputation, however, now lies in ruins.

Afterword

In November 2016 the company which owned the Lord Tonypandy pub announced that its name was being changed to The Fulling Mill.

Plaid Cymru leader and Rhondda AM Leanne Wood had organised a petition urging a name change after Thomas' betrayal of the people of Aberfan was explored in news coverage marking the 50th anniversary of the tragedy.

Describing the name change as a "victory for people power", Ms Wood added: "There was a palpable feeling in the Rhondda that local people were sick and tired of being associated with Lord Tonypandy. His role during the Aberfan disaster was appalling; not only to the people of that village but to the nation as a whole."

Then, in June 2017, the charity George Thomas Hospice announced that it was changing its name to City Hospice.

Explaining that such a move had been under consideration since September 2016, the charity issued a statement which said: 'By lending his name to the charity, George Thomas ensured the charity's early survival and prosperity, and the association with his name has undoubtedly brought great benefits.

'However, 20 years after his death the present generation knows little of his achievements, or of his relevance to this charity. The Hospice needs to appeal to that wider public where, increasingly, only a minority are familiar with George Thomas. We believe our new name – City Hospice – will be appealing, easily recognisable and remembered, and should over time attract great support and affection across the City, allowing the Hospice to engage better with those supporters to whom the name George Thomas has little significance.

'Although our existing supporters value the essential work the charity does, knowing that it has no connection other than by name with George Thomas, our new name will also distance the charity from any negative connotation that may now or in the future be associated with George Thomas' name.'

Index

INDEX

INDEX

INDEX

welsh academic press

ABERFAN
Government and Disaster
(Second Edition)

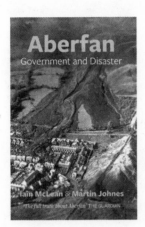

'The full truth about Aberfan'
The Guardian

'The research is outstanding...the investigation is substantial, balanced and authoritative...this is certainly the definitive book on the subject... Meticulous.'
John R. Davis, Journal of Contemporary British History

'Excellent...thorough and sympathetic.'
Headway 2000 (Aberfan Community Newspaper)

'Definitive...authoritative...anyone who wants to understand the process of government and its obsession with secrecy should read this book.'
Ron Davies, Secretary of State for Wales 1997-1998

'Intelligent and moving'
Planet

978-1-86057-133-6   192pp   £19.99   PB

GARETH JONES
Eyewitness to the Holodomor

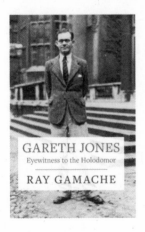

'Excellent ... serves as a warning to journalists not to be taken in by official sources and political ideology but to report what they actually learn through their own efforts. Gamache deserves commendation for his research and careful reconstruction of Jones' reportorial journeys.'
Prof. Maurine H. Beasley, Univ. of Maryland

'...meticulously researched book [that] returns Gareth Jones to his rightful status, as one of the most outstanding journalists of his generation'
Nigel Linsan Colley, www.garethjones.org

'Extraordinary ... Jones' articles ... caused a sensation ... Because [his] notebooks record immediate impressions and describe events as they were happening, they have an unusual freshness ... Jones' reputation has revived thanks to the Ukrainian government's broader efforts to tell the history of the famine ... the establishment of a Ukrainian state simply makes Jones seem less marginal, more central, more important.'
Anne Applebaum, The New York Review

978-1-86057-122-0   256pp   £19.99   PB

welsh academic press

The Financial Affairs of
DAVID LLOYD GEORGE

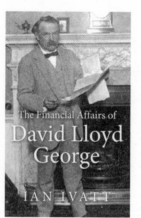

'In this important and pioneering study, Ian Ivatt has focussed his attention on a key theme rather neglected by historians and biographers of Lloyd George – his relationship with money and financial resources ... [these] compelling, engrossing themes, central to an understanding of Lloyd George's life, are dissected with a masterly touch by Mr. Ivatt. He has spared no effort to master the ever burgeoning published literature on David Lloyd George, has waded through the various scattered archival sources and scoured the newspaper columns too. He has also conducted personal interviews and undertaken research on the ground. All his enthralling discoveries have been deftly welded into a cohesive, absorbing account'
J. Graham Jones, from the Foreword

The Financial Affairs of David Lloyd George is the first serious and systematic study to examine, assess and analyse Lloyd George's attitude to money and finance and compellingly illustrates how he accumulated great wealth by fair and more questionable methods.

978-1-86057-125-1   128pp   £19.99   PB

JIM
The Life and Work of Jim Griffiths

'The remarkable story of James Griffiths takes us all the way from the origins of British Labour to the origins of devolved Wales. Ben Rees has crafted a highly-readable and authoritative account of the life and times of one of Wales' greatest statesmen'
Huw Edwards

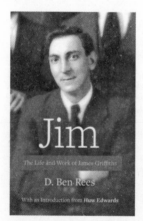

In this, the first full-length biography of James Griffiths in English, Dr D. Ben Rees provides a comprehensive yet very accessible and personal study of one of the towering figures of twentieth-century Welsh and British politics. As Minister for National Insurance in the Atlee post-war government, introduced the Family Allowance in 1946 and became Secretary of State for the Colonies in 1950.

A product of the Welsh radical political tradition, James Griffiths became a miner at 13 and was a conscientious objector during WW1. He rose to become President of the South Wales Miner's Federation, the MP for Llanelli for 34 years, Chairman and then Deputy Leader of the Labour Party and the first Secretary of State for Wales in 1964.

978-1-86057-120-6   400pp

welsh academic press

The Public Affairs Guide to WESTMINSTER

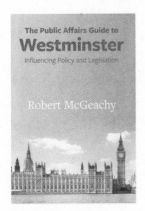

The Public Affairs Guide to Westminster is the essential handbook for organisations seeking to influence legislation and shape policy development in the UK Parliament and at UK Government level, and is packed with invaluable advice on devising cost effective public affairs strategies and campaigns that achieve success on a limited budget.

Robert McGeachy's step-by-step guide - for private, public and third sector organisations - expertly strips away the mysteries and misconceptions of engaging with the UK Government, Opposition parties, as well as with individual MPs, Peers and the civil service.

The Public Affairs Guide to Westminster will empower campaigners to maximise their influence and to ensure their voice is heard at Westminster.

978-1-86057-134-3 224pp £19.99 PB

The Public Affairs Guide to SCOTLAND

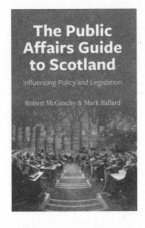

'[an excellent] guide for the newcomer and a 'memory stick' for the expert. It contains all a person needs to know to engage with the Parliament, the Government, local authorities and civic society in an effective and efficient way. This book shows how one can participate in that fast moving and interesting field and will become a tool for all who wish to get involved and achieve success in their endeavours.'
Michael P Clancy

'Effective and informed activity by MSPs, the Parliament, the Scottish Government and third sector bodies in taking forward legislation and promoting causes, whilst protecting the most vulnerable is the best way to ensure a truly participatory, power sharing democracy and that is why this guide will be so useful ... Mark Ballard and Robert McGeachy, through the pages of this important book, are therefore doing democracy a service.'
Michael Russell, MSP for Argyll & Bute
Professor in Scottish Culture & Governance,
The University of Glasgow

978-1-86057-126-8 224pp £19.99 PB

welsh academic press

SNP
The History of the Scottish National Party
(Second Edition)

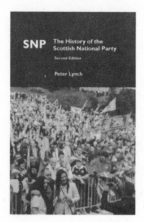

'lucid, comprehensive and balanced - an invaluable guide to the SNP"
David Torrance

'There is scholarship on every page. It will become the definitive reference work on the nationalist strand of Scottish politics and Scottish history...the early days in particular are extremely well done, with close attention to original sources...impressive and has never been so well set out before.'
Scottish Affairs

The first full-length history of the Scottish National Party which traces the fortunes of the SNP from its establishment in 1934 to winning power in the Scottish Parliament.

978-1-86057-057-5 319pp £19.99 PB

INDYREF TO SCOTREF
Campaigning for Yes

The Scottish independence referendum of 2014 was the most colourful, dynamic and longest political campaign Scotland has ever seen and which, in IndyRef to ScotRef, is lovingly recounted through the experiences of university lecturer turned Yes for Scotland activist, Peter Lynch, who shares his personal journey - one that will resonate with tens of thousands of Scots, from all backgrounds and walks of life, who found themselves drawn to Campaigning for Yes - from his early involvement with local Yes groups in his home city of Edinburgh to a deeper immersion in the grassroots campaign with leafleting, street stalls, door-to-door canvassing, public meetings, electoral registration and the many political carnivals held across Scotland in pursuit of a Yes vote.

In the final chapters of IndyRef to ScotRef, Peter Lynch analyses the huge political events that have occurred in Scotland and the rest of the UK since September 2014, which have seen the SNP's domination of Scottish politics and Britain voting for Brexit despite Scotland voting to Remain, resulting in the decision of the Scottish Parliament in March 2017 to call for a second independence referendum. With an eye on ScotRef, whenever it comes, Lynch warns 'Yessers' to be realistic and prepared, outlining what must be done to secure a Yes for Scotland.

978-1-86057-131-2 128pp £14.99 PB